M000206290

WANNSEE

WANNSEE

THE ROAD TO THE FINAL SOLUTION

PETER LONGERICH

TRANSLATED BY

LESLEY SHARPE AND JEREMY NOAKES

OXFORD
UNIVERSITY PRESS

OXFORD
UNIVERSITY PRESS

Great Clarendon Street, Oxford, OX2 6DP,
United Kingdom

Oxford University Press is a department of the University of Oxford.
It furthers the University's objective of excellence in research, scholarship,
and education by publishing worldwide. Oxford is a registered trade mark of
Oxford University Press in the UK and in certain other countries

First Edition published in 2021

Impression: 1

Published in the United States of America by Oxford University Press
198 Madison Avenue, New York, NY 10016, United States of America

British Library Cataloguing in Publication Data
Data available

Library of Congress Control Number: 2021932104

ISBN 978–0–19–883404–5

Printed and bound in the UK by
TJ Books Limited

Contents

Abbreviations

AA	Auswärtiges Amt (Foreign Ministry)
ADAP	*Akten zur deutschen auswärtigen Politik*
AO	Auslandsorganisation der NSDAP (NSDAP/AO)
APL	Archivum Panstwowe w Lublinie
BAB	Bundesarchiv, Abteilung Berlin
BAF	Bundesarchiv Militärarchiv, Abteilung Freiburg
BDC	Berlin Document Center
CDJC	Centre de documentaton Juive Contemporaine
DG	Durchgangsstraße
DNVP	Deutschnationale Volkspartei (German National People's Party)
EG	Einsatzgruppe
EK	Einsatzkommando
Gestapa	Geheimes Staatspolizeiamt
Gestapo	Geheime Staatspolizei
GG	*Geschichte und Gesellschaft*
HGS	*Holocaust and Genocide Studies*
HSSPF	Höherer SS- und Polizeiführer (Higher SS and Police Leader)
HZ	*Historische Zeitschrift*
IfZ	Institut für Zeitgeschichte, Munich
IMT	*International Military Tribunal*
KZ	Konzentrationslager (also Kl)
NSDAP	Nationalsozialistische Deutsche Arbeiterpartei (National Socialist German Workers' Party)
OA	Osobyi Archive, Moscow (special archive)
PAAA	Politisches Archiv des Auswärtigen Amtes, Berlin
RGBl.	*Reichsgesetzblatt*
RSHA	Reichssicherheitshauptamt (Reich Security Head Office)
SA	Sturmabteilung
SD	Sicherheitsdienst
SK	Sonderkommando

SS	Schutzstaffel
SSPF	SS- und Polizeiführer (SS and Police Leader)
StA	Staatsarchiv
StAnw	Staatsanwaltschaft
TNA	The National Archives, London
ToE	*The Trial of Adolf Eichmann*
TWC	*Trials of War Criminals Before the Nuremberg Military Tribunals*
VAA	Vertreter des Auswärtigen Amtes (Foreign Ministry representative)
VEJ	*Die Verfolgung und Ermordung der europäischen Juden durch das nationalsozialistische Deutschland 1933–1945*
VfZ	*Vierteljahrshefte für Zeitgeschichte*
VOGG	*Verordnungsblatt für das Generalgouvernement*
WVHA	SS-Wirtschafts- und Verwaltungshauptamt (SS Business and Administration Head Office)
YIVO	YIVO Institute for Jewish Research
ZStL	Zentrale Stelle Ludwigsburg

Prologue

A meeting followed by breakfast

On 20 January 1942 fifteen men met at a luxury villa on the Wannsee, a lake on Berlin's western outskirts. They had been invited by Reinhard Heydrich, head of the Reich Security Head Office (RSHA), and were almost all high-ranking representatives of the Nazi state, the Nazi Party, and the SS. They included four state secretaries,* two further senior officials of equivalent rank, and an undersecretary. The villa, now the House of the Wannsee Conference, occupies an exceptionally attractive position on the lake, its imposing approach road opening out onto a large circular drive in front of the house itself. The site still gives visitors today a clear impression of the original owner's ambition to create a grand, almost palatial, property in a striking setting. Its extensive, carefully designed park, its series of spacious and impressive rooms giving onto the park and the lake, its three terraces stretching the length of the garden side, and its conservatory complete with marble fountain were created to proclaim the success and refinement of its owner, a wealthy businessman, in the second decade of the twentieth century. The beautiful location contrasts starkly, however, with the purpose of that meeting in 1942. The villa had been taken over by the SS to provide accommodation for its guests, and the meeting was called to discuss the 'final solution to the Jewish question'. The surviving minutes of the meeting record that the aim was to discuss precisely who was to be targeted and how to deport a total of 11 million people, subject them to extremely harsh forced labour, and kill any who survived or were no longer capable of work by some other method. The meeting was to conclude with breakfast.

* Translators' note: the most senior civil servant in a ministry.

The fifteen men included ten university graduates, nine of them qualified lawyers, eight of whom had a doctorate.[1] The minutes suggest that they discussed these matters in a purposeful, business-like, and informed manner in comfortable surroundings and in a positively idyllic setting. While expressing a variety of different views on matters of detail, not a single one of them raised concerns about the project as a whole, namely the murder of 11 million Jews.

Today the minutes of the Wannsee Conference are seen as synonymous with the coldblooded, bureaucratically organized, and industrialized mass murder of the European Jews, as an almost unfathomable document capturing how the Nazi system's ideologically driven impulse to destroy was translated on the orders of the regime's highest authority into state action and mercilessly executed. In the words of the historian Wolfgang Scheffler at the opening of the House of the Wannsee Conference in 1992, 'No other document presents more clearly the overarching plan to exterminate the European Jews'.[2]

The immense importance of the minutes of the Wannsee Conference lies not only in the fact that they display the blatant cynicism and contempt for humanity of high-ranking representatives of the Nazi regime. The minutes are unique because, more than any other document, they demonstrate with total clarity the decision-making process that led to the murder of the European Jews. This decision-making process—in other words, the proposals, meetings, instructions, and arrangements in which Hitler, Himmler, Heydrich, and other leading Nazi political figures were involved—took place for the most part orally; to the extent that documents were generated at all, they were destroyed as far as possible or, if they survived, were written in the language of obfuscation. They did not survive, moreover, as a single corpus but were scattered far and wide. Those who initiated and organized this mass murder intended to cover their tracks systematically. Reconstructing the decisive sequences of events is thus a laborious task, for, although evidence is provided by many thousands of documents, some questions necessarily remain unanswered and thus there is considerable scope for interpretation.

The minutes of the Wannsee Conference are the exception, for here the master plan to murder the European Jews is discussed in fairly direct language and in a manner that demonstrates that the century's most appalling crime was not just the work of the SS, Security Police, and Security Service; rather, the Reich Chancellery, Ministry of Justice,

Interior Ministry, Foreign Ministry, civil occupation authorities, Four-Year Plan (the highest authority in the armaments sector), and Nazi Party were all actively involved and jointly responsible.

The fact that the minutes have not survived as part of a series of key documents reflecting the decision-making process from start to finish, but are more like a snapshot of an emerging decision being reached largely in secret, gives them their exceptional character. It also gives rise to problems and questions.

Contrary to first impressions, when the document is examined carefully it is clear that no 'decision' to murder the European Jews was made at the Wannsee Conference.[3] According to a widely held interpretation, however, various phrases in the minutes indicate that this was the crucial meeting at which the heads of the agencies responsible for carrying out the 'final solution' ordered by Hitler discussed how to organize it. There is mention of the fact that the deportations had begun the previous October after 'prior approval from the Führer'. On the basis of an authorization from Göring to prepare for the impending 'final solution', Heydrich, it is claimed, now aimed to create an overarching plan, which he outlined at the meeting.

On the other hand, at the time of the conference many hundreds of thousands of Jews had already been systematically murdered in the Soviet Union, in the district of Galicia in the General Government,★ in Serbia, and in the 'Warthegau', a district created from conquered Polish territory and incorporated into the Reich. It was here that the first extermination camp had been built. From 6 December 1941 onwards, in a building constructed for the purpose near the village of Chelmno, thousands of people had been herded into sealed containers mounted on specially adapted lorries and then murdered on the subsequent journeys by exhaust fumes fed into the containers. In the Lublin district of the General Government a permanent extermination camp had been under construction since November 1941 and in a number of other locations preparations were being made to murder large numbers of people using poison gas. If mass murder was to a great extent already underway, why was there any further need for 'preparations' for the 'impending final solution'? What in concrete terms would this 'impending final solution' involve? As the alternative interpretation argues, does the advanced state of the mass murder programme in

★ Translators' note: the non-annexed territory in occupied Poland.

January 1942 not suggest that the 'final solution' was far from the result of centralized decision-making and planning but rather had been set in motion in an uncontrolled and uncoordinated way on the initiative of lower-level authorities? These questions clearly indicate that the purpose and significance of the Wannsee Conference can be established only by careful interpretation and contextualization of the minutes—even if at first glance we are clearly confronted with an overall plan for mass murder formulated with striking precision.

A significant reason for the difficulties arising from analysis of the document, and the controversies among researchers provoked by it, lies in the different models that scholars have used as a basis for their interpretations. These have frequently been presented as being mutually exclusive. The following are the most important lines of interpretation. On the one hand, there is the view that the murder of the European Jews was the result of a long-term plan on the part of the Nazi leadership, Hitler in particular, and was set in motion and implemented stage by stage on the basis of centrally controlled decision-making. According to this 'intentionalist' interpretation, Hitler made a fundamental decision to murder the European Jews at a specific time, namely during the summer of 1941 or even earlier.[4]

Other historians take the view that Hitler made this fateful decision in the late summer,[5] the autumn,[6] or in December;[7] according to the various permutations of this theory, the expansion of the war caused Hitler to turn his idea of 'removing' the Jews one way or another into reality. This explanation is, in other words, an attempt to link Hitler's intentions with what we know about the structures and functions of the Nazi state. Thus, regardless of when Hitler and the Nazi leaders made their decision, the purpose of the Wannsee Conference, according to both of these approaches, must have been to implement it. The objection that mass killings were being carried out even before the conference and that, if the conference had been designed to implement the original order to murder the Jews, it was actually convened too late is countered by the claim that the conference's importance was more formal than practical: in this view, Heydrich's primary purpose in setting it up was to create a record of his 'appointment' as the man responsible for the 'final solution', even though the programme of killing he was directing had begun some time before.[8] Those who take the view that Hitler decided to implement the 'final solution' in December 1941, after declaring war on the United States, are faced with the question of why invitations to the Wannsee Conference were originally issued on 29 November. Their answer is to argue that at the outset the purpose of the conference, which was originally planned for 9 December, had been different.[9]

Opposing these views that emphasize a long-standing 'intention' and/or central decision-making is the idea that various agencies in the Nazi state, authorized only vaguely and in general terms by Hitler, had found themselves in competition to propose the most radical solution to the 'Jewish question'. By proceeding in an uncoordinated and precipitate manner (by intensifying the executions in the Soviet Union to the level of genocide and by beginning deportations from Germany before victory was won in the east), they had found themselves in a blind alley and could only escape through even more radical measures. According to proponents of this argument, frequently referred to as 'functionalists' or 'structuralists', the minutes of the Wannsee Conference are a precise reflection of the muddle that actually existed and the desire to remedy it by drastic action. These historians are primarily concerned to explain the mass murders as developing out of the structures of the Nazi state in a 'process of cumulative radicalization' (Hans Mommsen), in which the individual roles of Hitler and other leading functionaries were, by comparison, of secondary importance.[10]

This interpretative model has become more plausible in the last two decades as a result of a series of important studies of key geographical areas for the Holocaust in eastern Europe. These studies agree that the leading German functionaries in the occupied territories must be seen as enjoying considerable independence and freedom of action in initiating and implementing the murder of the Jews; in other words, they seem to confirm the 'functionalist' argument that the process of radicalization was driven by the regime's structures (in this case the occupation authorities on the 'periphery'). If one pursues the 'structuralist' interpretation, also taking into account the results of research into specific regions, the reason the conference was held would be primarily in order to place the programme of killing, already well underway under the auspices of the RSHA, once more under the control of a single organization.

In this book I present and develop an interpretation that uses the models outlined above but does not regard them as mutually exclusive, but rather as building blocks towards a more complex explanation.[11] I argue that the Holocaust was not set in motion by a single decision from the centre. It must instead be seen in the context of the National Socialists' anti-Jewish policies, which, while focused on the long term, were repeatedly subject to changes. The Holocaust was the result of a decision-making process in which Hitler, the key source of authority in the 'Third Reich', acting in close co-operation with other parts of the power structure, gradually developed what had previously been only a vague intention to destroy the Jews into a concrete programme to murder them. I aim to demonstrate how significant the meeting of these fifteen men on 20 January 1942 in fact was as part of this decision-making process.

The issue of the conference's historical significance leads us back to its geographical location: why did this important meeting take place specifically in this luxury villa on the Wannsee?

The location

The building where the Wannsee Conference was held is part of an exclusive villa development, originally called the 'Alsen Colony', which was being constructed on the shores of this Berlin lake from the 1870s onwards. It is close to Potsdam and from 1874 onwards had a direct rail link to the city. Successful Berlin bankers, entrepreneurs, businessmen, artists, publishers, and professors gradually settled there, including such notable people as the painters Max Liebermann and Anton von Werner, the surgeon Ernst Ferdinand Sauerbruch, the lawyer and politician Hugo Preuss, and the publisher Carl Langenscheidt.[12]

In 1914 Ernst Marlier, a businessman born in 1875 in Coburg and resident in Berlin since 1903, acquired a plot of land more than 30,000 square metres in size. The following year he engaged the architect Paul O. A. Baumgarten, who had also built a house nearby for the Liebermanns, to build him a villa with 1,500 square metres of living space. A larger-than-life character, Marlier had made his money from dubious medicines; he had a number of criminal convictions for acts of violence, clearly the result of his quick temper. In 1921 he sold the villa to the equally notable Friedrich Minoux, who was then forty-four. Formerly the business manager of the Essen Gas and Waterworks Company, in 1912 Minoux went to work for the entrepreneur Hugo Stinnes and, appointed chief executive in 1919, played a major role during the great inflation of 1921–3 in the Stinnes group's rapid expansion on the back of some highly speculative ventures. As a highly paid top manager with business interests on his own account, he could afford to buy the villa, which soon became a venue for large social gatherings and important business and political meetings. At the height of the inflation he put forward proposals for a currency reform and for a future economic policy based on massive state intervention. This political activity led to his parting company with Stinnes. In autumn 1923 his name repeatedly came up in connection with the 'directory' planned by right-wing conservative circles, which was to govern Germany through dictatorial powers. During the following years Minoux's business interests lay primarily in coal, while in the crisis years of 1930–3 he became known in the economic sphere for his idiosyncratic ideas on how to reduce unemployment.[13] Minoux was forced to sell the property after he was arrested in May 1940 on suspicion of long-term fraudulent dealings at the expense of the Berlin utility company Gasag, on whose supervisory board he sat. In August 1941 he was sentenced to five years' imprisonment and a hefty fine; he served his sentence up to the point where Brandenburg prison was liberated in April 1945 and died in October 1945 in Berlin.

The property was bought at the end of 1940 by the Nordhav Foundation, which was set up by Heydrich on 30 July 1939 'to establish and maintain recreation centres for members of the SS's Security Service and for their families'. In creating the foundation Heydrich had at first intended to buy the Katharinenhof estate on the island of Fehmarn, not far from his holiday home there, and in August 1939 he did so. 'Nordhav' had been the name of a farm that had had to make way for the estate in the eighteenth century and indicated the SS's interest in researching the island's Germanic–Nordic prehistory. From the start, however, Heydrich's probable aim had been to secure the Katharinenhof as a future holiday home for himself. The following year he also seems to have acquired the Wannsee villa via the foundation in order to use it in future as his official residence.

This suggests that the creation of the Nordhav Foundation was only a temporary measure.[14] However, we read in the gazette (*Befehlsblatt*) issued by Heydrich as Head of the Security Police and the Security Service (SD) for 18 October 1941 that the villa's accommodation was 'at the disposal of regional heads of Security Police and SD offices and their representatives when they wish to spend the night in Berlin'. Other Security Police and SD leaders were also allowed to stay. Bed and breakfast cost 5 Reich marks per night.[15] Four weeks later, the gazette stated that guests had the use of a number of 'public areas' such as a music room, a billiard room, a spacious hall, and also a conservatory and terrace overlooking the lake.[16]

The building was indeed used for this purpose. British Secret Service files concerning the situation in Germany and accessible today in the British National Archives contain a report from a high-ranking member of the Swedish police who confidentially informed the British in Stockholm in the middle of April 1942 that he had just been in Berlin on official business and while there had renewed contact with old acquaintances in the German police. The latter had assured him of their indignation at the brutal methods used by the Gestapo towards the Jews. In addition, he had had excellent accommodation, namely in an SS residence on the Wannsee. Neither the Swedish policeman nor his British contacts could have suspected that the murder of millions of European Jews had been discussed in this very place a few months earlier.[17]

As may be inferred from the information sheet from Office VI of the RSHA of 7 August 1942, however, the residence had at the same time been 'in great demand for official meetings and special occasions', in the course of which excessive amounts of alcohol had been consumed. Thus the residence's 'original purpose of providing the Security Police with a prestigious venue had not been respected'.[18]

It is certainly true that in the increasing greyness of day-to-day life in wartime Berlin the luxurious impression made by the building and its attractive situation were calculated to impart a special lustre to the meeting held on 20 January 1942 and give the participants a sense of occasion. The grandeur of the surroundings must surely have rather overawed Heydrich's guests and thus contributed to the conference passing off almost without a hitch.

The initial invitation

Heydrich's invitation of 29 November 1941 was sent to thirteen recipients; two copies have survived, namely those addressed to the undersecretary at the Foreign Office, Martin Luther, and to the head of the SS Race and Settlement Head Office, SS Gruppenführer Otto Hofmann. In addition to Luther and Hofmann, those invited were:

Governor General Hans Frank; Alfred Meyer, 'permanent representative' of the Minister for the East, Alfred Rosenberg; Georg Leibbrandt, the head of Main Section I (Politics) of the same ministry; the state secretaries Wilhelm Stuckart (Interior Ministry), Erich Neumann (Four-Year Plan), Franz Schlegelberger (Ministry of Justice), and Leopold Gutterer (Propaganda Ministry); Deputy Secretary Friedrich Kritzinger (Reich Chancellery); Gerhard Klopfer, who was responsible for state matters in the Party Chancellery and was addressed using his SS rank of Oberführer; the Higher SS and Police Leader (HSSPF) in the General Government, Friedrich-Wilhelm Krüger; and SS Gruppenführer Ulrich Greifelt, who was chief of the SS Head Office that Himmler had set up to carry out his responsibilities for 'consolidating the German ethnic nation'.[19]

In his invitation Heydrich referred to a task that Hermann Göring had delegated to him on 31 July 1941, namely 'to cooperate with the central agencies potentially involved to make all necessary organizational, practical, and material preparations for a total solution to the Jewish question in Europe and to provide him as soon as possible with a comprehensive plan'; he attached a photocopy of this assignment to the invitation. In view of the 'extraordinary importance' of this matter, Heydrich continued, and 'in the interests of reaching a uniform view on the part of the central authorities that will be involved in the additional tasks arising from this final solution', he was proposing a meeting, in particular because 'the evacuation of Jews to the east in continuous transports from Reich territory, including the Protectorate of Bohemia and Moravia', had already begun on 15 October 1941. This meeting was planned for 9 December at 12 noon in the offices of the International Criminal Police Commission (Interpol), which Heydrich had chaired since August 1940, at number 16, Am Kleinen Wannsee.[20] A few days later Heydrich's office amended the invitation: the meeting would take place at 56–58, Am Grossen Wannsee, the address of the residence.[21]

Heydrich's invitation reveals two aspects. On the one hand, his focus was the 'total solution to the Jewish question in Europe' and to fulfil Göring's wishes he was aiming to prepare for it and agree it with the other central authorities. He would of course be in charge. On the other hand, there was clearly a need to clarify how the mass deportations from Reich territory that had been proceeding since mid-October could be integrated into the 'comprehensive plan', which was

only in the process of emerging. The invitation thus contains two distinct levels: a European 'total solution', which lies in the future, and the
measures that had already been initiated to achieve this within the
so-called Greater German Reich.

Only two days later, on 1 December, the original list of invitees was
amended. For on 28 November Heydrich had had a meeting with
Krüger, the HSSPF in the General Government, at which they agreed
to act together to resist Frank's ambitions to 'assume complete control
himself of the measures to deal with the Jewish problem' in the General
Government.[22] After setting this matter straight, Heydrich could leave
Krüger to take appropriate measures in Cracow to rein Frank in and
thus avoid having to conduct the dispute that was looming with Frank
about the scope of his powers at a ministerial meeting in Berlin. Now
the latter's state secretary, Josef Bühler, was invited instead of Frank
himself, Frank being in any case too high-ranking for a 'meeting of
state secretaries'.[23] Krüger received a new invitation, worded in such a
way as to suggest that his attendance in person was not expected.[24]

Heydrich's late November invitation came at a time when the Nazi
regime's 'Jewish policy' had reached a critical stage. The original plan
had been to deport the European Jews to the newly occupied eastern
territories after the rapid defeat of the Soviet Union, but the military
situation made this a distant prospect. At the same time, the shootings
of Jewish civilians in the Soviet Union, and in Serbia too, had reached
such proportions that those responsible saw an opportunity to accom-
plish the 'final solution to the Jewish question' in these territories even
before the end of the war. In addition, the deportations that had begun
in the autumn from the German Reich to the ghettos of eastern
Europe created new problems, and some of those in authority on the
spot had begun to propose mass murder as a solution. There was therefore a distinct need to clarify how 'Jewish policy' should be taken
forward.

I

The background to the conference
The 'removal of the Jews', 1933–41

Right from the start, the 'removal of the Jews' from Germany had been one of Hitler's and the Nazi movement's central aims. On assuming power in 1933 the National Socialists found they had an opportunity to turn this aim, hitherto formulated only in vague terms, into reality. Indeed one of the most dynamic areas of Nazi policy in the 1930s consisted in discrimination against the Jews, forcing them out of public life, relentlessly harassing and intimidating them, exploiting them economically, and ultimately expelling them from Germany. The most important stages in this process were the boycott of Jewish businesses in April 1933, the Nuremberg Laws of September 1935, and the pogrom of November 1938.[25]

This 'Jewish policy' was driven forward on the one hand by the state authorities—led by the Ministry of the Interior, its most important agencies were the Gestapo and the police—and on the other by the Party organization, considerably supported by the Sturmabteilung (SA), which from 1934 onwards had largely been deprived of other functions. Since 1937, however, the Security Service (Sicherheitsdienst (SD)), the Party's intelligence service led by Reinhard Heydrich, had intervened increasingly in the articulation of 'Jewish policy'. The self-styled 'intellectuals' of the Security Service were concerned to develop a comprehensive plan for Jewish 'emigration' (meaning expulsion) that would counteract the prevailing trend for only wealthy Jews to succeed in fleeing Germany, leaving behind those who had next to no property or wealth (or who had lost what remained of them as a result of the Nazis' policy of plunder) as an impoverished underclass.[26]

In 1938, after the annexation of Austria, the Security Service managed to intervene effectively in 'Jewish policy' for the first time. Adolf

Eichmann, who in April had taken up a post as a divisional head in the newly established SD regional headquarters in Vienna, succeeded in persuading Josef Bürckel, the Reich commissar responsible for implementing the Anschluss, to create a 'Central Office for Jewish Emigration' in Vienna in August 1938, which officially reported to the SD.[27] This was the first time that the SD had managed to exercise executive powers itself on behalf of a state authority (the Reich commissar). At the Central Office Eichmann and his 'Jewish experts' immediately developed a kind of fast-track procedure to speed up the emigration of the Vienna Jews, financed by a special fund created by confiscating Jews' residual assets.

The Vienna office became a model for the 'Reich Office for Jewish Emigration', which Göring set up on 24 January 1939 in line with the proposals Heydrich had put forward in the immediate aftermath of the November pogrom.[28] Headed by Heydrich, its chief executive was Heinrich Müller, the head of the Gestapo,[29] but the Foreign Ministry and the Economic, Finance, and Interior Ministries were also represented there.[30] Göring was involved because as Hitler's Plenipotentiary for the Four-Year Plan he was the 'strong man' as far as the Third Reich's economic policy was concerned, and after the November pogrom he had been given the job of carrying out the final exclusion of the Jews from the German economy and of taking charge thereafter of 'Jewish policy'.[31]

This was not, in fact, the first task connected with 'Jewish policy' that Göring had delegated to Heydrich. Back in July 1936, at the height of a serious Reich foreign exchange crisis, he had appointed Heydrich as head of a 'Foreign Exchange Investigation Office' so that in conjunction with the Foreign Exchange Control Centres and the Tax Fraud Office it could plunder the assets of Jews 'suspected of having emigrated'.[32] Thus when Heydrich alluded in his invitation to the Wannsee Conference of 29 November 1941 to the authorization Göring had given him on 31 July 1941, this 'appointment' already had an extensive prehistory.

'Territorial solutions'

By the outbreak of the Second World War the Nazi regime had succeeded in driving about 250,000 Jews out of Germany.[33] The start of the war, however, initiated a completely new and more radical phase in 'Jewish policy'. Although pressure to 'emigrate' continued, the conditions of war made it impossible to 'remove' in this way the 190,000 Jews still living in the Altreich ('Old Reich'),[*] numbers augmented by the Jews living in the territories annexed in 1938/9.[34] More particularly, after victory over Poland, 1.7 million Polish Jews were now inside the expanded German territory—which, given the anti-Semitism fundamental to Nazi thinking, was a problem in need of a 'solution'. In addition to the severe conditions imposed on Polish Jews (in particular visible identification, forced labour, and confiscation of their property)[35] and further ramping up of measures against German Jews (which included a general curfew after 8 pm and an increase in forced labour),[36] a new measure was being considered: the organized deportation of all Jews under German control to a 'reservation' on the periphery of German-controlled territory.

Briefly, this so-called territorial solution to the 'Jewish question' developed as follows: first of all, the Nazi regime attempted in autumn 1939 to set up a 'Jewish reservation' in the Lublin district in the east of the General Government for all Jews under its jurisdiction.[37] In October the so-called Nisko action began, an initiative to deport more than 70,000 Jews from Upper Silesia and thousands more from Mährisch-Ostrau in the Protectorate as well as from Vienna to this area via a provisional transit camp near Nisko on the San, immediately on the border of the Lublin district.[38] According to comments made at the time by Eichmann, who was responsible for the Nisko action, the latter was a pilot project for the deportation of all Jews under German control to this area and Hitler had approved it. As no preparations at all had been made to accommodate large numbers of people, it must be assumed that Eichmann and his colleagues intended either to force those deported via the Nisko camp to cross the line of demarcation into the Polish territories occupied by the Soviet Union, or simply to abandon them, which would have resulted in the majority perishing in appalling conditions during the following winter.

In fact, the Nisko action had to be discontinued after only a few days, by which time a total of 4,700 people had been deported, because it clashed logistically with the mass resettlement that had begun simultaneously of ethnic Germans from the Baltic region to the annexed

[*] Translators' note: Germany as defined by its 1937 borders.

Polish territories. The Germans then had the idea of forcing the Jews in their territory across the demarcation line with the Soviet Union; at the end of 1939 or beginning of 1940 a request to that effect for Soviet government consent was issued to the Soviet Foreign Ministry by the Berlin and Vienna Emigration Offices, which at this point were headed by Eichmann and Franz Josef Huber (the head of the Security Police and SD in Vienna). The Soviets' response was, however, negative.[39]

The second variation on the idea of a 'territorial solution' on Nazi-controlled soil was developed by the Reich Security Head Office (RSHA) and Foreign Ministry after the German victory over France in summer 1940: the so-called Madagascar Plan.[40] All Jews within the German sphere of influence (the estimate was between 4 and 6.5 million) were to be shipped to the island, then under French colonial rule, and be subject to a German police regime. According to Franz Rademacher, the 'desk officer for Jewish affairs' in the Foreign Ministry, this plan was linked to the idea that the Jews would act as a kind of 'bargaining chip to guarantee the Germans the future good behaviour of members of their race in America'. 'Appropriate punitive measures would be taken against them if provoked by the hostile actions of Jews in the United States towards Germany'.[41] Such threatening scenarios and more particularly the fact that in Madagascar there were no foundations on which millions of European settlers could build a life (and the new masters were not planning to create them) reveal that the Madagascar alternative was not a plan to establish a place where the European Jews, though isolated, might build a lasting home. On the contrary, what was planned for this territory amounted to the physical annihilation of the deported European Jews in the medium to long term by a combination of desperate living conditions, suppression of the birth rate, and 'punitive measures'.

When, in the summer of 1940, Madagascar had to be abandoned as the envisaged destination—the island remained inaccessible because Britain was continuing the war against Germany—Heydrich, as head of the RSHA and hence the key figure at this point in the persecution of the Jews, worked out a third possible 'territorial solution'. In January 1941 he presented Hitler with a detailed plan for a Europe-wide 'final solution' for the post-war period. Heydrich had received Hitler's instruction to do this via Himmler and Göring, and the powers and responsibilities of both these leading Nazi figures with regard to 'Jewish policy' had been taken into account. Although Heydrich's plan has not survived, its contents can be deduced from two surviving documents.[42] He proposed settling the European Jews as a body in a 'territory yet to be determined'. In using this form of words Heydrich was presumably masking his intention to deport the Jews in the medium term to the Soviet Union, which the Nazi regime was secretly preparing to conquer at the time. At first, the preparatory work in the RSHA focused on the General Government as the target destination for this new deportation project, though from the outset it was probably only an interim solution. In January 1941, at any rate, Heydrich announced his intention to deport more than 800,000 people by the end of the year to the General Government, primarily Poles and Jews from the territories incorporated into the Reich but also 60,000 Viennese Jews.[43] These deportations did in fact begin in February 1941, but they had to be discontinued after only a few weeks in mid-March 1941 as a result of preparations for the Wehrmacht's deployment in the east.[44]

Heydrich then concentrated deportation plans on the territory that from the start had been central to his thinking, namely the Soviet Union. This became clear when at the end of March 1941 he presented Göring with a draft authorization.[45] Göring, however, told him he needed to take account of Rosenberg's responsibilities, the latter having been chosen to be head of a department with oversight over the occupied eastern territories (subsequently the Ministry for the East).[46] So Heydrich revised his plan and submitted it once again to Göring, who signed it on 31 July. He duly tasked Heydrich with 'making all necessary organizational, practical, and material preparations for a total solution to the Jewish question in the German sphere of influence in Europe', with involving other 'central authorities' if necessary (an allusion to Göring requiring Heydrich to take account of Rosenberg), and then finally with presenting him with a 'comprehensive plan' of the appropriate 'preliminary measures'. This authorization is therefore the one Heydrich was to allude to six months later at the Wannsee Conference.[47]

Thus the preconditions had been created for a mass deportation of European Jews after victory over the Soviet Union. Early in 1941, Himmler had asked Viktor Brack, the organizer of the 'euthanasia' programme, to prepare a plan for the mass sterilization of Jews. Significantly, however, he did not in fact pursue this project further, even though detailed plans were sent to him in March 1941.[48] In June 1941, a few days before the attack on the Soviet Union, Frank, the Governor

General, received an assurance from Hitler that in the foreseeable future the Jews would be 'removed' from the General Government. In mid-July Frank gave instructions that no new ghettos were to be created, as the General Government would soon be no more than 'a kind of transit camp'.[49]

The deportations 'to the east' were in fact to begin in autumn 1941 but without the original precondition, namely victory over the Soviet Union. This 'anticipation' of the deportation plan has to be seen against the background of the escalation of 'Jewish policy', which, after the German invasion of Soviet territory, soon expanded into genocide.

Mass shootings and genocide in the Soviet Union in summer 1941

From the outset, the war against the Soviet Union,[50] which began on 22 June 1941, was conceived as a racially motivated war of conquest and annihilation. The mass of the Soviet population, which in Nazi terms consisted of 'racially inferior' Slavs or members of a 'crossbred race' with Asiatic characteristics, was to be enslaved, expelled, or starved to death in their millions.[51] By such methods 'living space' was to be created for German settlers and for people from 'Teutonic' countries such as the Netherlands and Scandinavia.[52]

The war was, however, particularly aimed at the Jewish population; what was alleged to be 'Jewish bolshevism' was to be deprived by violence of its demographic base. As the Germans prepared for war, one of their main aims from the outset was to kill systematically the members of an only vaguely defined Jewish-communist elite.

During the preparations for war at the beginning of March, Hitler issued an instruction to 'remove' the 'Jewish-bolshevist intelligentsia' and warned the generals all through March that the 'intelligentsia established by Stalin' had to be 'destroyed' for this was a 'struggle between two ideologies'. Consequently, the troops were required not only to 'wipe out' Soviet commissars as 'originators of barbaric Asiatic fighting methods' but also to take 'ruthless and vigorous action against bolshevist agitators, francs-tireurs, saboteurs, Jews, and to eliminate root and branch every trace of active or passive resistance'.[53] Criminal acts perpetrated by German soldiers on the Soviet civilian population were as a matter of principle no longer to be punished through courts-martial.

Above all, however, the Reichsführer SS, Himmler, was given 'special tasks on behalf of the Führer' in the army's theatre of operations that resulted from 'the decisive struggle that must finally take place between two opposing political systems'; in carrying out these assignments, the Reichsführer SS would be acting 'independently and on his own authority' but always in close co-operation with the Wehrmacht. The four Security Police and Security Service task forces ('Einsatzgruppen') and also twenty-three battalions of the Order Police and three SS Death's Head brigades (as Himmler's reserve) were earmarked for these special duties.[54]

In the run-up to the war the leaders of the Einsatzgruppen were given orders for their 'deployment' that amounted to shooting all Jews who could be regarded as part of the Soviet system or who represented 'radical elements'.[55] There is evidence that by the end of June or in July, almost all Einsatzkommandos or special units (Sonderkommandos) and a number of battalions had conducted mass shootings of Jewish men of military age; depending on the unit or battalion, the numbers were in the hundreds or even thousands.[56]

During July and the first half of August, the Kommandos and police units began killing Jewish men of military age indiscriminately and systematically. At the same time Himmler ordered the mass murder of women and children too: he assigned two of the three SS Death's Head brigades, which were directly subordinate to him, to the Higher SS and Police Leaders for Central Russia and Southern Russia, instructing them to carry out massacres involving several thousand Jewish civilians—men, women, and children. These mass murders spurred on the leaders of the Einsatzkommandos and police battalions during the following months to begin murdering the Soviet civilian population across the board. The number of Jewish civilians killed by the end of 1941 was most probably at least 500,000.[57]

Himmler, who made sure that he had permanent backing from Hitler for his actions,[58] was using this unprecedented radicalization of the persecution of the Jews in the east to regain political ground that he had lost. Up to this point he had left Jewish persecution to a great extent to Heydrich. Charged by Hitler in October 1939 with 'Germanizing' extensive conquered territories, he had regarded his main task in this 'new racial order' as being the forcible expulsion of the Poles.[59] In summer 1941, however, this changed dramatically. When on 16 July Hitler established the various spheres of responsibility for

the occupied eastern territories, Himmler was disappointed; he had
been put in charge only of 'police security' and not, as he had hoped,
'police and political security', in other words of laying the foundation
for the 'living space' programme.[60] After this humiliating setback, however, Himmler made use of his powers as Reich Commissar for the
Consolidation of the German Ethnic Nation responsible for settlement policy and applied these, in spite of resistance from other authorities, to the new eastern territories. One of these powers was the
'elimination of the damaging influence... of alien elements in the
population'.[61] Himmler immediately began to extend the extermination of Jewish men that was already taking place to the whole of the
Jewish population, thus bringing together his powers in the areas of
'police' and 'settlement'. In the course of this gradual extension of mass
shootings to the point of genocide, Himmler changed the locus of the
operation from the Security Police, which with its Einsatzgruppen had
originally been responsible primarily for the 'elimination' of 'Jewish
bolshevists', to the Higher SS and Police Leaders, who as his regional
'plenipotentiaries' could use all branches of the SS and Police organization to carry out this comprehensive genocide. In so doing Himmler
had activated a second chain of command in addition to the one that
had established itself in the previous years and led from Hitler via
Göring to Heydrich. With authorization from Hitler, Himmler could
now intervene decisively in 'Jewish policy' via the Higher SS and
Police Leaders.[62]

Deportations

During the first months of the 'eastern campaign', Hitler and the
RSHA under Heydrich were still intending to deport the European
Jews to the conquered eastern territories after their victory in the war.
In mid-August 1941 Goebbels pressed forward with the plan, already
discussed in 1938, of making Jews wear some kind of identifying mark.
At an inter-ministerial meeting at his ministry to discuss this plan, the
RSHA representative Adolf Eichmann also brought up the matter of
the deportation of German Jews: according to Eichmann, the RSHA
assumed that Hitler was still opposed to 'evacuating' the German Jews
during the war; Heydrich, however, intended to try to persuade Hitler
of the need to conduct a 'partial evacuation of the larger cities'.[63]

Three days later, on 18 August 1941, Goebbels discussed the questions of an identifying mark and deportation with Hitler. Hitler immediately agreed to the first point and also gave Goebbels permission to deport the Berlin Jews 'to the east as quickly as possible, as soon as the opportunity of transporting them presents itself'. There they should 'be subjected to harsher conditions'. This would happen 'immediately after the eastern campaign' and Berlin would become a 'city free of Jews'.[64] Hitler also declared to Goebbels that his 'prophecy' about the 'annihilation of the Jews' was coming true 'in these weeks and months with an almost uncanny certainty. In the east the Jews must pay the price; in Germany they have already paid in part and will have to pay more in future'. He was referring here to his speech to the Reichstag on 30 January 1939, when, assuming the mantle of 'prophet', he had declared that if 'the Jews controlling international finance inside and outside Europe should succeed in plunging the nations once again into a world war', then the consequence would be 'the annihilation of the Jewish race in Europe'.[65]

This was a very clear warning to the United States not to intervene in the event of a European war; in other words, not to expand the future war into a 'world war'. With the increasing probability in summer 1941 that the United States would enter the war, Hitler's 'prophecy' was becoming more and more of a reality.

Four weeks after this meeting, however, Hitler had changed his mind about when to begin the deportations. He was now unwilling to wait for the war to end but rather preferred to have the Jews immediately deported 'to the east'. At the beginning of September Himmler had already had exploratory talks. First of all, he had approached the Higher SS and Police Leader (HSSPF) for the General Government, Friedrich-Wilhelm Krüger, and then his colleague in the Warthegau, Wilhelm Koppe, on the subject of the deportation of German Jews. Whereas Krüger's response was negative, Koppe seemed to be prepared to receive 60,000 Jews in the Lodz ghetto.[66]

While Himmler's soundings were still in progress, an event occurred that presented the German leadership with the perfect excuse to set the deportations in motion. On 28 August the Soviet government had decided to resettle the Volga Germans in Siberia,[67] and on 8 September this became known to the German leadership.[68]

Rosenberg, who assumed that the deportation of the Volga Germans was tantamount to an intention on the Soviet leadership's part to murder them, presented Hitler with a 'very hard-hitting statement', which, according to Rosenberg, Hitler made even more hard-hitting. In addition, on 11 September he produced a proposal 'to inform Russia, England, and the United States by radio that if this mass murder were to go ahead Germany would make the Jews of Central Europe pay the price'.[69] He gave this proposal to Hitler for his authorization and the latter decided to discuss it with the Foreign Minister, Joachim von Ribbentrop.[70]

A series of meetings during the following days suggests that things were beginning to move: on 16 September Hitler met Otto Abetz, the German ambassador in Paris, for lunch with Himmler. We know that at this meeting Abetz put forward proposals for the deportation of French Jews to the Soviet Union and that Himmler's response was positive.[71] The same day Himmler, in his capacity as Reich Commissar for the Consolidation of the German Ethnic Nation, discussed the 'Jewish question' and 'eastern settlement' with Greifelt, his most important departmental colleague, and the next day Hitler and Himmler finally met with Ribbentrop to discuss Rosenberg's proposal.[72]

On 18 September it became clear that Hitler had made his decision, for the same day Himmler informed the Gauleiter of the Warthegau, Arthur Greiser, in writing that Hitler wished 'the Altreich and the Protectorate to be cleared and made free of Jews as soon as possible from the west to the east'. He, Himmler, therefore intended 'as a first stage' to transport the Jews from the Reich, including the Protectorate, 'to the eastern territories that became part of the Reich two years ago, and then to deport them further east next spring'. As a first step he was minded, he said, to transport 'about 60,000 Jews from the Altreich and the Protectorate for the winter' to the Lodz ghetto.[73]

Two days later, on 20 September, Werner Koeppen, Rosenberg's liaison officer in the Führer headquarters, was told that, with regard to 'reprisals' against the German Jews as proposed by Rosenberg on 13/14 September in response to Soviet measures against the Volga Germans, Hitler 'was holding back pending America's possible entry into the war'.[74] This meant that within a few days the reason for threatening to deport German Jews had shifted: the target was no longer the Soviet Union (where the enforced resettlement of the Volga Germans had meanwhile been carried out) but the United States.

Germany's relationship with the United States had gone downhill rapidly during the course of the summer. Most recently, President

Franklin D. Roosevelt had issued the 'Shoot on Sight Order' on 11 September; henceforth the US navy was to attack any warship of the Axis Powers found in waters essential to American defence. At this point Hitler was assuming that it was virtually inevitable that the United States would enter the war.[75] The anti-Semitic propaganda campaign that Goebbels launched immediately after his meeting with Hitler on 18 August to prepare the population to accept the introduction of the yellow star for Jews also had a strong anti-American element; given that for months there had also been virulent propaganda against 'Jewish bolshevism', Hitler and Goebbels were already waging a comprehensive propaganda 'war against the Jews'.[76]

In addition to his intention to use the Jews as hostages in the event of the United States's entry into the war, Hitler's decision to proceed with deportations before defeating the Soviet Union can be explained by four motivations:

1. The escalation of mass shootings of Jewish civilians in the Soviet Union, which prompted a general shift towards a radicalization of 'Jewish policy'.

2. The military situation, which was developing in September in such a way as to make Hitler assume that he could defeat the Soviet Union to all intents and purposes before the year was out and thus resume the planned deportations to the Russian interior after a few months.[77]

3. The deportations of Jews from the big cities of the Reich, which were taking place in full view of the public and were accompanied by an intense anti-Jewish propaganda campaign,[78] were to be used to create a connection in people's minds between 'the Jews' and British air raids. As the German air-raid defences were weakened through the deployment of the Luftwaffe on the eastern front, British bombing was becoming heavier and was naturally worrying people. 'The Jews' were now pilloried as the 'string-pullers' behind the bombing war and their deportation presented as a fitting response (though no precise details about the real purpose of the deportations were made known), while the German population profited from this retaliation because through it Jewish homes were 'freed up' more quickly[79] and household goods owned by Jews were auctioned off.[80] During these weeks, other Gauleiters, in addition to Goebbels, pressed Hitler to step up the deportation of Jews from their districts.[81]

4. Three months after the start of the war against the Soviet Union, resistance movements, led in particular by communists, began to form across Europe and to oppose the German occupation regime. The latter as a rule responded by shooting hostages: in July the commander-in-chief in Serbia, for example, had begun shooting large numbers of hostages;[82] in France the first executions as 'reprisals' for attacks by the resistance took place on 6 September, in Belgium on 15 and 26 September, and in Norway in mid-September also.[83] Immediately on taking office, Heydrich, who had been Deputy Reich Protector in Prague since the end of September, imposed a state of emergency and set up drumhead courts-martial. During the state of emergency between 27 September and 29 November, 404 men and women were shot.[84] In Greece also the resistance movement carried out a series of assassinations in late August and September.[85] On 16 September the military high command issued an order concerning the 'communist insurgence movement in the occupied territories', issuing the general rule that fifty to a hundred communists should be executed for one German soldier killed.[86] As the Nazi leadership assumed that communism and Jewishness were more or less identical, they regarded it as logical in a war against 'Jewish bolshevism' that was becoming increasingly brutal to step up measures against Jewish minorities outside eastern Europe as well; in other words, against the spectre of a Europe-wide Jewish-communist resistance movement. In autumn 1941 German occupation authorities began to focus reprisals for attacks carried out by the resistance movement on the Jewish minority: in Serbia, for example, from October 1941 onwards the Wehrmacht systematically shot Jewish men as 'retribution' for attacks, while in France the military authorities began in November to imprison Jews and communists first and foremost instead of shooting hostages.

Even though various motives lay behind Hitler's decision to begin deportations, they have one thing in common: in autumn 1941 the Nazi leadership began to conduct the war on every level as a war 'against the Jews'. Above all, the Nazi leadership appeared determined not to be deterred by the course of the war from its original intention, pursued from autumn 1939 onwards, of deporting the Jews to a remote area and leaving them there to their fate.

During the weeks following his basic decision to begin the deportations, Hitler underlined his determination to remove the Jews finally and completely from Central Europe. On 23 September he told Goebbels that Berlin, Vienna, and Prague would be made 'free of Jews' first. It therefore seemed that the plan of 'partial evacuations' pursued by Goebbels and Heydrich in August would soon become a reality, as Heydrich had assured him immediately before his meeting with Hitler: as soon as the military situation permitted, he told Goebbels, the Berlin Jews would 'all be transported [to the] camps set up by the bolshevists'.[87] On 6 October 1941 Hitler announced to his lunch guests that all Jews had to be 'removed' from the Protectorate, though not to the General Government but rather 'directly further east', though he conceded that as yet there was no transport available for this. Along with the 'Protectorate Jews', the Jews from Vienna and Berlin were to 'disappear' as well.[88] As Heydrich explained at a meeting in Prague on 10 October, Hitler wished the Jews as far as possible to be 'removed from Reich territory' by the end of the year.[89]

The deportations did in fact begin on 15 October. The original plan to deport 60,000 Jews to Lodz had meanwhile been modified. After resistance on the part of the Lodz authorities to these mass arrivals on the grounds that they contravened the designation of Lodz as a 'work ghetto',[90] the Reich governor Greiser and Himmler reached a compromise: the number of people to be deported to Lodz was reduced to 25,000 and in return Greiser clearly obtained agreement for 100,000 Polish Jews to be murdered.[91] In July the Reich governor's office had already considered 'finishing off' the Jews 'no longer fit for work' by means of 'some fast-acting substance', for they could in any case no longer be fed during the coming winter.[92] In addition to Lodz, Riga and Minsk were earmarked to receive 25,000 deportees each.[93] Between 15 October and 5 November some 10,000 Jews from the Altreich and 5,000 each from Prague and Vienna, along with 5,000 Sinti and Roma from Burgenland, were in fact transported to Lodz.[94] A further 8,000 Jews from the Reich were transported to Minsk, where on 7 November 12,000 inhabitants of the ghetto there were murdered in order to vacate accommodation for Jews arriving from the Reich. At the end of November the transports to Minsk had to be suspended because of the military situation.[95] By the beginning of February 1942, around 25,000 Jews had finally been deported to the Riga area.[96]

During November 1941, Heydrich told Goebbels in confidence at a meeting that the RSHA was already planning a third wave of deportations for the following spring.[97] The State Archive in Shitomir in the

Ukraine contains a document that sets out the concrete preparations for further deportations to German-occupied territory in the Soviet Union: on 12 January 1942, in other words only a few days before the Wannsee Conference, the Higher SS and Police Leader for the Ukraine instructed the General Commissars in Brest, Shitomir, Nikolajev, Dnjepropetrovsk, and Kiev to begin at once setting up ghettos to 'accommodate Jews from the Altreich in the course of 1942'.[98]

The deportations in the coming spring were not, however, to include only Jews from the 'Greater German Reich' but were also to be extended to the occupied countries. Himmler had already agreed this on 16 September with the German ambassador in Paris, Abetz, with regard to the French Jews.[99] In a letter of 6 November to the Quartermaster General, Heydrich gave the reason for his agreement to a series of attacks by French anti-Semites on Paris synagogues (they were carried out on the night of 2/3 November) as being that 'Jewry was being assigned prime responsibility by the highest authority as the cause of conflagration in Europe and it must finally be banished from Europe'.[100] On 4 October Heydrich had spoken even more explicitly of the 'plan to remove and resettle all Jews from the territories we occupy'.[101]

Significantly, the ban on emigration that the RSHA issued on 23 October applied to the whole territory under German control. It was provoked by a proposal hatched by the Foreign Ministry to deport the Spanish Jews currently in France to Spanish Morocco. From the point of view of the RSHA, however, this would have threatened the 'measures to be taken after the end of the war to solve the Jewish question fundamentally', as they would have been too far 'beyond immediate reach'.[102]

There is evidence that during autumn 1941 the Germans were intending to carry out deportations and that concrete preparations were being made in a number of countries. From December onwards, Jews (and communists) in France were imprisoned en masse and earmarked for deportations 'to the east', which after being postponed at first because of transport problems were in fact to begin in March 1942.[103] Franz Rademacher, the head of the Jewish desk at the Foreign Ministry, was also assuming at the end of October that those Serbian Jews who survived the shootings carried out by the Wehrmacht would be 'deported by boat to the reception camps in the east', as soon as 'the technical means' existed 'as part of the overall solution to the Jewish question'.[104] On 20 October 1941 Himmler had a meeting, also attended by Ribbentrop, in the Führer headquarters with the Slovakian

President Joseph Tiso, the latter's Prime Minister and Foreign Minister Vojtech Tuka, and the Minister of the Interior Alexander Mach, and offered to deport the Slovakian Jews to a specially designated area in the General Government.[105]

At the beginning of November 1941, at a meeting with Hitler (according to notes made by Hitler's Army adjutant Engel), Himmler proposed deporting not only the Jews from Riga, Reval (Tallinn), and Minsk, but also those from Saloniki, a place that posed a particular danger, given that a series of assassinations had recently taken place there. In response Hitler demanded that the 'Jewish element be removed from S.' and gave Himmler the special powers he needed for this. In fact, however, deportations of Jews from Saloniki were not to take place until 1943.[106] These examples show that during autumn 1941, preparations for the imminent deportation of the Jews began throughout the German sphere of control. It was primarily Himmler, who had already played and continued to play a decisive role in the expansion of mass executions in the Soviet Union, who was pressing ahead with this development, on Hitler's instructions and with his support. A further important fact is that the deportations began during autumn 1941, before Heydrich had worked out the great plan to deport all European Jews that he had been due to present to Göring since the end of July 1941.

Regional 'final solutions'

Closely coordinated with the timing and location of the deportations, various technologies for killing people en masse by gassing were developed and/or procured in late summer and autumn 1941. Three strands of development can be identified.

First, in the Warthegau the 'Sonderkommando Lange' under the control of HSSPF Koppe had been using a gas van to murder the mentally ill since late 1939/early 1940. In 1941 the criminal police developed a new model of gas van that was designed in the first instance for the occupied Soviet territories. This was prompted by a visit Himmler made to Minsk on 15 August 1941, where he ordered that new methods of killing be found that were less harrowing for the perpetrators than mass shootings.[107] After conducting gruesome experiments with explosives and carbon monoxide fed into sealed chambers on patients in Soviet institutions for the mentally and physically disabled,[108] the Criminal Police Institute developed a gas van in which the exhaust fumes from the vehicle itself, rather than carbon monoxide in bottles, were fed into the sealed box.[109] In an experiment carried out in early November 1941 at Sachsenhausen concentration camp, around thirty prisoners were killed in such a vehicle.[110] It is presumed that by the end of the year five gas vans in all were being used by the four Einsatzgruppen to murder people in the occupied Soviet territories,[111] and three by the 'Sonderkommando Lange' in the Warthegau.[112]

Second, after Hitler had decided in August 1941 to discontinue the 'euthanasia' killings carried out during the 'T4 programme' and to carry on with them in a more disguised and decentralized form, the specialists in murder by gassing were redeployed for other operations. There is evidence to show that from the end of 1941 onwards Brack, the 'euthanasia' organizer from the Führer Chancellery, had provided a total of ninety-two specialists to develop and operate extermination camps in the General Government; gas chambers were built there which were fed by deadly exhaust fumes from engines.[113]

Third, in Auschwitz, concentration camp experiments were being conducted with Zyklon B, a highly toxic disinfectant, as a means of murdering prisoners. These experiments were independent of the development of gas vans and gas chambers but it is striking that these activities were happening at the same time.

The development of these different technologies led to the creation from autumn 1941 onwards of a series of murder centres. While transports from Reich territory composed of 25,000 Jews in total plus Sinti and Roma had been arriving since the middle of October in the Lodz ghetto, the 'Sonderkommando Lange' under the command of HSSPF Koppen had, as Greiser and Himmler had agreed the previous month, begun to murder the local Jews in Konin district. At the end of November, the Sonderkommando, which during 1940 and 1941 had murdered Polish asylum inmates by means of a gas van, now used the more sophisticated second-generation model to murder Jews.[114] From 8 December 1941 onwards Rudolf Lange's unit used a building in Chelmno to gather up Polish Jews from various ghettos in the Gau, who were then killed while being transported in the gas van. In a first wave of deportations between 16 and 29 January, the first 10,000 inhabitants of the Lodz ghetto were taken off to Chelmno and murdered in this manner.[115]

In Riga, the second target destination for deportations from Reich territory, the Security Police had since the beginning of October been pursuing the plan of setting up a large concentration camp for Jews deported from Central Europe,[116] expressly citing Hitler's approval.[117] As the camp could not be completed by the time the first transports arrived, at the end of October, Erhard Wetzel, the official responsible for racial issues in the Ministry for the East, offered Reich Commissar Hinrich Lohse, head of the civil administration for the whole of occupied 'Ostland' (in other words, the Baltic States and western Belarus), an alternative: 'Director Brack from the Führer Chancellery' had, he said, agreed 'to contribute to providing the necessary accommodation and gassing equipment'. According to information from Eichmann, camps were to be set up for Jews in Riga and Minsk 'that might also be used for Jews from the Altreich'. There should be 'no hesitation in using Brack's facilities to get rid of Jews who are unfit for work', while 'those fit for work will be transported further east and put to work'.[118] In fact, however, no 'accommodation' (most probably meaning gas chambers) was to be constructed in Riga but rather from the end of 1941 onwards gas vans were used, at first to murder the Jews from the local area rather than Jews from the Reich.[119]

The officials responsible on the spot solved the accommodation problem by murderous means: in the second half of November the first five transports bound for Riga and made up of a total of about 5,000 people from Berlin, Munich, Frankfurt am Main, Vienna, and Breslau were diverted to Kaunas, where all deportees were shot on arrival in so-called Fort IX by Einsatzkommando 3.[120] On 30 November, however, Himmler gave the order by telephone that a further 1,000 Berlin Jews arriving in Riga that day were not to be shot.[121] The order came too late; those people had already been shot on 30 November in the course of a 'Sonderaktion' aimed at the Riga ghetto, in the course of which 4,000 Latvian Jews were killed.[122] Friedrich August Jeckeln, the HSSPF responsible for the murders, was now given a strict warning by Himmler to abide by the 'guidelines' in force governing the treatment of 'Jews being deported there from other territories'.[123]

The fact that Jeckeln was reprimanded by Himmler but not punished shows that, although by shooting German Jews Jeckeln had not contravened an explicit command of the Reichsführer SS, he had nevertheless exceeded his own authority in interpreting the 'guidelines' (the exact wording of which is unknown). After Himmler's intervention, the systematic murder of deportees to Latvia was temporarily halted: the Jews who arrived by February on the following nineteen transports were as a rule confined in the Riga ghetto or in the Salaspils camp, which was still being built, or in the Jungfernhof camp, which was designated a temporary overflow camp, even though it was much too small.[124]

During autumn 1941, preparations were clearly also being made to construct an extermination camp close to Minsk, the third deportation destination. In Mogilev (Mahiljou), a good hundred kilometres from Minsk, the HSSPF for Central Russia, Erich von dem Bach-Zelewski, ran a forced labour camp for 'suspect' Soviet civilians that was also used for murdering Jews from the local ghetto. Mogilev was the scene of a barbaric experiment in which inmates of a psychiatric institution were killed in a sealed chamber with exhaust fumes. After Himmler visited the labour camp on 23 October with Bach-Zelewski, Topf and Sons, a firm specializing in crematoria, received a commission in November to build a gigantic crematorium with thirty-two chambers in the camp. As construction was never completed, however, the ovens were taken in 1943 to Auschwitz.[125] There is some evidence to suggest that the original plan was to create this crematorium complex as part of an extermination camp for Jews from all over Europe.[126]

Preparations were also made in autumn 1941 in the General Government to create a further extermination camp, in this case in the Lublin district. It was envisaged that Lublin and the neighbouring district of Galicia would both be in the vanguard when the 'final solution' was set in motion in the General Government.

The Galicia district was made up of territory that up to 1939 had been Polish and thereafter occupied by the Soviets. It came into being on 1 August and was incorporated into the General Government. The Security Police had carried out mass shootings of Jewish civilians in this territory, as it had done across the Soviet-occupied territories. These mass shootings continued even after these territories were reorganized.[127] Here, too, from the beginning of October onwards, the Security Police began murdering Jewish men, women, and children indiscriminately. The policy of comprehensive genocide had thus reached the eastern part of the General Government.[128]

In the directly adjacent district of Lublin, which had been earmarked as a 'Jewish reservation' as early as 1939 and to which further transports were to be sent in spring 1942, the SS and Police Leader

(SSPF) there seized the initiative: on 13 October Odilo Globocnik met Himmler[129] to discuss proposals he had made two weeks before to step up the 'Jewish persecution' in his district.[130] As a result Himmler gave Globocnik the task of building the first extermination camp in the General Government.[131]

Since spring 1941 the 'government' of the General Government under Hans Frank had in the main assumed that after Germany's imminent victory over the Soviet Union, the Jews on their territory would be deported there. In July 1941 Frank was hoping that the Pripjet Marshes in conquered Soviet territory would be added to the General Government so that the Jews of the General Government could be used there as forced labour. This marshland was, however, assigned to the Reich Commissariat of the Ukraine.[132] On 13 October, in other words on the same day Globocnik met Himmler, Frank again urged Rosenberg to deport the 'Jewish population of the General Government to the occupied eastern territories'. Rosenberg agreed in principle but dismissed the proposal as being impractical at that time.[133]

Immediately after he had returned to the General Government, Frank set up a series of meetings of his government in the district capitals at which a more radical course was adopted in dealing with the 'Jewish question'. There was an obvious determination now to cross the line and embark on mass murder, as is shown, for example, by the decision taken at this time to introduce the death penalty for leaving the ghetto.[134]

At the beginning of November, work started in Belzec in the Lublin district on the construction of a camp, at first consisting of nothing more than a group of huts.[135] The history of its construction (it was significantly extended in spring 1942)[136] supports the view that at first it served a limited purpose, namely the murder of Jews from the Lublin district, and possibly also from the neighbouring district of Galicia, who were 'unfit for work', and that it was not until spring 1942, when the extermination camps Sobibor and Treblinka were also built, that the murder of the General Government's entire Jewish population was envisaged.[137]

In his capacity as Commissar for the Consolidation of the German Ethnic Nation, Himmler had been enforcing a resettlement programme in the east of Upper Silesia, which had been annexed in 1939. As a result of the Wehrmacht's deployment in the east, however, this had ground to a halt in spring 1941. Thousands of Poles who had been expelled from their homes were in so-called Polish camps, while the Jewish population of eastern Upper Silesia had been 'concentrated' in particular cities.[138] From October 1940 onwards the Jews had been used as forced labour as part of the 'Schmelt Organization' (so named after the head of this initiative, the chief of police in Breslau, Albrecht Schmelt, who had become district president).[139] In November 1941 the Schmelt Organization had begun deporting Jews 'no longer fit for work' (as a result of the appalling living conditions and exhausting work in the forced labour camps) to Auschwitz to be murdered.[140] There is some evidence to suggest that from around the start of 1942 at least some of the 'Schmelt Jews' were not shot but rather killed with Zyklon B.[141] Zyklon B is presumed to have been used first in early September 1941 to murder 600 Soviet prisoners of war in the camp who were classed as 'fanatical communists' and also 250 sick prisoners. In mid-September a further 900 Soviet POWs were killed in this way, after makeshift alterations had been carried out to the morgue in the crematorium.[142]

On 21 and 22 October 1941, as part of the planned expansion of the Auschwitz complex, the heads of the construction department there had discussions with representatives of Topf and Sons about building a new and significantly larger crematorium complex consisting of a total of fifteen furnaces.[143] It is unclear whether the plan at this stage was to turn one of the morgues into a gas chamber or whether the decision to do this was not made until September 1942. Even if the decision to build a gas chamber was already made in 1941, this does not constitute solid evidence of a 'Führer decision' to murder the European Jews.[144] The building of a gas chamber in the new crematorium was the logical extension of the makeshift changes already carried out to the old crematorium, while at this point Jews were not the main victims of murder in Auschwitz. In addition, the building of the crematorium did not begin right away, in fact not until August 1942, and not in the old camp but in Birkenau. It was finally ready for use in March 1943. Similarly, the decision to extend the crematorium's capacity significantly and to construct a second crematorium along similar lines in the new Birkenau complex was not taken until August 1942. Furthermore, Auschwitz did not feature in the 1941 plans to murder the European Jews and appears not to have assumed importance for those advocating a radical 'Jewish policy' until January 1942, when Himmler gave the order for Jews from Germany to be confined in concentration camps.[145]

Finally, I have already mentioned that in October 1941 the Wehrmacht also began systematically murdering Jewish men in Serbia using the excuse of reprisals. By the beginning of November the death toll was 8,000. The families of these victims were interned in concentration camps and in spring 1942 a gas van was used to murder them.

Threats of extermination

After the start of deportations in mid-October, it is striking that many members of the Nazi regime commented openly on the imminent 'extermination' of the Jews. These statements were clearly designed to give sustained impetus to the radicalization of 'Jewish policy' that had been set in motion by the deportations and regionally based 'final solutions'. Germany's deteriorating relations with the United States played a significant role in the background to these developments. In the final months of 1941 it became increasingly evident that the United States was likely to enter the war soon, and, as a result, Hitler became increasingly preoccupied with the 'reprisals' aimed at the Jews that he had been keeping in reserve for this eventuality. What began as a threat was turning more and more into a firm intention to exact revenge if the United States continued to ignore the unmistakable warnings Germany was convinced it had issued through the increase in Jewish persecution in autumn 1941. The spectre of a Jewish world conspiracy that dominated Hitler's vision of the world and that of the Nazi leadership was now increasingly dictating their political actions. The 'war against the Jews' was to become a reality. On 25 October at table Hitler told Himmler and Heydrich that the Jews had the German dead of the First World War on their consciences as well as those of the present conflict. Nobody was to say to him, 'We can't send them off into a swamp'. On the contrary, it was good 'if the terror precedes us that we are exterminating the Jews'.[146]

On 16 November 1941 Goebbels published a leading article titled 'The Jews are to blame' in the weekly *Das Reich*. In it he referred back to Hitler's 'prophecy' of 30 January 1939, thus supplying in retrospect a barely disguised public avowal of the deportations from the Reich that had begun four weeks previously: 'We are now seeing the fulfilment of this prophecy. The Jews are suffering a fate that, though harsh, is amply deserved. Pity or regret are completely out of place'. 'World Jewry', Goebbels claims, 'is now undergoing a gradual process of annihilation'.

On 15 November Rosenberg had had discussions lasting several hours with Himmler that included 'Jewish policy'.[147] Three days later, at a press conference designated as 'confidential', he spoke of the 'biological eradication of the entire Jewish population of Europe'; European Jews, he said, had to be 'driven beyond the Urals or eradicated by some other method'.[148]

At a meeting on 28 November 1941 with the Grand Mufti of Jerusalem, who had taken refuge with the Axis Powers, Hitler announced that Germany was 'determined to demand that the European nations step by step, one after another, solve the Jewish problem'. In addition, he intended 'when the time is right' to issue 'the same challenge to nations outside Europe too'. In the foreseeable future German troops would reach the southern gateway to the Caucasus. Germany was not, however, pursuing any imperialist goals in the Arab world but 'merely aiming to exterminate Jews living on Arab soil under the protection of Britain'.[149]

'Action needed': the close of 1941

Hitler's decision in mid-September 1941 initially to deport the Central European Jews to the east and his growing determination during the following weeks to extend these deportations to other countries as well did not in itself represent a 'fundamental decision' to murder all the European Jews. Rather, his order to begin the deportations must be regarded as a further escalation in the process of deciding to commit mass murder. This process started immediately after the outbreak of war in September 1939, but by autumn 1941 it was not yet complete. As early as autumn 1939 the Nazi leadership had developed the (admittedly still vague) idea of consigning the Jews to the periphery of German-dominated territory and then over the medium or longer term letting them perish there. A number of deportation projects were developed. In the 'Eastern Campaign', which from the start had been planned as a racially motivated war of annihilation, Hitler and his regime had already crossed the line into genocide. His decision of mid-September 1941 in the medium term to deport all Jews from the territory he controlled to these already very blood-soaked regions was a clear indication of how things would develop, even if there was as yet no overall plan or agreed timescale for the murder of the European Jews. Until these matters were finally determined, the first waves of deportations were destined for the ghettos. Ghettos were seen as 'transit camps' until the military situation permitted people to be transported further to the east. The idea Hitler pursued for a short time in September of using the deported Jews as hostages to prevent the Americans from entering the war shows that the decision to deport these people did not amount to a decision to murder them immediately.

As we have seen, the decision to deport them very soon prompted positively feverish preparations to establish facilities in which to murder local Jews 'no longer fit for work' by means of gassing. They were to be constructed close to all the ghettos selected as destinations for the first waves of deportations from the Reich: in Riga, in the Lodz area, in Belzec (Lublin), and in Mogilev, not very far from Minsk.

The fact that even in late summer and autumn 1941 those involved still had no order to kill all European Jews as quickly as possible by gassing, and that this enterprise only took on firmer contours in the course of the following months, points up above all how complicated was the development of the technology of murder as described here. The specific technical means and the complex organization required to implement mass murder had basically been developed in 1939/40 in connection with the 'euthanasia' programme, and these were available from August 1941 onwards for other tasks. This tried-and-tested equipment and organization was not, however, transferred to eastern Europe en bloc and used in the systematic murder of the Jews; instead, only part of the staff of the T4 organization was gradually moved to the General Government. In Riga it was offered but refused; simultaneously, a 'second-generation' gas van was being developed further as a mobile instrument of murder.

In Lodz, Riga, Mogilev, and also in the construction of the camp at Belzec, Himmler's guiding hand is evident. In all four locations he worked with the responsible HSSPF or SSPF (SS and Police Leader); in other words, with the same people with whose help he had extended the mass shootings in the Soviet Union to genocidal levels. However uncoordinated were the measures taken in the key areas described, in the final analysis all the various strands came together in the

Reichsführer SS, who in autumn 1941 was pursuing the plan of having some of the local Jews murdered in these territories in order to be sure of the deportations from the Reich. It was Himmler who in September and October 1941 demanded that the second-tier regional agencies come up with their own initiatives to cope with their particular 'Jewish question', intervened to give direction, and thus consolidated the 'solutions' he was offered into a unified policy. This development was fully in line with Hitler's intentions when he gave impetus to a further radicalization of 'Jewish policy' in his public and private utterances.

At the same time, however, in autumn 1941 Heydrich's project of deporting the remaining Jews after the end of the war to the occupied Soviet territories still existed. This was also a plan for a 'final solution' involving the physical annihilation of the European Jews, but one that was designed to be realized in the long term and not primarily by means of immediate campaigns of murder. At the end of 1941, therefore, there was from the point of view of those directly involved a need to reconcile the two strands of 'Jewish policy' represented by the names Himmler and Heydrich.

2

The Wannsee Conference

The Nazi leadership's original intention to leave the 'final solution to the Jewish question' until after the war had therefore already been abandoned by 29 November 1941, the day that Heydrich issued his invitation to a meeting on 9 December[150] to discuss in detail the plan for a 'total solution to the Jewish question in Europe'.[151] The Nazi regime had already murdered several hundred thousand people, even though 'Jewish policy' had not yet come to be officially designated a 'final solution'.

Heydrich's evident intention in convening the meeting was to strengthen his authority as the man responsible for preparing the 'final solution'. He also wanted to create the impression that the current deportations and the resulting mass murders of local Jews that had taken place or were planned in various regions were experiments that fitted into an overall programme for a 'final solution' that he was controlling. At the same time, by revealing details of the plans for a 'final solution', he intended to make senior representatives of the government bureaucracy officially complicit, as it were, and jointly responsible, while also achieving clarity about the still open question of how wide the scope of the deportations should be.

Forced by events in the war to postpone this important meeting at short notice to 20 January,[152] Heydrich had six weeks to reconsider his strategy for it. Germany's declaration of war on the United States had changed the entire war situation and this may have been an important factor in further radicalizing his attitude. If, in autumn 1941, Hitler was considering using the deported Jews as hostages to prevent the United States from entering the war and Goebbels in particular was making use of this thinly veiled threat by publicly referring to Hitler's 'prophecy', the declaration of war on America had made this threat redundant. Even after his blackmail attempt had been unsuccessful, however, Hitler was far from ready to take back his threat of annihilation—quite the reverse.

On 12 December 1941, one day after the declaration of war on the United States, Hitler spoke again of his 'prophecy' of 30 January 1939 when addressing the Gauleiters and Reichsleiters. As Goebbels noted in his diary,[153]

As far as the Jewish question is concerned, the Führer is determined to make a clean sweep. He prophesied to the Jews that if they caused another world war they would see themselves annihilated. That was not just empty talk. The world war is happening and the annihilation of Jewry must be the inevitable consequence. We have to consider this matter without any sentimentality. It's not our job to have sympathy with the Jews but to have sympathy with our own German nation. In the eastern campaign the German nation has now once more sacrificed some 160,000 dead and so the originators of this bloody conflict must pay with their own lives.

The fact that the world war was 'happening' lent particular weight to Hitler's prophecy, one he had repeated frequently since 1939. What he had originally intended as a threat to blackmail the United States he was now presenting as the inevitable fulfilment of a fateful 'prophecy'. It nevertheless seems an exaggeration to see Hitler's speech of 12 December as the announcement of his 'fundamental decision' to murder the European Jews.[154] Rather, it was a further call to speed up and radicalize the policy of annihilation that had already been set in train. In its radical rhetoric this call echoes (in part word for word) the statements Hitler made on 25 October, as well as Goebbels's article of 16 November and Rosenberg's press conference of 18 November; in other words, statements made before Germany declared war on the United States. Neither can Himmler's brief note in his office diary about a discussion with Hitler on 18 December be regarded as additional evidence of a 'fundamental decision', allegedly reached a few days beforehand.[155] The words 'Jewish question' and 'to be exterminated as partisans' that occur in it rather represent Hitler's renewed confirmation that the mass murders of Soviet Jews should be continued and stepped up using the pretext given hitherto.[156]

On 14 December Hitler agreed with Rosenberg that, now that war had been declared on the United States, there should be no more public threats of 'exterminating' the European Jews, but in a confidential discussion he assured him that that was precisely his intention.[157] In his New Year address, however, he referred once more to his 'prophecy' of 30 January 1939, which was, he said, being fulfilled.[158] 'The Jew will not annihilate the European nations, however, but will be the victim of his own attack'. He made similar statements at the end of January and in February 1942.[159]

Hans Frank, head of the Party's Legal Department (Reichsrechtsamt) and Governor General in occupied Poland, had also heard Hitler's address to the Gauleiters and Reichsleiters. On his return from Berlin he announced to his most senior colleagues at a meeting on 16 December that the Jews had to be got rid of 'one way or another'. He then referred to Hitler's 'prophecy' and warned against having inappropriate feelings of pity towards the Jews—words that sound like an echo of Hitler's address of 12 December. Thus, Frank went on, as far as the Jews were concerned, he simply 'presumed that they would disappear'. He notified his colleagues of the postponed Wannsee Conference and, concerning what was in store for the Jews, he told them: 'In Berlin people said to us, "Why make all this fuss and bother? We can't do anything with them in the Ostland or in the Reichskommissariat [Ukraine] either. Liquidate them yourselves!"'

These words quite clearly refer to the attitude of the Ministry for the East; on 13 October in Berlin Rosenberg had told Frank in no uncertain terms that any move to deport the Jews from the General Government to 'his' territory was impossible, and he may have made this plain again during Frank's most recent visit to Berlin.[160] Frank's standpoint was at least clear: 'We must destroy the Jews wherever we find them and when-ever possible, in order to maintain the overall integrity of the Reich here.' He had not, however, returned from Berlin with any greater clarity about how he should proceed. There was a total of 2.5 million Jews in the General Government (perhaps as many as 3.5 million counting all family members): 'we can't shoot them, we can't poison them, but we will be able to take steps to ensure that they are successfully exterminated—as part of the more extensive measures that are to be discussed in relation to the Reich. The General Government must be made just as free of Jews as the Reich. Where and how this happens is a matter for the official agencies we must establish and deploy here and I will keep you posted about their effectiveness in due course.'[161] It was now clear to State Secretary Josef Bühler, who was to deputize for Frank at the Wannsee Conference, that the postponed meeting was going to focus on what form the 'final solution' everyone was trying to effect should take and what the General Government's role in it should be. On 16 December 1941, at any rate, Bühler forbade any further 'removals or resettlements' of Jews and in particular 'the creation of new ghettos or alterations to existing ones' (apart from minor adjustments).[162]

Heydrich's invitation to the rescheduled conference on 20 January stated that its purpose was to deal with 'all the issues relating to the final

solution of the Jewish question' and referred to the initial invitation
with its more wide-ranging agenda.[163] The final paragraph of the invitation, which referred to 'the circle of invitees included in my previous
letter of invitation' as being 'unchanged', was not entirely accurate: in
addition to Bühler deputizing for Frank, the Gestapo chief Müller and
Walther Stahlecker, the head of the Security Police and the Security
Service in the Ostland, were invited, though in the end the latter was
represented by Rudolf Lange, the head of the Security Police and
Security Service in Latvia.[164] Including the Ostland Security Police was
an obvious move, as two out of the three ghettos to which German
Jews were now being deported (Minsk and Riga) were in the 'Ostland'.

The participants: a 'final solution' based on a division of labour between the SS and the bureaucracy

Heydrich's lists of invitees from November 1941 and January 1942
indicate that he was aiming to bring together a group of people who
represented those 'central authorities' and SS departments that had
been working with him since early 1941 on his plan for a 'final solution'. That their joint project of deporting the German Jews (and in
the medium to long term the European Jews also) to 'the east' would
ultimately lead to the death of these deportees must have been evident
to the conference participants by the end of 1941 at the latest: the mass
shootings in the Soviet Union, the execution of Jewish men in Serbia
by the Wehrmacht, and the murder of 6,000 German Jews from the
Reich in Riga and Kaunas at the end of November did not take place
in secret;[165] it was quite obvious that mass deportations to already
overcrowded ghettos or non-existent 'reception camps' would have
catastrophic consequences.

Viewed in this context, the unmistakable warnings of annihilation
coming from representatives of the regime such as Hitler, Goebbels, and
Rosenberg indicate that they were not simply indulging in rhetoric.
Heydrich's motive in calling the conference, and thus creating written
records of what was said by representatives of the ministerial bureaucracy concerning the planned murder of the deportees, was certainly to
make the participants officially complicit in an atrocity of staggering
proportions. At the same time, those invited were neither ignorant nor
innocent, for their actions had long since made them accomplices.

This can be demonstrated in detail for every participant. As a group, they can be split into three categories: 1. Representatives of the (mostly state) 'central authorities' in the Reich; 2. Representatives of the civil occupation authorities (General Government and Ministry for the East); 3. SS functionaries representing either SS head offices or branch offices in the occupied territories.

Representatives of the 'central authorities'

The members of the first group were in the main both highly qualified top civil servants and longstanding and active National Socialists—the embodiment of the Nazi state.

Admittedly, the representative of the Foreign Ministry was distinctly under-qualified to be a top civil servant (and in that regard he was an exception). Martin Luther, the undersecretary and head of the Germany desk at the Foreign Ministry (born 1895), was anything but a career civil servant, but nor was he one of the 'Alte Kämpfer' (Party veterans). He had left grammar school in 1914 to enlist as a volunteer. At the end of the war he had been successful in various jobs, including working in a removals company and running a house clearance business. When he began to get involved with the Nationalsozialistische Deutsche Arbeiterpartei (NSDAP) in 1932, he met Joachim von Ribbentrop, a spirits wholesaler who at this point was trying to form connections with the leading figures in the Party. Luther was a down-to-earth individual and during the following years he took care of alterations and renovations to various private and business properties owned by Ribbentrop, at the same time making himself indispensable in the so-called Ribbentrop Office (the office Ribbentrop maintained from 1933 onwards for his various special foreign policy assignments and ambitions). Luther gathered around him a group of young, ambitious co-workers in the 'Party liaison office' he set up: their overly brash approach, however, quickly led to Ribbentrop temporarily disbanding the office. Luther, however, survived this crisis unscathed.[166]

When Ribbentrop was appointed Foreign Minister in February 1938, Luther managed in autumn 1938 to take over the new Party department in the Foreign Ministry in addition to regaining his position in the Ribbentrop Office. In May 1940 he was appointed as head of the Germany desk in the Foreign Ministry, which was now responsible for all the liaison work with the Party and the SS, for the 'Jewish question', and for other tasks besides. In the course of the next few months he also assumed responsibility for monitoring all the Foreign Ministry's propaganda work and, by setting up a 'special organization department', he attempted to structure the Ministry more effectively.[167]

In June 1940 Luther's newly created Jewish department under Franz Rademacher began to play an active role in the regime's 'Jewish policy', whereas up to this point the Foreign Ministry had tended to act more as an observer in this area. In particular, in summer 1940 Rademacher was instrumental in pushing the 'Madagascar Project', though as far as the persecution of the Jews in the occupied or allied countries was concerned, the Foreign Office for the time being was only to play a secondary role.

When the war against the partisans broke out in Serbia in late summer 1941, the embassy recommended the deportation of all the Serbian Jews to Romania, as they were all suspected of supporting the partisans. When the Foreign Office objected, the embassy recommended that at least the Jewish men be deported to the General Government or the occupied Soviet territories. When Rademacher put the request to Eichmann on 13 September, however, he turned it down, recommending instead that these Jews be shot where they were.[168] While Ribbentrop intended to discuss deporting this group to eastern Poland,[169] Luther and Heydrich joined forces to send Rademacher and two of Eichmann's team to Belgrade to find out whether the problem of the 'Jewish rabble-rousers' could be 'dealt with on the spot'.[170] Once there, the delegation discovered that at the beginning of October the Wehrmacht had already started shooting the captive Jewish men en masse as 'reprisals' for attacks by partisans on its members.[171] The families of these men had also already been put into camps, and on 25 October Rademacher proposed that they should be deported 'by boat to the reception camps in the east'.[172] In November Luther began an initiative, prompted by Eichmann, to persuade the governments of Romania, Croatia, and Slovakia to agree to take back their Jews who were resident in Germany if they wished to prevent their being included in the deportations; all three governments had no objections to this, however.[173] Luther was made aware at the latest from mid-November onwards of the murderous activities of the Einsatzgruppen in the occupied Soviet territories, in particular via their reports, which were circulated in the Foreign Ministry and also shown to him.[174]

After the first invitation to the Wannsee Conference arrived, the Jewish desk in the Germany department produced a briefing document for Luther headed 'The Foreign Ministry's requests and suggestions regarding the planned comprehensive solution to the Jewish question in Europe'.[175] The Croatian, Slovakian, and Romanian Jews resident in Germany were to be deported 'to the east'. In addition, Germany should indicate to these governments as well as to those of Bulgaria and Hungary that it was willing also to deport all the Jews living in these countries to the east. Furthermore, all German Jews living in the occupied territories (who had meanwhile become stateless), all Serbian Jews, and all Jews 'handed over to us by the Hungarian government'[176] were to be deported, while pressure should be put on the governments of European countries, starting with Bulgaria and Hungary, to introduce 'Jewish laws on the model of the Nuremberg Laws'. All these measures should be implemented 'as hitherto in close cooperation with the Secret State Police [Gestapo]'. This document makes it clear that in November Luther was preparing for a comprehensive, Europe-wide deportation programme.

Among the remaining top civil servants, State Secretary Wilhelm Stuckart, representing the Ministry of the Interior, was to play a particularly prominent role at the Wannsee Conference. During the years after 1933 this Ministry was the central authority responsible for 'Jewish policy'. Even though in 1941 it was still officially 'in charge' of anti-Jewish legislation,[177] from 1939 onwards it had effectively lost control over the 'Jewish question' and been forced to cede most of its power in this area to Göring, Himmler, and Heydrich. When viewed in the context of the struggles, so typical of the 'Third Reich', to gain and retain areas of responsibility, Stuckart's contribution to the Wannsee Conference therefore appears to be part of a rearguard action on the part of his Ministry.

Born in 1902, Stuckart completed his legal studies in 1928 with a doctorate in commercial law. He then became a judge but left the judiciary, probably as a result of his involvement with the NSDAP, which by his own admission had begun in 1923, and became a lawyer in Stettin. For a short time in 1933 he was acting NSDAP Oberbürgermeister there, as well as state commissioner for Pomerania, after which he was appointed to the Prussian Ministry of Culture, becoming state secretary shortly afterwards (a post that continued when the Ministry became part of the Reich Ministry of Education in May 1934). After a dispute with his minister, Bernhard Rust, he was forced

into temporary retirement, but during the following months he managed, amongst other things by appealing directly to Hitler, to get himself accepted back into government service, resulting in his appointment
as ministerial director with the title of state secretary to head the constitutional department of the Interior Ministry. In this capacity he once
more became a fully fledged state secretary from 1938 onwards.[178] In
1935 Stuckart was in charge of producing the Nuremberg Laws; he
personally led the subsequent negotiations for the Ministry with other
agencies over the complex regulations for their implementation.

The controversial issue of how people were to be treated who were
descended both from Jews and non-Jews led to the creation of the category of the 'Jewish Mischling' [lit. 'mongrel']. This was primarily
Stuckart's initiative. Anyone who had two Jewish grandparents but did
not belong to the Jewish religious community was classified as a
'1st-degree Mischling' and not as a Jew; anyone who had one Jewish
grandparent was a '2nd-degree Mischling'. The members of this new
'intermediate race', whose numbers were estimated at several hundred
thousand,[179] were not to be allowed to reproduce amongst themselves;
as Stuckart and his colleagues reasoned, their 'Jewish blood' would in the
course of generations be neutralized by the 'German blood' of the
majority population and thus be eliminated. By contrast with the 'full
Jews', who were to be driven out of Germany, the 'Mischlinge', according to the line taken by Stuckart in the mid-1930s, would be allowed to
remain, though subject to a wide range of discriminatory measures.[180]

As a departmental head, Stuckart had become prominent through
his numerous publications on legal matters. He had staked his reputation on this approach to the 'Mischling' question by allowing his name
to appear as one of the authors of the official commentary to the
Nuremberg Laws.[181] In addition, since March 1936 he had been chair
of the Reich Committee for the Protection of German Blood, which
in exceptional cases dealt with permissions for 'Mischlinge' and 'people
of German blood' to marry. When the census of 1939 established that
in what was by then the 'Greater German Reich' there were in fact
only 72,000 '1st-degree Mischlinge' (including 8,000 who, as adher-
ents of the Jewish religion, 'counted as Jews') and 42,000 '2nd-degree
Mischlinge', the Interior Ministry could chalk this up[182] as confirmation of the correctness of its 'moderate' approach to the 'Mischling
question'. This concern about the treatment of the 'Mischlinge' should
not, however, obscure the fact that Stuckart and his colleagues

advocated very tough measures as far as the rest of 'Jewish policy' was concerned.[183]

The idea of a German-Jewish intermediate race was in danger of collapsing, however, as the Interior Ministry increasingly lost the initiative in the 'Jewish question' and was confronted with powerful institutions that aimed to treat the vast majority of '1st-degree Mischlinge' as Jews, in other words to deport them, and in the case of the '2nd-degree Mischlinge' to establish their status on a case-by-case basis. If this hard line had prevailed, it would have meant a serious loss of prestige for the Interior Ministry and above all for Stuckart as its state secretary.

Stuckart's most important opponents were also represented at the Wannsee Conference: apart from Heydrich, there was above all Gerhard Klopfer, representing the Party Chancellery. Born in 1905 and with a doctorate in law, he joined the NSDAP in 1933 and entered the Prussian Agriculture Ministry, moving at the end of 1934 to Gestapo headquarters. In 1935 he became a member of the Staff of the Führer's Deputy, first as private secretary to Martin Bormann, the chief of staff. He quickly advanced until in May 1941 he became head of Department III, which was responsible for the involvement of the Führer's Deputy's office in state matters, in particular in the fields of legislation and the appointment of civil servants.[184]

The Staff of the Führer's Deputy, which after Rudolf Hess's flight to Britain in May 1941 became the Party Chancellery headed by Bormann, regarded one of its key tasks as encouraging discrimination against and the removal of rights from German Jews in every sphere of life. It therefore not only forbade most contacts between Party comrades and Jews, but was also active from the mid-1930s onwards in creating a comprehensive set of laws expressly for Jews and putting pressure on the government bureaucracy to interpret legal provisions in the most anti-Jewish way possible; it persisted in trying to bring about the dismissal of civil servants married to Jewish women or to women classed as 'Jewish Mischlinge' and to prevent the appointment of such civil servants in all cases.[185]

Erich Neumann, state secretary in the office for the Four-Year Plan, represented an agency at the conference that had also been advocating a radical anti-Jewish policy for years. Particularly in the period immediately preceding the conference, it was one of the forces that had opposed the position of the Interior Ministry regarding 'Mischlinge' and 'mixed marriages'.[186] Born in 1892, Neumann was a law graduate, had fought in the First World War, and was a career civil servant who had originally been a member of the right-wing Deutschnationale Volkspartei (DNVP). In 1933 he joined the NSDAP and in 1934 the SS. After the Four-Year Plan organization was set up in 1936, he became head of the foreign currency section and in 1938 was made one of the state secretaries in the organization.[187]

When appointing Göring as his special commissioner for the Four-Year Plan in 1936, Hitler had issued the express order that Jewish property should be used to finance rearmament, and from the start Göring had accorded this task high importance.[188] Furthermore, the fact that Heydrich's assignment to prepare the 'final solution' required authorization by Göring, officially the 'second man' after Hitler, indicates that Göring's central role in the development of 'Jewish policy' was not simply a formality. In fact, Göring and the Four-Year Plan, particularly with regard to the exploitation of Jewish labour and the looting of Jewish property, were so integral to 'Jewish policy' that even several months after the Wannsee Conference they were still demanding a crucial role in the 'final solution'. When in spring 1942 the Four-Year Plan Organization set about producing a concluding report on the period 1936–40, the following key sentences were put on the front page to indicate the broad scope of its activities: 'I. Purpose of the Four-Year Plan as mandated by the Führer. Four-Year Plan: Means to an end, platform for the Final Solution; II. Today the German nation is in the midst of the Final Solution...'.[189] Neumann's function at the Wannsee Conference was primarily to be Göring's eyes and ears; he undoubtedly relayed to him afterwards how Heydrich was carrying out his assignment.

Another of the 'hard-liners' in 'Jewish policy' was the state secretary in the Propaganda Ministry, Leopold Gutterer, who was invited to the conference but was unable to attend as a result of other commitments. On 15 August 1941[190] at an inter-ministerial meeting in the Propaganda Ministry, Gutterer, echoing precisely the views of his minister, had demanded 'immediate measures' to be taken against the Berlin Jews: they should be sent to camps and those unable to work should be 'carted off to Russia'; special 'Jewish shops' should be set up; above all and as a 'basic precondition' for these measures, the Jews must be required to wear a distinguishing mark, a move approved by Hitler a few days later when Goebbels discussed the matter with him.

The Justice Ministry (State Secretary Roland Freisler) and the Reich Chancellery (Ministerial Director Friedrich Kritzinger) were two

further bodies represented at the Wannsee Conference that throughout 1941 had taken part in negotiations over nationality and property
issues as well as in discussions on the subject of 'Mischlinge'.

State Secretary Freisler, born in 1893, a First World War volunteer and
a prisoner of war in Russia from 1915 to 1920, had gained his doctorate
in law in 1924 and then practised as a lawyer in Kassel, where he became
an active member of the National Socialists. At the time of the 'seizure of
power' he was deputy NSDAP Gauleiter of Hesse-Nassau. That same
year he became state secretary in the Prussian Justice Ministry and in
1934 he took over the same role in the Reich Justice Ministry. As a state
secretary, Freisler, who in August 1942 became president of the People's
Court, was a prominent advocate of radically overhauling constitutional
law along National Socialist lines and in accordance with racial doc-
trines.[191] At the conference Freisler represented the institution that,
along with the lead ministry, namely the Interior Ministry, had played
an important role throughout the development of anti-Jewish legislation. It was clear to those in the Justice Ministry that the phase of legal
measures dealing with the 'Jewish question' was drawing to a close. For
example, on 29 October 1941 it responded to a question from the Party
Chancellery dating back to March 1941 concerning protecting debtors
against 'unjustified demands' from Jews by asserting that 'particularly in
view of probable developments in the Jewish question' it was unneces-
sary to provide the courts with special instructions about how to handle
such cases. The Party Chancellery specifically endorsed this view at the
end of November 1941.[192]

Friedrich Kritzinger, born in 1890, was a lawyer who had been in
the army from 1913 to 1920. In 1921 he entered the Reich Justice
Ministry, where he pursued a successful career as a high-ranking civil
servant, interrupted temporarily while he served in the Prussian
Ministry of Commerce. In 1938 State Secretary Hans Heinrich
Lammers brought him into the Reich Chancellery, where he became
Lammers's most important colleague, as is shown by Kritzinger's
appointment as deputy state secretary (early 1942) and state secretary
(end of 1942). During the Weimar period he had had ties to the DNVP
and did not join the Nazi Party until 1935. He was the only person
involved in the Wannsee Conference who after 1945 frankly admitted
what was discussed there and showed remorse.[193] In an official statement from late 1940, however, even Kritzinger assumed that 'in the not
too distant future Jews will have disappeared from Germany'.[194]

At the Wannsee Conference the top civil servants briefly presented here were representing 'central authorities'. Since the beginning of 1941, when Hitler had given Heydrich the task of drawing up a comprehensive plan to deport the Jews, these authorities had held a series of meetings to discuss how, as part of the planned deportations, legally to deprive Jews of their German citizenship so that their property would be 'forfeit' to the state.[195] The Reich Interior Minister's proposal to declare the Jews in the Reich (as was the case with Poles and Czechs) to be 'protected residents', in other words second-class citizens, was rejected by Hitler.[196] Herbert Reischauer, representing Hess's office and supported by the representatives of the SS Office of the Reich Commissar for the Consolidation of the German Ethnic Nation and also the Reich Security Head Office, proposed at an inter-ministerial meeting in mid-January 1941 that the Jews be deprived of citizenship; '1st-degree Mischlinge' and Jews living in 'privileged mixed marriages' should be included in this ruling. The property of these Jews should be forfeit to the state the moment they moved 'their normal place of residence to a foreign country'.[197]

When further discussions failed to produce agreement, however,[198] a 'Führer decision' was sought. Hitler informed the Interior Ministry on 7 June 1941 that he would regard as sufficient a ruling that 'deprived Jews who are normally resident abroad of their German citizenship and declared their property to be forfeit to the Reich'.[199]

Lammers told Bormann in confidence that Hitler had rejected the Interior Ministry's proposed ruling 'primarily . . . because he takes the view that after the war there will be no more Jews in Germany anyway'.[200]

The discussions about the German Jews' loss of citizenship and forfeiture of property had also raised the issue of the future treatment of the 'Mischlinge'; although the 11th decree implementing the Reich Citizenship Law of 25 November 1941 settled the issue of the forfeiture of property to Hitler's satisfaction, it referred to 'Jews' in general.[201]

Meanwhile, the 'central authorities' dealing with the matter had begun to discuss the 'Mischling question' as an independent problem and to work towards a solution. In August and September a series of meetings took place to clarify the matter at which differing approaches collided: whereas the Interior Ministry wished to hold to the Nuremberg Laws, the Party Chancellery, Four-Year Plan office, and Reich Security Head Office, supported by the NSDAP's Racial Policy Office, took the line that, as far as deportation was concerned, 'Mischlinge' were in principle to be treated as Jews.[202] The negotiations were hampered by the fact that there was a written statement from Hitler to the effect that half-Jews were definitely not to be regarded as Jews, whereas the RSHA and the Party Chancellery claimed that 'in respect of the final solution' Hitler's view on the 'Mischling question' was the precise opposite, though they were not prepared to produce any written statement from the 'Führer'.[203]

Eventually, an inter-ministerial 'working party',[204] formed on Eichmann's initiative, seems to have reached agreement on the proposal that '1st-degree Mischlinge' should in principle be treated in the same way as Jews as far as deportation was concerned, but in exceptional cases where political factors were involved '1st-degree Mischlinge' were to be sterilized.[205] This compromise applied only to 'Mischlinge' in the Reich, however; the 'working party's' original task of examining 'issues pertaining to the protection of blood *in Europe*' was evidently never fulfilled. On the contrary, in the negotiations over the 'Mischling question' an increasing tendency emerged to make the definition more stringent in the occupied territories and thus to create a series of faits accomplis. In the Interior Ministry it was feared that 'the Altreich would be encircled, so to speak' and thus subject to pressure to introduce the more stringent definition here as well.[206]

Thus, months before the Wannsee Conference, a clear direction was being set for the future and at the conference itself it was taken for granted that the 'Mischlinge' issue would be confined to the Reich. At the meeting on 13 August, at which negotiations on the 'Mischling question' began, Eichmann, emphasizing the leading role assumed by the RSHA, read out the well-known 'authorization' from Göring of 31 July, which Heydrich in turn was to include in the invitation of 29 November. This meant that for most of the participants of the conference Heydrich's 'appointment' was old news.

Finally, in August officials involved with the 'Mischling question' and the problem of removing citizenship and property from the Jews also discussed making Jews wear an identifying mark. The initiative for this move, which led to the introduction of the 'Jewish star' on 1 September 1941, came in particular from the Propaganda Ministry and the RSHA, which were using it to put pressure on the Interior Ministry, originally the lead ministry with regard to the 'Jewish question'.[207]

Thus the representatives of the state 'central authorities' invited to the Wannsee Conference—the Reich Chancellery, Interior Ministry, Justice Ministry, Propaganda Ministry, and Foreign Ministry—together with the Party Chancellery and representatives of further ministries had been in continuous close contact with Eichmann and other RSHA functionaries throughout 1941. Through a series of meetings and correspondence they endeavoured to clarify the essential preconditions for and consequences of the prospective deportations, in particular: definition of the group of people designated for deportation, which involved discussion of the status of 'Mischlinge' and of 'mixed marriages' as well as the treatment of foreign Jews; deprivation of citizenship for German Jews and—closely bound up with this—forfeiture of property; and, last but not least, the identifying mark to be worn by those affected.

Although differing views certainly emerged—for example, on the contentious matter of the treatment of 'Mischlinge'—these should not obscure the fact that the deportation of the Jews living in Germany and the future deportation also of those living in the rest of Europe was a project pursued jointly and largely consensually by the 'central authorities' named above and was in the end realized almost without a hitch. Neither the Reich Chancellery nor the Foreign Ministry, Justice Ministry, or the Interior Ministry advanced any fundamental objections or attempted to obstruct or delay the deportation project as a whole in any way. Civil servants involved such as Bernhard Lösener (Interior Ministry) or Friedrich Kritzinger (Reich Chancellery), who after the war stressed their private reservations about the regime's 'Jewish policy', were in fact operating primarily within a bureaucratic machine that created the administrative preconditions for the deportations.

Representatives of the civil occupation authorities

The second group of institutions represented at the Wannsee Conference was made up of representatives of the civil occupation authorities in Poland and the Soviet Union. The Ministry for the Occupied Eastern Territories under Alfred Rosenberg was responsible for the latter, and it was represented at the conference by Rosenberg's permanent deputy Alfred Meyer and by the head of the Main Department I (Political) in the Ministry for the East, Georg Leibbrandt.

Born in Göttingen in 1891 as the son of a government construction official, Meyer completed his school leaving examination (Abitur) in Soest, to which his father had been transferred, in 1911. He then began a career as an army officer and was made a lieutenant in 1913. He fought in the First World War until he was captured by the French in 1917. On his release he was discharged with the rank of captain and began to study law. In 1922 he gained his doctorate in political sciences at Würzburg with a dissertation on 'The people's war in Belgium', in which he justified the brutal reprisals meted out by the German occupying forces to Belgian civilians engaged in acts of resistance. In 1923 he sat the state examinations in politics and economics, political economy, and international law. He then became an employee at the Bismarck mine in Gelsenkirchen. In 1928 he joined the NSDAP and after six months became leader of the local Gross-Gelsenkirchen branch. In 1930 he was elected to the Reichstag and in 1931 became the Nazi Gauleiter for Westphalia North. In May 1933 he was appointed Reich governor of the two small states of Lippe and Schaumburg-Lippe and from 1938 onwards was also president of the Province of Westphalia. When in April 1941 Rosenberg became the commissioner heading the office responsible for dealing with eastern Europe matters, he appointed Meyer as his permanent deputy. Meyer retained this post when Rosenberg's planning staff became the Ministry for the East in summer 1941. He was not subsequently appointed state secretary, as in his capacity as a Reich governor (Reichsstatthalter), a position he retained, he already held a higher rank.[208]

Georg Leibbrandt, born in 1899 in a Swabian German settlement near Odessa, attended the grammar school in Dorpat and Odessa, fleeing after the October Revolution to Berlin, and from 1920 onwards studied theology, philosophy, and economics in Marburg, Tübingen, Leipzig, and London. In 1927 he gained his doctorate with a dissertation on the Swabian emigration to Russia in the early nineteenth century. After working as a junior academic at Leipzig University and then at the Reichsarchiv in Potsdam, in 1931 he went to Washington on a scholarship from the Rockefeller Foundation. In 1933 he became a member of the NSDAP and joined its Foreign Policy Office under Alfred Rosenberg.[209] There he became head of the department for the east. In July 1941 Rosenberg appointed Leibbrandt head of the Main Department I (Political) in the Ministry for the East, which at that time was still being set up.

As the highest civil authority in the occupied eastern territories, the Ministry for the East had from the outset assumed particular responsibility for the measures by which the civil administration had marginalized and isolated the Jews living there: definition, documentation, visible identification, accommodation (in other words, ghettoization), economic exploitation, theft of property, and forced labour. By these means the civil administration, with the Ministry for the East at its summit, had created the crucial preconditions for the murder of the Jews (the murders themselves being primarily the responsibility of the SS).[210]

At the beginning of October Leibbrandt and Meyer had already had one session with Heydrich. They had discussed the appointment of 'Jewish experts' in the Ministry and in the occupation authorities, a plan Heydrich opposed because he feared that the administration might use this as a means of laying claim to more Jewish workers and thus 'the plan for a total resettlement [of the Jews] from the territories we occupy' might be frustrated. The representatives of the Ministry for the East had, however, shown little inclination to accommodate Heydrich on this matter.[211]

On 15 November Rosenberg and Himmler met to discuss the fundamental, though as yet unresolved, issue of who was 'responsible' for the Jews in the occupied Soviet territories.[212] There was disagreement over whether 'dealing with' the 'Jewish problem' was a police matter, as Himmler claimed, or whether, as Rosenberg insisted, it had to be managed 'in the context of overall policy'. In the end both agreed to subordinate the SS and Police Leaders (SSPFs) to the General Commissars and the Higher SS and Police Leaders (HSSPFs) to the Reich Commissars, in addition to their still being under the command of the Reichsführer SS, thus making them effectively responsible for the police within the civil administration. The 'officials responsible for the Jews' on the staffs of the HSSPFs could thus also take on the equivalent role on the staffs of the Reich Commissars, combining the two roles in one person.[213]

This 'dual subordination', so typical of the Nazi system, did not of course provide a solution to the problem of who had authority, and as the mass murders went on, the SS inevitably began to get the upper hand over the civil administration.[214] The SS was thus able to get its way in particular over the conflict surrounding the preservation or murder of Jewish workers. When in mid-November Reich Commissar Lohse asked the Ministry for the East if the official position was that 'all Jews in the eastern territories' were to be 'liquidated' and if this were to be carried out regardless of age, sex, and economic interests (such as the Wehrmacht's need for skilled workers in the armaments industry),[215] he received the answer on 22 December that 'oral discussions' had taken place (probably an allusion to Himmler's meeting with Rosenberg), leading to the conclusion that 'in dealing with the problem economic concerns were as a matter of principle to be ignored'. Any queries arising were to be clarified directly with the HSSPF.[216]

In the General Government in 1940, responsibilities relating to the 'Jewish question' had generally been shared between the civil administration and the SS bureaucracy. The civil administration was responsible for defining Jews and making them wear an identification mark, as well as for their ghettoization, removal from the economic sphere, and forced labour. Its measures against epidemics and the black market were primarily directed at the Jews, who were blamed for both phenomena. The various levels of the civil administration contained 'Jewish sections' (though Heydrich was aiming to prevent this for the occupied eastern territories). The HSSPF and the SSPFs in the General Government demanded to be in charge of all 'police' issues, which amounted in practice to the police authorities not only carrying out the administration's instructions but also acting on their own initiative.[217]

When work had begun on the construction of the first extermination camp in Belzec in autumn 1941, the government of the General Government in its turn introduced increasingly stringent residence provisions for the Jews, who were to be prevented under any circumstances from leaving the ghettos. First of all, the 'order to shoot' mentioned earlier of 15 October imposed the death penalty on anyone leaving the ghetto without permission.[218] As the special courts responsible for criminal prosecutions quickly became overloaded, on 21 November 1941 the commander of the Security Police and the Security Service, Karl Georg Eberhard Schöngarth, issued the additional order 'to shoot on the spot any Jews found wandering about', if they put up the slightest resistance or attempted to run away—reactions that were generally to be expected.[219] On 16 December, in other words on the day that Frank was getting his staff accustomed to the idea of liquidating the Jews in the General Government as required by Berlin, State Secretary Josef Bühler made all movement of people within and out of the General Government, and in particular the creation or alteration of ghettos, dependent on approval from the Department for Population and Welfare, which was responsible for all Jewish matters. On 20 January, the day of the Wannsee Conference, the government of the General Government circulated the draft of a revised and significantly more stringent set of provisions banning residence, stating that the absence of reasons given for these bans was intentional.[220]

Thus, even though in the occupied eastern territories and in the General Government there were significant rivalries and conflicts over powers and jurisdiction between the civil administration and Himmler's empire, it is nevertheless evident that precisely in the matter of preparing for the murder of the Jews both authorities were in the final analysis working together. The presence of Meyer, Leibbrandt, and Bühler at the Wannsee Conference was therefore fully in line with an established practice of close cooperation.

SS functionaries

The third group attending the Wannsee Conference consisted of a series of high-ranking SS men who were already heavily implicated in dealing with the 'Jewish question'. The crucial role played by the man who hosted it, Reinhard Heydrich, in planning and initiating the 'final solution' has already been described in detail. In January 1942 SS Obergruppenführer Heydrich, who was also General of the German Police as well as Deputy Reich Protector of Bohemia and Moravia, was thirty-seven years old. After completing the school leaving examination in 1921, he had embarked on a career as an officer in the German navy but had been forced to leave in 1931 after he violated its strict moral code by breaching a promise of engagement. The former lieutenant then became a member of the NSDAP and the SS, in which Himmler gave him the task of creating a special organization for gathering intelligence that came to be known as the Security Service (Sicherheitsdienst or SD). As part of Himmler's entourage, Heydrich rose through the ranks after 1933: head of the Political Police in the Munich Police Headquarters; head of the Bavarian Political Police; from 1934 onwards head of Gestapo headquarters in Berlin, which, after Himmler took over as Chief of the German Police, he built up into the central office of a Reich-wide secret police. This made Heydrich a key figure in combatting opponents of the Nazi state, an activity he extended to encompass all potential 'enemies of the Reich' (among them Jews, Freemasons, and priests). In 1939 he was made head of the RSHA, which brought together the Gestapo, the Criminal Police, foreign espionage, and the Security Service. In September 1941 Hitler sent him to Prague as Deputy Reich Protector of Bohemia and Moravia in order to take draconian measures against the growing unrest among the Czech population and to prepare the 'Protectorate' for future 'Germanization'.[221]

Ulrich Greifelt, who was head of the unit responsible for implementing Himmler's measures as Reich Commissar for the Consolidation of the German Ethnic Nation, and Otto Hofmann, who was in charge of the SS Race and Settlement Head Office, had been invited to the conference as they had responsibility for matters that the SS, in their plans for a new European order along racial lines, regarded as complementary to the 'final solution'. These included the 'racial' examination and 'resettlement' of all 'undesirable elements' from the conquered colonial territories in eastern Europe and the establishing of 'German' and 'Germanic' settlers in this 'living space'.

Greifelt was unable to attend on 20 January 1942 and did not send a representative, whereas his colleague Otto Hofmann was present. Born in 1896, he was a volunteer in the First World War and afterwards joined the Free Corps. During the Weimar Republic he worked in the wine trade, and after initially joining the NSDAP in 1923, he became an active member of the Party from 1929 onwards and of the SS from 1933 onwards. In 1933 he became a full-time SS leader and, after holding various posts, in early 1939 he took over as head of the SS Clan Office and at the end of the year became first acting head and then regular head of the Race and Settlement Head Office. While there, he organized amongst other things the programme of 'racial registration' in occupied Poland.[222]

Finally, Adolf Eichmann and Heinrich Müller attended the conference as representatives of the RSHA. Born in Solingen in 1906, Eichmann grew up from 1914 onwards in Linz, after his parents moved there. He left technical school early and also failed to complete an apprenticeship as a mechanic. He worked in a variety of jobs up to 1933, when he moved to Germany after the NSDAP, which he had joined the previous year, was banned in Austria. In Germany he first of all joined the Austrian Legion, an organization set up for Nazi emigrants. In 1934 he became a member of the Party's Security Service in Berlin. There Eichmann worked first in the Freemasonry and then in the Jewish department. After the Anschluss he was transferred to Vienna, where, as described earlier, he set up the Central Office for Jewish Emigration. In July 1939, after the occupation of Czechoslovakia in March of that year, he assumed the equivalent role in Prague. In 1940 Eichmann became head of the Reich Headquarters for Jewish Emigration in Berlin and in the new RSHA he took over as head of the corresponding department (IV D 4, later IV B 4), namely Jews and Clearance Issues. In this capacity he was responsible for the planning, preparation, and implementation of Jewish deportations and thus one of the key figures in the organization of the systematic murder of the Jews.[223]

Eichmann had had the task of arranging what would be covered in the meeting and thus it was logical that he would show the draft minutes to Heydrich. Following on from the many inter-ministerial meetings of the previous months, he knew the views of the various bodies represented at the Wannsee Conference concerning the next steps to be taken with regard to the 'Jewish question', and he was versed in the terminology being used for the mass murder being planned and indeed already being implemented. There is evidence that the day before the conference he visited Theresienstadt,[224] and while in the Protectorate he probably used the opportunity to discuss how it should proceed with Heydrich, who was based in Prague.

Eichmann's superior, the head of the Gestapo, Heinrich Müller, was born in Munich in 1900. In 1917 he joined the Bavarian Army as a volunteer, moving in 1919 to the police force, in which from 1929 onwards he specialized within the political police in combatting communism. In 1933 he was recruited into the Bavarian Political Police, which Himmler and Heydrich were re-establishing. In spring 1934, after Heydrich was appointed chief of the Gestapo head office, he followed his boss to Berlin. Müller's Catholic conservative background did not impede his rapid rise in the Gestapo. In 1939 he was made chief executive of the Reich Central Office for Jewish Emigration, and from autumn 1939 he was head of Office IV (Gestapo) within the RSHA.[225] In this capacity, despite appearing somewhat nondescript, he was in fact involved in all the essential measures connected with the persecution of the Jews. Thus in October 1939 Müller had given Eichmann the task of implementing the 'Nisko Action'—the expulsion of 70,000 to 80,000 Jews mainly from the Kattowitz district[226]—and from 1940/1 he was a leading figure in the expulsions of Poles (Jews and non-Jews) to the General Government.[227] In spring 1941 he was in charge of negotiations on behalf of the RSHA with the Quartermaster General of the army concerning the activities of the Einsatzgruppen in the Soviet Union.[228] He played a leading role in the selection and liquidation of Soviet prisoners of war, non-Jews as well as Jews.[229] In April 1940 he signed off the guidelines for 'Jewish emigration' and in October 1941, on Himmler's authority, the final ban on emigration.[230]

When, a few days after the Wannsee Conference, Müller received via Luther an anonymous letter sent to the Foreign Office about the 'solution to the Jewish question in the Warthegau', he replied, 'You can't make an omelette without breaking eggs.★ That's unavoidable'.[231]

★ Translators' note: lit.: 'If you're planing a piece of wood, there will be shavings'.

After the conference Müller was also to play a key role in organizing the deportations from the occupied territories[232] and implementing the expulsion of Jews from concentration camps in the Altreich to the camps at Lublin and Auschwitz.[233]

Karl Georg Eberhard Schöngarth and Rudolf Lange were two attendees already actively involved in the mass murder of the Jews. Schöngarth was the commander of the Security Police in the General Government; Lange was the commander of the Security Police and Security Service in Latvia and was representing Walther Stahlecker, the commander of the Security Police and the Security Service in the so-called Ostland.

Born in 1903, Schöngarth joined the NSDAP in 1922 and in 1929 completed a doctorate in employment law. In 1935 he joined the Gestapo, holding various high-ranking posts before taking up his position in the General Government on 30 January 1941. After the German invasion of the Soviet Union, he established an 'Einsatzkommando for special purposes' from Security Police units in the General Government, which carried out mass murders of Jews in the Soviet Union.[234] Schöngarth was also actively involved in preparations for the mass murder of Jews in the General Government. His command 'to shoot on the spot any Jews found wandering about' was referred to earlier.[235]

Born in 1910, Lange had a doctorate in law and began a career in the Gestapo in 1936, becoming acting head of the Gestapo headquarters in Berlin in 1940. In the run-up to the attack on the Soviet Union, Lange took over responsibility for Gestapo and Criminal Police matters in Einsatzgruppe A, which was deployed in the Baltic States and Belarus. He was thus a key player in the murder of the Jews in this region in the second half of 1941.[236] At the beginning of December 1941 he assumed command of Einsatzkommando 2 and thus was commander of the Security Police and Security Service in Latvia.[237]

The suggestion that Heydrich invited him to the conference as a 'practitioner of mass murder'[238] in order to give those present an idea of the reality and feasibility of the murders, as has been claimed, is highly dubious. It is pure speculation that Lange actually spoke about murders in the region he was responsible for. The minutes of the conference contain not a single comment from Lange, and even if Eichmann's claim that methods of killing[239] were discussed there in concrete terms is accurate, whether he is referring to anything Lange said is a completely open question. Apart from that, it was unlikely to have been in line with Heydrich's strategy for the conference to go into too much gory detail about the reality of the 'final solution'.

The historians Andrej Angrick and Peter Klein, who have researched the murders in the Riga area in detail, are nevertheless convinced that important general conclusions can be drawn from the presence of this mass murderer at the conference. They cite the fact that on 19 January, the day before the conference, Lange was responsible for the shooting of around 900 Jews from a transport from Czechoslovakia to the Riga area and deemed 'unfit for work'. This action was, they claim, a clear contravention of Himmler's ban of 30 November and draw the conclusion that 'between 30 November 1941 and 20 January 1942 the scope of the murders carried out as part of the "final solution" had been extended'.[240] In other words, Himmler and Heydrich had in the meantime given permission for Jews from the Reich 'unfit for work' to be systematically murdered.

Leaving aside the fact that the Riga area massacre cannot be proved beyond doubt,[241] if it did in fact happen, it would have been an exception, for as a rule those deported in the total of nineteen 'Riga transports' between December and February were placed in the ghetto and work camps there.[242] Also, the evidence that Angrick and Klein advance of selections of Reich Jews 'unfit for work' in the Latvian camps of Salaspils and Jungfernhof before the Wannsee Conference[243] does not require any far-reaching conclusions to be drawn about any fundamental change in the orders in operation regarding the 'final solution'.[244]

Lange was himself admitting murdering allegedly small groups of deported Jews in early 1942 when, presumably at the beginning of February, he wrote in a report that 'in isolated cases' he had had Jews who had fallen ill executed in the ghetto and the two camps in order to prevent epidemics. He had also 'separated out a number of mentally ill Jews in the same way'.[245] The fact that he gave particular justifications for murdering Reich Jews is a clear indication that he regarded Himmler's general ban of 30 November 1941 as still in force (presumably in reality interpreting the 'justifications' for such 'isolated cases' generously). Had Himmler's ban in the meantime been lifted, Lange would certainly not have hesitated to carry out murderous 'selections' from all the transports and would by the same token have referred to the new orders when writing his report.

Even after the Wannsee Conference, however, Lange was to assume that all Jews who survived the winter could be sent in the spring to the now finally completed camp of Salaspils; the same report expressly states that the construction of the 'new camp for Jews from the Reich' was 'being continued by all Jews fit for work'. The camp would be 'finished by the spring to the extent that all evacuated Jews who survive the winter can be sent to it'. At the same time, Stahlecker, Lange's superior, reported to the RSHA that near Salaspils the construction 'of a large camp for c. 15,000 prisoners' was underway and would be completed 'around the end of April', and was earmarked 'in the first instance for Jews coming from the Reich'. The 'deportation of the Jews' was scheduled for about the middle of the summer. Thus after the Wannsee Conference Lange and Stahlecker were clearly still assuming that Heydrich's plan to deport the Reich Jews to the occupied eastern territories would go ahead.[246]

Finally, there is the question of which high-ranking functionaries from the SS and police were not invited to the Wannsee Conference—and why Heydrich kept them away. It is particularly striking that none of the Higher SS and Police Leaders were summoned to attend; yet these were Himmler's representatives on the ground in the various regions, who on the orders of the Reichsführer SS had played a decisive role in the preceding months in the mass murders in the Soviet Union, the first deportations, and the measures to extend the 'final solution' to Polish territory. It is even more striking in the case of Wilhelm Koppe, who was responsible for the murders using poison gas begun a month previously in Chelmno, Friedrich-Wilhelm Krüger (General Government), whose attendance had been forestalled by 'diplomatic' means, and the HSSPFs in the occupied eastern territories, especially Friedrich Jeckeln, who was responsible for the 'Ostland'. The same applies to SSPF Odilo Globocnik, who played a central role in Himmler's future plans by virtue of his task, begun in November, of establishing the extermination camp Belzec in the Lublin district.

Had Heydrich intended to convey to the conference participants an authentic impression of the state of the 'final solution', he would have been bound to bring in these people as the actual organizers of the deportations and mass murders. But that is precisely what Heydrich did not want. In inviting people to the conference he was still assuming he could push through his own plan for the 'final solution'. He was thus reluctant to acknowledge that Himmler and his colleagues had long since made his plans obsolete by their active interventions; those who had initiated what at the conference he was to describe dismissively as 'stop-gap solutions' would not be given the chance to attend his event.[247]

Top Secret!

30 copies
Copy 16

Minutes of the meeting

I. The following persons were present at the meeting concerning the final solution of the Jewish question that took place in Berlin, 56/58 Am Grossen Wannsee, on 20 January 1942:

Gauleiter Dr Meyer and Reichsamtsleiter Dr Leibbrandt	Reich Ministry for the Occupied Eastern Territories
State Secretary Dr Stuckart	Reich Ministry of the Interior
State Secretary Neumann	Plenipotentiary for the Four-Year Plan
State Secretary Dr Freisler	Reich Ministry of Justice
State Secretary Dr Bühler	Office of the Governor General
Undersecretary Luther	Foreign Ministry
SS Oberführer Klopfer	Party Chancellery
Ministerialdirektor Kritzinger	Reich Chancellery

The minutes

The so-called 'minutes of the meeting' written by Eichmann and approved by Heydrich provide the principal source for the conference. Of the original thirty copies, so far only copy number 16 has been found. It was discovered along with a covering letter dated 26 February in the files of Martin Luther, undersecretary in the Foreign Ministry. There is evidence that the minutes were also received by another ministry. On 7 March Goebbels, the Propaganda Minister, whose state secretary Leopold Gutterer had been unable to attend on 20 January, noted that on the previous day he had read a 'detailed memorandum from the Security Service and Police about the final solution to the Jewish question'. Further details noted closely match those found in the Wannsee Conference minutes.[248] Copy number 16 was discovered by the Allies in March 1947 during their search for documents in preparation for the so-called 'Wilhelmstrasse Trial' and produced in evidence at the trial. It is now kept in the Foreign Ministry's Political Archive in Berlin.[249]

The 'minutes of the meeting' consist of fifteen pages summarizing what was said at the conference, which, according to Eichmann, lasted approximately an hour to an hour and a half. They are therefore not a transcript. According to Eichmann, Heydrich heavily edited his minutes,[250] though this cannot now be demonstrated in detail. During his trial before the Jerusalem District Court Eichmann was at any rate concerned to pin responsibility for the document on Heydrich and to talk down his own role in the conference.

We should base our reading of the 'minutes' on the assumption that they are not a direct reproduction of what was said but a document summarizing the main lines of discussion and decisions reached from the standpoint of the Reich Security Head Office (RSHA). It is still unclear whether the underlinings visible in the typescript are the work

SS Gruppenführer Hofmann	Race and Settlement Head Office
SS Gruppenführer Müller SS Obersturmbannführer Eichmann	Reich Security Head Office
SS Oberführer Dr Schöngarth Commander of the Security Police and the SD in the General Government	Security Police and SD
SS Sturmbannführer Dr Lange Commander of the Security Police and the SD for the General District of Latvia, representing the Commander of the Security Police and the SD for the Reich Commissariat of the Ostland	Security Police and SD

II.   The Chief of the Security Police and SD, SS Obergruppenführer Heydrich, began by announcing that the Reich Marshal had appointed him to take charge of preparations for the final solution of the Jewish question in Europe and indicated that this meeting had been called to clarify fundamental matters. The Reich Marshal's request to receive an outline of the organizational, practical, and material issues connected with the final solution of the Jewish question in Europe required that all the central authorities directly involved in these matters should deal with them jointly in advance, in order to coordinate the lines to be taken.

of the recipient of the minutes (the Foreign Ministry as represented by Undersecretary Martin Luther) or were added after 1945.[251]

Following the list of participants on the first two pages of the minutes Heydrich states, as he had done already in his invitation, 'that the Reich Marshal had appointed him to take charge of preparations for the final solution of the Jewish question in Europe'. The purpose of the conference was to 'clarify fundamental matters'; Göring wished him, Heydrich, to produce 'an outline of the organizational, practical, and material issues connected with the final solution of the Jewish question in Europe' and this required that 'all the central authorities directly involved in these matters should deal with them jointly in advance, in order to coordinate the lines to be taken'. Heydrich's phrase 'preparations for the final solution' and the mention of an 'outline' that he still had to work out are clear indications that the actual order to implement the 'final solution' was not yet in his hands. His 'outline' had first to be approved.

What is immediately striking about Heydrich's choice of words is that, as in the second letter of invitation, he no longer refers to Göring's commission as a 'total solution' but as a 'final solution'. There is no doubt that this choice of expression reflects a radicalization of the prospective 'solution', now presented as definitively final. Also, the development of 'Jewish policy' in the most recent months as well as the pronouncements by Hitler and leading functionaries on the subject suggest only too plainly that, even if the details had not yet been decided, this 'final solution' would be a murderous one. Heydrich's intention was to wait until the conference itself to provide more detail about what would actually be involved.[252]

In the second paragraph of the minutes Heydrich refers to a central concern, namely his demand that 'overall control of the implementation of the final solution of the Jewish question' should lie 'with the Reichsführer SS and Chief of the German Police (Chief of the Security Police and the SD)'—in other words, with him—'regardless of geographical borders'.

In referring to the Reichsführer SS, namely Himmler, Heydrich is introducing a second source of authority in addition to Göring—one who will guarantee Heydrich's central role in the implementation of the 'final solution'. The reference to the unlimited scope of his commission is directed in particular at the representatives at the conference of the Ministry for the East and of the General Government. With

Regardless of geographical borders, overall control of the implementation of the final solution of the Jewish question lay centrally with the Reichsführer SS and Chief of the German Police (Chief of the Security Police and the SD).

The Chief of the Security Police and SD then gave a brief review of the struggle thus far against this enemy, the essential points being:

a) the exclusion of the Jews from every sphere of German life,

b) the exclusion of the Jews from the German nation's living space.

As the only feasible temporary measure to achieve these goals, Jewish emigration from Reich territory was being further accelerated and pursued methodically.

In January 1939, on the orders of the Reich Marshal, a Reich Central Office for Jewish Emigration had been established under the authority of the Chief of the Security Police and SD. Its main tasks were

a) to make all necessary arrangements to <u>prepare</u> for an increase in Jewish emigration,

b) to <u>direct</u> the flow of emigration,

c) to accelerate emigration in <u>individual cases</u>.

The objective was to cleanse German living space of Jews in a legal manner.

regard to powers and responsibilities, in the run-up to the conference the SS leadership had agreed a compromise with the Ministry for the East in a form of words that did not in essence really resolve the matter of who had overall control of the 'Jewish question' but rather left it up in the air.[253] Heydrich's evident fear before the conference that Frank was seeking the dominant role in the persecution of the Jews for the General Government was not confirmed at the conference itself. On the contrary, at the end of the conference Frank's representative, Bühler, was to acknowledge that Heydrich was in charge.

The minutes then report Heydrich's fairly lengthy review of 'Jewish policy' up to that point: the 'exclusion of the Jews', first of all 'from every sphere of German life', then 'from the German nation's living space'. In this context Heydrich makes special reference (page 62) to the 'Reich Central Office for Jewish Emigration' (also created on Göring's instructions), of which the Reich Marshal had appointed him head in January 1939.

Heydrich goes on to highlight, on the one hand, the achievements of the emigration programme—a total of 537,000 Jews (the figures are somewhat exaggerated) from the Reich, including the Ostmark (Austria) and the Protectorate of Bohemia and Moravia, had been 'induced' to emigrate by the end of October 1941[254]—while on the other hand also emphasizing the 'drawbacks' and thus the provisional nature of emigration as a solution; 'in the absence of alternative solutions' there had been no other choice at the time. The situation had changed as a result of the introduction of Himmler's ban (dating from 23 October 1941) on emigration, a measure that, as Heydrich expressly states, was introduced 'in view of the hazards of emigration in wartime and of the possibilities opened up by the East' (page 66).

The minutes then move on to a new (specially numbered) section of Heydrich's remarks, focusing on future 'Jewish policy'. Every single word in the minutes has special importance for the interpretation of this passage.

'In place of emigration, with prior approval from the Führer', Heydrich's presentation continues, 'the evacuation of the Jews to the East has now emerged as a further possible solution'. These 'Aktionen' (meaning the evacuation) 'must, however, be regarded merely as stop-gap solutions [...] providing practical experience that will be very important for the impending final solution to the Jewish question'.

All the agencies involved recognized the drawbacks of such accelerated emigration. In the absence of alternative solutions, however, for the time being these drawbacks had to be accepted.

Subsequently, dealing with emigration had not been only a German problem, but also a problem confronting the authorities in the countries to which Jews were emigrating. Financial difficulties, such as increases in charges for visas and landing fees by the various foreign governments, a lack of berths on ships, ever tighter immigration quotas, or even bans on immigration had greatly added to the difficulties of emigration. In spite of these difficulties, c. 537,000 Jews in all had been induced to leave the country between the takeover of power [30 January 1933] and 31 October 1941. Of these

from 30.1.1933 from the Altreich	c. 360,000
from 15.3.1938 from Austria	c. 147,000
from 15.3.1939 from the Protectorate of Bohemia and Moravia	c. 30,000

The Jews themselves, or Jewish political organizations, financed the emigration. In order to avoid proletarianized Jews remaining behind, the principle was adopted of wealthy Jews having to finance the emigration of Jews with no property; accordingly, a contribution or emigration fee, graded according to wealth, was required and used to pay the financial costs of emigration for Jews without assets.

Heydrich is careful here to distinguish between 'the impending final solution' (in other words, the project he is heading and laying the groundwork for, which is supposed to be the real focus of the conference) and the 'Aktionen', namely the evacuations that have already started. The latter must be regarded as 'stop-gap solutions' and therefore only provisional, though they provide experience that will support the 'impending final solution'. Even though they are only a temporary measure and should not be confused with the actual 'final solution', Heydrich considers it necessary to emphasize the fact that they have been authorized by Hitler ('prior approval from the Führer'). This is notably the only place in the text where the 'Führer' is explicitly mentioned; the fact that in speaking of the 'impending final solution' Heydrich does not refer to Hitler reveals that at this point the latter had not yet provided formal authorization, nor could such authorization exist, for Heydrich had first to seek approval for his 'outline' of 'preparations' for the 'final solution'.

Heydrich then returns to *his* project, the 'final solution of the European Jewish question', stating that 'around 11 million Jews will be involved'.

The list of the numbers of Jews in individual countries raises a number of questions. We do not know, for example, whether Heydrich read out the figures as they are written, whether they were handed out for perusal at the meeting, or whether they were inserted later into the minutes in tabular form.[255] What is striking is that the table contains figures for countries that were either neutral or at the time at war with Germany: The British, Irish, Portuguese, Swedish, Swiss, Spanish, and Turkish Jews who form part of the 11 million could only have fallen into Nazi hands after a total German victory. The same is true of the estimated 5 million Jews in the Soviet Union, a clear indication that the 'final solution of the European Jewish question' was a project that could have been carried out in its entirety only after the end of the war.

The figures for France have prompted some speculation. In addition to the 165,000 Jews in occupied France, the 700,000 given for 'unoccupied territory' must comprise Jews from France's North African colonies. Even so, the figure is too high.[256] It may be a simple arithmetical mistake. As we already know, the *Frankfurter Zeitung* of 4 December 1941 published the following figures and there is evidence that they had been given to Eichmann: 165,000 Jews in occupied France, 170,000 in unoccupied France, plus about 360,000 in its North African

Apart from the sums required in Reich marks, foreign exchange had also been needed to pay for visas and landing fees. In order to protect German foreign exchange reserves, Jewish financial institutions abroad were requested by Jewish organizations in the Reich to ensure the provision of the required foreign exchange. Up to 30.10.1941 these Jews abroad had donated a total of around 9,500,000 dollars.

In the meantime, in view of the hazards of emigration in wartime and of the possibilities opened up by the East, the Reichsführer SS and Chief of the German Police had banned Jewish emigration.

III.   In place of emigration, with prior approval from the Führer, the evacuation of the Jews to the East has now emerged as a further possible solution.

These actions [Aktionen] must, however, be regarded merely as stop-gap solutions, although they are providing practical experience that will be very important for the impending final solution to the Jewish question.

Around 11 million Jews will be involved in the final solution of the European Jewish question, distributed as follows among the individual countries:

possessions. It is conceivable that the figure of 700,000 given for the 'unoccupied territory' arose in error from the addition of the three numbers, the total (695,000) then being rounded up.

It is therefore in principle altogether plausible that North African Jews were included in the 'final solution of the European Jewish question' at the Wannsee Conference. In fact, from spring 1942 an Einsatzkommando was being created to accompany Rommel's Panzer army as it advanced across the Suez Canal; when this plan failed the Einsatzkommando was deployed from the end of the year in Tunisia, where it began to segregate the local Jews from the rest of the population, introduce forced labour, and impose levies.[257] The fact that only the Jews living in the European part of the Soviet Union and Turkey were included in the table cannot be taken to indicate that the manic destructiveness of a victorious Nazi Germany would have stopped at the Urals or the Bosphorus. Had Rommel's troops crossed the Suez Canal, the Jewish population of Palestine would have been targeted also. These inconsistencies reveal the extent to which at the start of 1942 much of the 'final solution' was a project for the longer term.

Also striking are the figures given for Latvia and Lithuania and the fact that Estonia is stated as being 'free of Jews'. According to *Der Grosse Brockhaus*, the standard encyclopaedia at the time, in the pre-war period there were 5,000 Jews in Estonia, 100,000 in Latvia, and 155,000 in Lithuania rather than the figures of 3,500 for Latvia and 34,000 for Lithuania that appear in the table.[258] The RSHA had therefore taken into account the numbers of Jews already murdered and had evidently had no qualms about revealing this fact in the official minutes.

The impression of precision and purposefulness created by the list of figures is, however, quickly modified as the minutes continue. One instance is the comment that the figures apply primarily to 'practising Jews', as the definition of being Jewish based on the racial criteria of the Nuremberg Laws has not been introduced throughout Europe; another is the reference to the 'difficulties' expected 'particularly' in the implementation of 'Jewish policy' in Hungary and Romania. The 'employment structure' of the Soviet Jews that follows on from this somewhat inconsequentially is probably there to restore the impression of a project based on statistical analysis.

At the bottom of page 70 we find the critical passage in the minutes in which the 'final solution' itself is described in more detail: 'Jews fit

68 WANNSEE

Country	Number
A. Altreich	131,800
Ostmark	43,700
Eastern territories	420,000
General Government	2,284,000
Bialystok	400,000
Protectorate of Bohemia and Moravia	74,200
Estonia – free of Jews –	
Latvia	3,500
Lithuania	34,000
Belgium	43,000
Denmark	5,600
France / Occupied territory	165,000
Unoccupied territory	700,000
Greece	69,600
The Netherlands	160,800
Norway	1,300
B. Bulgaria	48,000
England	330,000
Finland	2,300
Ireland	4,000
Italy including Sardinia	58,000
Albania	200
Croatia	40,000
Portugal	3,000
Romania including Bessarabia	342,000
Sweden	8,000
Switzerland	18,000
Serbia	10,000
Slovakia	88,000
Spain	6,000
Turkey (European part)	55,500
Hungary	742,800
USSR	5,000,000
Ukraine 2,994,684	
White Russia excluding Bialystok 446,484	
Total: over	11,000,000

for work will be taken to these territories in large work gangs. Men and women will be segregated and made to construct roads, in the course of which the majority will doubtless succumb to natural wastage'.

The following sentence leaves no doubt that 'natural wastage' means death on a massive scale as a result of inhumane working conditions. 'The remaining Jews who survive', who are 'doubtless the toughest', will, to quote the expression used at this point, 'have to be dealt with accordingly'. Given that they represent 'a natural selection, they would, if released, be the germ cell for a new Jewish regeneration', as the 'experience of history' had shown. In plain language: not only would those who survived forced labour be murdered in an unspecified manner ('dealt with accordingly' is in itself a clear example of Gestapo jargon), but, as the remarks on preventing a 'new Jewish regeneration' reveal, the rest of the Jews not 'fit for work'—in other words, the women and children—would by no means escape this mass murder, while the segregation of men and women was designed to prevent any future progeny.

In older research this key passage has been read as a veiled reference to the mass murder of deported Jews that was to begin a few months later in the gas chambers of the extermination camps[259] (a system under which Jews were indeed designated either as 'fit for work' or 'unfit for work'). In more recent studies, however, it has become increasingly apparent that in talking about constructing roads Heydrich was pursuing concrete plans. At the start of 1942 large numbers of Jews from the local population were being used as forced labour in road construction projects in the occupied eastern territories. Himmler himself was putting serious effort into the plan for a link road (Durchgangsstrasse IV) between Lemberg (Lviv) and the Donets region.[260]

The 'control of the implementation' of the final solution that Heydrich wished to secure once and for all by means of the Wannsee Conference was designed to give the SS authority to use the Jews deported to the east as forced labour without restriction. As we have already seen, only a few days before the conference the Higher SS and Police Leader (HSSPF) in the Ukraine was preparing the Regional Commissars for the arrival of more Jews from the Reich in the course of 1942 and was planning to have them accommodated in special ghettos.[261] Also, only a few days before the conference Himmler had

The numbers of Jews given for the various foreign states refer only to practising Jews, for in some countries there are as yet no definitions of Jewishness based on racial principles. Dealing with this problem in certain countries will give rise to difficulties arising from people's attitude and outlook, particularly in Hungary and Romania. For example, Jews in Romania today can still buy documents officially confirming that they are foreign nationals.

The Jews' influence in all spheres of the Soviet Union is well known. In the European part there are about 5 million, in the Asiatic part just under ¼ million Jews.

The employment structure of Jews living in the European

Agriculture	9.1%
Urban workers	14.8%
Commerce and trade	20.0%
State employees	23.4%
Private occupations – medicine, the press, theatre etc.	32.7%

part of the Soviet Union was approximately as follows:

As part of the final solution the Jews are now to be deployed for labour in the East in an appropriate manner and under suitable supervision. Jews fit for work will be taken to these territories in large work gangs. Men and women will be segregated and made to construct roads, in the course of which the majority will doubtless succumb to natural wastage.

initiated the establishment of the SS Business and Administration Head Office (WVHA), which would bring together the planning for the SS's gigantic building projects and for the most effective exploitation of concentration camp prisoners as forced labour under one roof.[262] A few days after the Wannsee Conference Himmler ordered 150,000 Jews from Germany to be sent to concentration camps with the aim of creating a pool of forced labour for the SS's ambitious construction plans in the eastern territories.[263] On 4 February 1942 in a confidential address to members of the government of the Protectorate, Heydrich, on the other hand, was to describe the 'Russian concentration camps' in the Arctic Circle as the 'ideal homeland' for the 11 million Jews deported from Europe,[264] thus making it clear once again that he had not yet given up his original plan. Himmler too was still pursuing this idea in February.[265]

Back to the minutes: Heydrich then describes how 'in the course of the implementation of the final solution Europe will be combed from West to East', although 'Reich territory, including the Protectorate of Bohemia and Moravia, will of necessity anticipate future developments'. Use of the word 'anticipate' once again indicates that Heydrich considered the current deportations from Reich territory to be merely 'stop-gap solutions' that did not represent the actual 'final solution'. Heydrich provides a specific explanation for this anticipatory move by citing the 'issue of housing and other socio-political exigencies' (page 72). It is true that a number of Gauleiters in the previous months had justified the accelerated 'expulsion' of the Jews from cities by pointing to housing problems, and, not least as a result of increased bombing raids, the vacated 'Jewish accommodation' was to become highly sought after.[266] 'The evacuated Jews', Heydrich continues, 'will first be transported in stages to so-called transit ghettos and from there further eastwards'. Jews over the age of sixty-five, 'severely disabled Jewish war veterans and Jews with war decorations' will be excused from the deportations; a special 'old people's ghetto'—Theresienstadt in the Protectorate was the camp envisaged—will be established for them.[267]

Heydrich goes on to say that the 'start date of individual large-scale evacuations' would depend on 'military developments', thus making it clear that the next round of deportations and the beginning of the large-scale programme of evacuations, the 'impending final solution', would not take place before the following spring.

The remaining Jews who survive, doubtless the toughest among them, will have to be dealt with accordingly, for, being a natural selection, they would, if released, be the germ cell for a new Jewish regeneration (see the experience of history).

In the course of the implementation of the final solution Europe will be combed from West to East. Reich territory, including the Protectorate of Bohemia and Moravia, will of necessity anticipate future developments, if only because of the issue of housing and other socio-political exigencies.

The evacuated Jews will first be transported in stages to so-called transit ghettos and from there further eastwards.

A vital precondition for any evacuation, SS Obergruppenführer Heydrich continued, is to define precisely which people are to be affected.

It is not intended to evacuate Jews over the age of 65 but rather to transfer them to an old people's ghetto. Theresienstadt is envisaged for this.

In addition to this age group – of the roughly 280,000 Jews remaining on 31.10.1941 in the Altreich and the Ostmark around 30% are over 65 years of age – severely disabled Jewish war veterans and Jews with war decorations (Iron Cross First Class) will also be accommodated in the Jewish old people's ghettos. This expedient solution will put an end to numerous interventions at a stroke.

With regard to countries 'occupied or influenced' by Germany, 'the desk officers in the Foreign Ministry' would liaise with the 'responsible desk officer of the Security Police and SD' (meaning Eichmann, who was present at the meeting).[268]

Heydrich then describes the situation in respect of individual countries. His assessment of Slovakia and Croatia is positive: deportations from Slovakia had in fact already been agreed with the Slovak government, while the Croatian government had already taken the initiative in October in asking the Germans to begin preparations for the deportation of Jews there (the RSHA refused, however).[269] Heydrich notes with approval that the Romanian government has already appointed 'someone to be responsible for Jewish affairs' (a reference to Radu Lecca,[270] who had just been appointed and was cooperating closely with the Germans). By contrast, it would 'shortly be necessary to impose an adviser for Jewish questions on the Hungarian government', though this plan was not to be realized until 1944.

Regarding Italy, Heydrich advocates liaising with the Police Chief there, masking the fact that the Italians had no interest in adopting German 'Jewish policy'.[271] In the case of France, Heydrich can see no particular difficulties. Months earlier Himmler had made a clear declaration of intent to deport the French Jews and the military administration was already planning transports of hostages.

At this stage Undersecretary Luther, who was head of the Germany section at the Foreign Ministry and responsible for the 'Jewish question', intervenes and points out that in several countries, for example the 'Nordic states' (in other words, in occupied Denmark and Norway and in Finland, Germany's ally), there were still some 'difficulties' to overcome. Given the 'small numbers of Jews' there (page 74), this was not a significant problem. The Foreign Ministry did not anticipate 'any major difficulties' in dealing with south-east and western Europe.

Luther's statement provides the bridge to a general discussion among the participants focusing first of all on the precise definition of those to be affected. Although the minutes emphasize that the Nuremberg Laws are to form 'the basis for carrying out the final solution project', the following statement that the precondition for a 'comprehensive resolution of this problem' is finding a 'solution to the issues of mixed marriages and the Mischlinge' indicates that precisely in these matters Heydrich intended to ride roughshod over the prevailing legal provisions.

The start date of individual large-scale evacuations will depend to a great extent on military developments. As far as dealing with the final solution in those European territories occupied or influenced by us is concerned, it was proposed that the Foreign Ministry's desk officers would liaise with the responsible desk officer of the Security Police and SD.

In Slovakia and Croatia the matter is no longer all that difficult as the key issues in this respect have already been resolved there. In Romania the government has meanwhile also appointed someone to be responsible for Jewish affairs. In order to deal with the question in Hungary it will shortly be necessary to impose an adviser for Jewish questions on the Hungarian government.

With regard to the initiation of preparations for dealing with the problem in Italy, SS Obergruppenführer Heydrich considers liaison with the Police Chief over these matters to be appropriate.

In occupied and unoccupied France the registration of Jews for evacuation can probably go ahead without undue difficulties.

Undersecretary Luther commented that if this problem is dealt with thoroughly then difficulties will arise in some countries, for example in the Nordic states, and it would therefore be advisable to exclude those countries for the time being. In view of the small numbers of Jews involved there, this postponement would not in any case represent a significant restriction.

The Nuremberg Laws and the subsequent provisions for their implementation had turned the '1st-degree Mischlinge' into that 'intermediate' race whose members, while suffering discrimination, were not subject to the regulations governing 'full Jews'. From 1938/9 onwards the Nazi state had begun to concede certain 'privileges' to some of the roughly 20,000 'mixed marriages', in particular if the children of such marriages had not been brought up as Jewish and thus did not automatically 'count' as Jews. Their privileged status consisted above all in the fact that families were allowed to remain in their homes, their property could be transferred to the non-Jewish partner, and in 1941 they were not forced to wear the yellow star.[272]

In the run-up to the Wannsee Conference, however, and in view of the impending deportations, as described above, a coalition of the NSDAP's Office for Racial Policy, the RSHA, and the Party Chancellery had made persistent efforts to remove the distinction between 'half-Jews' and Jews. In particular, regulations to that effect were introduced in the occupied territories that were designed to create a fait accompli that would then be repeated in Reich territory. Significantly—and this is always overlooked in analyses of the minutes—at the Wannsee Conference Heydrich addressed the issue of 'mixed marriages' and 'Mischlinge' solely in relation to the 'Greater German Reich'; in doing so he succeeded from the outset in separating the clarification of this issue in the Reich from that in the rest of Europe and in frustrating the efforts of the Ministry of the Interior to create a single 'definition of Jewishness' in Europe.[273] As a result, the Ministry for the East in particular gained a free hand in its aim to introduce a largely arbitrary 'definition of Jewishness' in the occupied eastern territories. As early as 29 January it called an inter-ministerial meeting to discuss the 'definition of Jewishness' in the occupied eastern territories. The invitation and draft plan were sent out on 22 January; in other words, deliberately 'ahead of any announcement about the outcome of the state secretaries' meeting' with its anticipated stipulations regarding the 'Mischling question'.[274]

As far as clarifying the issue in the Reich was concerned, the head of the Reich Chancellery had issued a written statement in August 1941 claiming that Hitler had explicitly stated that he was fundamentally against categorizing 'Mischlinge' as Jews, whereas the RSHA and Party Chancellery asserted that they possessed an instruction to the

The Foreign Ministry does not, on the other hand, envisage any major difficulties with south-east and western Europe.

SS Gruppenführer Hofmann intends to send a representative of the Race and Settlement Head Office to Hungary for the purpose of general orientation when things are set in motion there by the Chief of the Security Police and SD. It was agreed that this representative of the Race and Settlement Head Office, who should not play an active role, would be provisionally officially assigned to the police attaché as an aide.

IV.   The Nuremberg Laws will form, so to speak, the basis for carrying out the final solution project; a precondition for the comprehensive resolution of this problem is, however, to find a solution to the issues of mixed marriages and the Mischlinge.

The Chief of the Security Police and the SD discussed – in the first instance theoretically – the following points relating to a letter from the head of the Reich Chancellery:

1)   <u>Treatment of 1st-Degree Mischlinge</u>

As far as the final solution of the Jewish question is concerned, 1st-degree Mischlinge are to be treated as Jews.

contrary from Hitler regarding the planned 'final solution', though they did not produce it in writing.[275] The formulation in the minutes that Heydrich had begun a 'theoretical' discussion of a series of points 'relating to a letter from the head of the Reich Chancellery' shows that at the time of the conference this issue had not yet been unequivocally decided in line with Heydrich's thinking, for otherwise any further discussion would have been superfluous.

Heydrich was therefore being deliberate in using the formulation, 'As far as the final solution of the Jewish question is concerned, 1st-degree Mischlinge are to be treated as Jews' (page 76), going on, however, to specify two exceptions, namely 'Mischlinge' with non-Jewish spouses and children from such marriages, and also those 'to whom the highest authorities in the Party or the state have hitherto granted exemptions'.[276] After careful examination of each individual case, both of these groups were to be 'voluntarily' sterilized. On the other hand, '2nd-degree Mischlinge' were to be treated as persons of German blood 'as a matter of principle', though Heydrich gives details of particular exceptions to this ruling.

With regard to marriages between 'full Jews and persons of German blood' (page 80), a decision had to be reached in each individual case over whether or not to deport the Jewish partner. In addition, Heydrich refers to marriages of '1st-degree Mischlinge'; deportation in their case was to depend on the status of the spouse (whether of 'German blood', Jewish, or a '1st-degree or '2nd-degree Mischling') and whether there were children (pages 80/82).

The comment that follows from Hofmann, the head of the Race and Settlement Head Office, that there should be 'extensive use of sterilization' as the people concerned would prefer this to being deported (page 82) makes it clear once more that the entire discussion was conducted on the basis that deportation meant death.

In an attempt to preserve 'Mischling' (a category he had taken the lead in creating) as a category at least in the Reich, while also salvaging his personal prestige and that of his ministry, Stuckart, state secretary in the Ministry of the Interior, takes up Hofmann's suggestion. He insists that the fine distinctions Heydrich proposes in the regulations would involve 'an immense amount of administrative work' and suggests compulsory sterilization in all doubtful cases and compulsory divorce for couples in mixed marriages.[277]

The following will be exceptions:

a) 1st-degree Mischlinge married to persons of German blood whose marriage has produced children (2nd-degree Mischlinge). These 2nd-degree Mischlinge are essentially to be treated as Germans.

b) 1st-degree Mischlinge to whom the highest authorities in the Party or the state have hitherto granted exemptions in any particular spheres of life.

Every case must be examined individually and there can be no guarantee that the decision will not go against the Mischling this time.

Any exemption must always be based on the intrinsic merits of the Mischling in question rather than on the merits of a parent or spouse of German blood.

To prevent any progeny and solve the Mischling problem once and for all, 1st-degree Mischlinge exempted from the evacuations will be sterilized. Sterilization will be voluntary but will be a precondition for remaining in the Reich. Sterilized 'Mischlinge' will subsequently be released from all restrictions that have hitherto been imposed on them.

2) Treatment of 2nd-degree Mischlinge

2nd-degree Mischlinge will as a matter of principle be treated as persons of German blood except in the following instances, in which they will be treated as Jews:

Neumann, the representative of the Four-Year Plan, interjects that Jews involved in work essential to the war effort cannot be deported. Heydrich counters this by pointing out that in practice this request is already being met.

Towards the end of the meeting there is quite a long statement from Bühler, the state secretary in the General Government, the significance of which is clearly underestimated in many interpretations of the Wannsee Conference. Bühler proposes that 'the final solution of this question' should begin in the General Government, as 'there is no significant transport problem there' (page 84) and the operation 'would not be impeded by labour issues' (in any case, the majority of the Jews were, he claimed, 'unfit for work'). The risks of epidemics and black-market activity were already reasons why the Jews should be 'removed as quickly as possible from General Government territory'. This removal did not, however, refer to the deportation of Jews to the occupied Soviet territories, for which Governor General Frank secured Hitler's agreement in spring and summer 1941, for in view of the military situation and the transport crisis this 'removal' was now impossible.

What Bühler meant by 'removed' is instead hidden within the formulation of the paragraph further down the same page, which states that 'Finally, the various possible types of solution were discussed'. Both Bühler and Alfred Meyer, his colleague from the Ministry for the East, advocate 'that certain preliminary measures for the final solution should be carried out right away in the relevant territories themselves'. Bühler and Meyer may well have been referring to the methods of murder that had been used or developed in their territories in the previous months: mass executions in the occupied eastern territories and in Galicia, gas vans in Meyer's territory, and the construction of the extermination camp Belzec in the Lublin district, which began in November 1941. These mass murders that had already taken place or were being planned in detail were aimed primarily at Jews 'unfit for work', who were to be selected from the Jewish population as a whole and immediately murdered. The remainder (in any case a minority) would first of all be subjected to forced labour and then 'dealt with accordingly', as Heydrich had explained in his remarks.

This interpretation and contextualization of the minutes based on the actual wording of the text can be summed up as follows: in the meeting Heydrich was still presenting the plan for a solution involving

a) If a 2nd-degree Mischling is the offspring of a bastard marriage (in which both partners are Mischlinge)

b) If a 2nd-degree Mischling's appearance is particularly unfavourable racially and already makes him/her look like a Jew.

c) If particularly negative police or political assessments indicate that a 2nd-degree Mischling feels and behaves like a Jew.

Even in cases such as these, exceptions should not be applied if the 2nd-degree Mischling is married to someone of German blood.

3) <u>Marriages between full Jews and persons of German blood</u>

These must be handled on a case-by-case basis to determine if the Jewish partner is to be evacuated or if, in view of the impact of such a measure on the German relatives in this mixed marriage, he/she should be transferred to an old people's ghetto.

4) <u>Marriages between 1st-degree Mischlinge and persons of German blood</u>

a) Without children.

If there are no children from the marriage the 1st-degree Mischling will be evacuated or transferred to an old people's ghetto. (The same treatment as in the case of marriages between full Jews and persons of German blood. See point 3) large-scale deportation to the occupied Soviet territories that he had been developing since spring 1941 and which for the most part could not have been realized until after the war. As his comments suggest, the plan was to be activated on the basis of an outline he had prepared after consultation with the 'central authorities'. It would have amounted to 11 million European Jews being deported to the periphery of the new German empire and, over a period of time as yet unspecified, physically exterminated through a combination of exhausting forced labour, catastrophic living conditions in camps, and direct large-scale killings, while births would also be prevented.

As a result of a decision by Hitler, deportations from Reich territory, with intermediate stops in the occupied eastern territories, had already commenced, thus partially 'anticipating' this plan, although the necessary groundwork and planning had not yet been completed. The scope of those affected by the deportations had not yet been defined, nor were there arrangements for exemptions in the case of older people and those severely wounded in war, though without such arrangements it was completely implausible that the deportations to the east were being carried out in order to put people to work. In addition, the 'central authorities' involved in the programme had not yet committed to it.

As Berlin had intended, the deportations in autumn and winter 1941 had led to a chain reaction, in the course of which the regional authorities in Lodz, Belzec, Riga, and Minsk/Mogilev had begun carrying out or preparing for mass murders of local Jews on the spot. Bearing in mind that the 'anticipatory' deportations had been urged by Himmler in particular, who went on to encourage those responsible locally to draw the 'correct' (i.e. the most radical) conclusions from the chaos caused by those deportations, we can begin to discern two increasingly competing lines being taken in 'Jewish policy' in these decisive months. On the one hand, Heydrich was still pursuing a solution through massive deportation on the basis of a fully worked-out overall plan, and, on the other, Himmler was aiming to boost by all available means the murder process that had been set in motion in particular key areas by the deportations, without waiting for an overall plan. In this situation Bühler was alluding in his comments to the possibility that the majority of the Jews in the General Government, the largest Jewish population under German rule, could be murdered on the spot by being declared 'unfit for work'.

b) With children.

If the marriage has produced children (2nd-degree Mischlinge) and <u>these children are being treated as Jews</u>, they will be evacuated along with the 1st-degree Mischling or transferred to a ghetto. If these children <u>are being treated as Germans</u> (the normal case) they are to be exempted from evacuation, as is the 1st-degree Mischling also.

5) <u>Marriages between 1st-degree Mischlinge and 1st-degree Mischlinge or Jews</u>

In the case of these marriages, all parties, including children, will be treated as Jews and therefore evacuated or transferred to an old people's ghetto.

6) <u>Marriages between 1st-degree Mischlinge and 2nd-degree Mischlinge</u>

Both partners will be evacuated or transferred to an old people's ghetto, regardless of whether there are children, as, racially speaking, any children will as a rule have a greater proportion of Jewish blood than 2nd-degree Jewish Mischlinge.

SS Gruppenführer Hofmann took the view that there must be extensive use of sterilization, in particular because any Mischlinge faced with the choice of being evacuated or sterilized would rather submit to sterilization.

State Secretary Dr Stuckart commented that the practical implementation of the solutions to the issues of mixed marriages and Mischlinge just announced would in its present form involve an immense amount of administrative work. On the other hand, to take the biological realities fully into account, State Secretary Dr Stuckart proposed that compulsory sterilization be adopted.

Furthermore, in order to simplify the issue of mixed marriages, thought should be given to the possibility of the legislator simply declaring, for example: 'These marriages <u>are</u> hereby dissolved'.

Thus the Wannsee Conference set in motion a process of redefining the when, how, and where of the 'final solution'. The extermination of the European Jews now turned into a project that was no longer to be carried out mainly after the war but completed during the war itself. The 'final solution' of the European 'Jewish question' was no longer to take place in the occupied Soviet territories; instead, the main activity was to be moved to occupied Poland. Instead of killing the European Jews by means of catastrophic living conditions and shootings, new possibilities of using various technologies for killing people by gassing had developed in the previous few months. As a result, at the Wannsee Conference an alternative to the programme for the 'final solution' proposed by Heydrich was emerging. The precise method by which the 'final solution' would be carried out was decided not at the conference itself but rather in the months that followed.

Concerning the issue of the economic impact of Jewish evacuation, State Secretary Neumann stated that Jews currently working in industries vital to the war effort could not be evacuated while no replacements were available.

SS Obergruppenführer Heydrich pointed out that, according to the guidelines he had approved for the implementation of the evacuations currently in progress, these Jews were not in any case being evacuated.

State Secretary Dr Bühler stated that the General Government would welcome it if the final solution of this question <u>were to begin in the General Government</u> because there was no significant transport problem there and the running of this operation would not be impeded by labour issues. Jews should be removed as quickly as possible from General Government territory because it was here in particular that the Jew as a carrier of epidemics presented a serious threat and in addition was constantly destabilizing the country's economic structure by continuous black market activities. Moreover, of the c. 2.5 million Jews in question most were <u>unfit for work</u>.

State Secretary Dr Bühler further stated that the solution to the Jewish question in the General Government was the responsibility of the Chief of the Security Police and SD and his initiatives would be supported by the authorities in the General Government. He had only one request, namely that the Jewish question be resolved as quickly as possible in this territory.

Finally, the various possible types of solution were discussed. Both Gauleiter Dr Meyer and State Secretary Dr Bühler expressed the view that certain preliminary measures for the final solution should be carried out right away in the relevant territories themselves, though without causing concern among the population.

The meeting closed with the Chief of the Security Police and SD's request to the participants to give him appropriate support in implementing the solution.

3

The 'final solution' becomes a reality

The day after the Wannsee Conference Heydrich informed Himmler by telephone of the most important outcomes.[278] Only a few days later Heydrich felt obliged to emphasize once again his central role in the future 'final solution' by sending copies of his 'appointment' by Göring of 31 July 1941 to a fairly large circle of leading functionaries in the Security Police and the Security Service and also to the head of the SS Personnel Head Office and to Governor General Frank (who had of course been represented at the Wannsee Conference by Bühler).[279] All these letters conclude with the sentence 'The preparatory work has begun', which was designed to emphasize Heydrich's commitment to carrying out the task Göring had given him without further delay.

After the Wannsee Conference Hitler for his part made explicit public announcements that the European Jews would be murdered during the war. On 30 January, ten days after the Wannsee Conference, in his speech at the Sportpalast on the anniversary of the 'seizure of power', he declared, 'We are fully convinced that the war can end only with the extermination of the Aryan nations or the disappearance of the Jews from Europe'.[280] In a declaration on the twenty-second anniversary of the founding of the Party on 24 February 1942 he said, 'my prophecy will be fulfilled. The Aryan peoples will not be destroyed by this war but rather the Jews will be exterminated'.[281]

'Extermination through labour'

The events of the weeks and months following the Wannsee Conference show that the two competing strands of the SS's 'Jewish policy', as represented by Heydrich and Himmler, were now being merged and combined with Bühler's proposals into a comprehensive programme to bring about a European 'final solution'. A key component in this was the issue of Jewish 'labour deployment'. Heydrich's idea of moving the Jews to the occupied eastern territories 'to construct roads' and thereby to decimate them was now transformed into the plan for concentration camp prisoners to carry out forced labour, again with the deliberate intention of destroying the Jews. Above all, the removal of the Jews who were 'unfit for work', which Heydrich had addressed only indirectly, was turned into a systematic plan to murder them. Identifying Jews who were not suitable for 'labour deployment' or seemed surplus to needs amounted to a decision to kill them by means of poison gas.

To explain the significance of Jewish 'labour deployment' in the context of planning for the 'final solution', it is necessary to outline how it developed in the months before and after the Wannsee Conference. As early as summer 1941 Himmler had initiated preparations to use large numbers of concentration camp inmates in the large-scale settlement projects the SS was planning for eastern Europe. First of all, he had a camp set up in Lublin for 25,000 to 50,000 prisoners to provide the basis for this forced labour.[282] In September 1941, after the Wehrmacht had agreed to transfer responsibility for Soviet prisoners of war to him, he ordered a further prisoner of war camp to be set up in Birkenau, close to Auschwitz concentration camp.[283]

Between January and March 1942 Himmler created the organizational basis for the most effective exploitation of prisoners' labour. He established the SS Business and Administration Head Office (WVHA) under Oswald Pohl, which combined responsibilities for construction programmes, budgets, and administrative affairs with control of the concentration camps.[284] The principal task of the new Head Office was first to prepare a grandiose SS 'peace-time construction programme', whose development can be traced from December 1941 to March 1942. Instructed by Himmler to make the project as large-scale as possible, the SS head of construction Hans Kammler produced a programme costing between 20 and 30 billion Reich marks that included in particular the planned settlements in the 'eastern territory' earmarked for development. In order to realize this project Kammler planned to establish SS construction squads totalling 175,000 people and composed of 'prison inmates, POWs, Jews etc.'.[285]

By the New Year of 1942 it was, however, already evident that the Soviet POWs originally earmarked for the SS construction projects would not be available. Their health had been undermined by the inhumane conditions in the camps and those who were still alive were completely debilitated.[286] On 26 January 1942 Himmler therefore assigned new duties to the head of the Concentration Camp Inspectorate (which under the title of Office Group D had been incorporated into the WVHA as it was being formed): 'Now that Russian POWs will not be available in the immediate future, I shall send to the camps a large number of Jews and Jewesses who have emigrated from Germany. Make ready to receive 100,000 Jews and up to 50,000 Jewesses into the concentration camps in the next four weeks. The concentration camps will acquire important economic tasks in the coming weeks'.[287]

At the end of March Himmler made it clear to Pohl that he saw 'an immense labour resource' in the individual capacity of prisoners. The 'potential to draw on them has been entrusted to the Head of the WVHA because the Concentration Camp Inspectorate has been transferred to it'.[288] Pohl acted on Himmler's words by issuing an order to concentration camp commandants making them responsible for 'the deployment of labour': 'This deployment must exhaust, in the true sense of the word, the available labour in order to achieve the maximum output'.[289]

Now that Soviet POWs were no longer available, Majdanek and Auschwitz-Birkenau, at that time being expanded, were the main camps available to absorb Jewish slave workers. During the following months deportees from the Reich were in fact sent to the Lublin district, where some of those Jews deemed 'fit for work' were subjected to forced labour in Majdanek and other camps. However, several thousand Slovakian and French Jews were deported to Auschwitz and put to work there as forced labour.[290] The prospect, however vague, of using this labour later in the occupied eastern territories nevertheless continued to be kept alive: Heydrich spoke on 4 February 1942 of the 'Arctic seas camps' as being the 'ideal future homeland of 11 million European Jews'. In February Himmler presented Hitler with a 'Report on the Arctic seas camps', which Hitler read.[291] On 5 April 1942 Hitler's table talk reports him as saying that Himmler should not get his hopes up of 'replacing Russian gulags on the Murmansk canal with his concentration camp inmates'. He needed these prisoners more urgently 'to build the requisite armaments factories across the expanses of Russia'.[292]

In the meantime, pressure was increasing on the Jews still working in German industry. An order from Göring issued in March 1942 forbidding the deportation of this group[293] had been largely ignored, as the Reich Security Head Office (RSHA) interpreted the provisions for the exemption of Jews in work camps 'carrying out labour vital to the war effort' in increasingly restrictive terms.[294] As he assured Goebbels when pressed at the end of May, Hitler had made up his mind to give Speer the task 'of seeing to it as quickly as possible that Jews working in the German armaments sector are replaced by foreign workers'.[295]

The increased numbers of Jews now being deported to concentration camps and forced labour camps were at first used in particular in construction, Himmler's ambitious plans for an 'eastern settlement programme' having turned out to be unrealistic.[296] Above all, however, the use of Jews 'fit for work' provided an excuse for getting rid of those who were 'unfit for work': the elderly and sick, and in particular children and their mothers, were now separated out at the beginning or end of the transports and earmarked for death in the gas chambers.

Deportations and mass murder in spring 1942

A few days after the conference, the RSHA began to prepare for a new wave of deportations from the Reich. On 31 January 1942 Eichmann informed the regional Gestapo headquarters in the Reich that 'the evacuation of Jews to the east that has been taking place recently in various regions' marked 'the start of the final solution of the Jewish question in the Altreich, the Ostmark, and the Protectorate of Bohemia and Moravia'. 'Particularly pressing plans' would be carried out first, but new 'accommodation' was being prepared so that further 'batches' of Jews could be deported. All Jews were to be included who fitted the definition contained in the First Decree implementing the [Nuremberg] Reich Citizenship Law, with the exception of those who were living in 'mixed marriages', were foreign nationals, were in work camps and 'carrying out labour vital to the war effort', were over sixty-five years of age, or were between fifty-five and sixty-five but particularly infirm. There was no mention here of a general deportation of Jewish 'Mischlinge' as discussed by Heydrich at the Wannsee Conference.[297]

Eichmann was therefore trying to present this 'start' to the 'final solution' in the Reich as still being a provisional arrangement that was not to be confused with the coming European 'total' or 'final' solution. For negotiations continued concerning the final criteria that would define the range of those to be deported. Indeed, in February Heydrich announced to conference participants receiving the minutes that only when these criteria had been established and other open questions had been clarified in a series of 'discussions of matters of detail' would he be in a position to complete the plan to implement the 'final solution' that Göring had requested the previous July. In fact, however, he appears not to have completed the documentation before his death early in June 1942.[298]

A few weeks later the RSHA had firmed up its future plans to the extent that on 6 March Eichmann was able to announce an additional deportation programme at a meeting with Gestapo officials from the entire Reich; 55,000 people from Reich territory, including the Ostmark and the Protectorate, were involved,[299] making up the 'third instalment', which Heydrich had already made known in November, after the previous year's first two waves of deportations (Lodz and Riga/Minsk).[300]

In addition, on 6 March Eichmann announced the plan to deport the majority of Jews remaining in the Altreich to Theresienstadt in the course of the summer or autumn; in the meantime, '15–20,000 Jews from the Protectorate' would 'move there temporarily'. Eichmann explained that the plan for an 'old people's ghetto' for Jews from the Altreich that Heydrich had introduced at the Wannsee Conference had been 'for appearances' sake': the official reason for the deportations, allegedly to provide 'labour in the east', could only be credible if there were exemptions for the old and sick and for those whose service to the country was beyond question.

On 6 March Eichmann chaired a further meeting. It was attended by representatives of the top Reich authorities, in this case desk officers, to discuss the question of 'mixed marriages' and 'Mischlinge', which had not been finally clarified on 20 January in relation to the deportations. The starting point was Stuckart's proposal to exempt the majority of '1st-degree Mischlinge' but to sterilize them in most cases. Most of those present opposed this proposal and thus supported Heydrich's intention of deporting 'Mischlinge' as a matter of principle, except in certain exceptional cases. The issue was to be decided once and for all by Hitler. There was agreement, however, that if Hitler should decide in favour of comprehensive compulsory sterilization, those affected should be 'assembled in a particular town' following the pattern of 'Theresienstadt, the old people's ghetto'.[301] With regard to 'mixed marriages' it was agreed that, rather than dissolving them across the board, for form's sake an accelerated process should be devised to allow the courts to treat each case individually.[302]

After various written statements had been exchanged,[303] on 27 October 1942 another inter-ministerial meeting was held on the issue of the 'Mischlinge' and mixed marriages and resulted in agreement to accept the plan originally put forward by Stuckart of compulsory sterilization of 'Mischlinge' remaining in the Reich and the compulsory dissolving of 'mixed marriages'. Although in the following months several draft laws were produced, the project had come to a standstill by autumn 1943[304] and plans for compulsory sterilization were evidently not pursued in practice. On 29 January 1942 a meeting was held in the Ministry for the East about introducing a directive designed to tighten the 'definition of Jewishness' in the occupied eastern territories. This plan was scotched at the end of July 1942, however, after disagreements between the SS and the Ministry for the East, by a ruling from Himmler, who feared there was a danger of 'tying our own hands' with 'all these stupid definitions'.[305]

The third wave of deportations from the Reich, which had been discussed on 6 March, did in fact take place between mid-March and mid-June 1942. There is evidence of forty-three transports, though the number may have been over sixty, and thus the total given by Eichmann of 55,000 victims of deportation was probably reached.[306] The transports that can be verified came above all from the regions of the Altreich 'in danger of air attack' (twenty-three trains), Vienna (six trains), and from the Protectorate (fourteen trains from Theresienstadt and one from Prague); their destination was a series of ghettos in the Lublin district (in particular Izbica, Piaski, and Zamość), and in April four transports arrived at the Warsaw ghetto.[307] The majority of the trains from the Reich interrupted their journey in Lublin, where men classed as 'fit for work' were removed from the wagons and taken as forced labour to Majdanek, as Himmler had instructed at the end of January 1942.[308]

In March 1942 it was also becoming clear that the SS was already seeking to turn the European scope of the deportation programme, as outlined by Heydrich at the Wannsee Conference, into reality. In contrast to Heydrich's announcements, however, these transports from territories outside the 'Greater German Reich' did not terminate in the occupied Soviet territories but in concentration camps in Poland. This expansion of deportations beyond the Reich affected two countries in particular in the first instance, namely Slovakia and France, but the Netherlands and Belgium soon also came within the purview of those planning mass murder.

In October 1941 Himmler had offered the leaders of the Slovakian government the option of the Slovakian Jews being deported to a particular region of the General Government. Early in 1942 he went to work on the Foreign Ministry, prompting it in February 1942 to request the Slovakian government to provide the Reich with 20,000 Jewish workers to be deployed 'in the east'.[309] Once the Slovakian authorities had assembled Jews aged between sixteen and forty-five and deemed 'fit for work' in special camps,[310] the deportations began on 25 March. The original plan, in line with the projected segregation of the sexes, provided for around 13,000 men to be deported to Majdanek in the Lublin district and 7,000 women to Auschwitz.[311] And, in fact, four transports of around 3,800 young women arrived in Auschwitz and four transports with some 4,500 young men arrived in Majdanek between 26 March and 7 April.[312] At the end of March the Slovakian government responded to a request from the Foreign Ministry, prompted shortly before by Himmler, by officially agreeing to hand over all Slovakian Jews (in other words, a further 70,000 people) to Germany.[313] On 10 April Heydrich explained to the Slovakian prime minister Tuka in Bratislava that the envisaged deportation of the Slovakian Jews was only 'part of the programme'. A 'resettlement' of a total of 'half a million' Jews 'from Europe to the east' was, he said, taking place at that time, affecting the Reich, the Protectorate, the Netherlands, Belgium, and France, as well as Slovakia.[314]

Heydrich's remarks are an important indication that he had by then reached agreement with Himmler on a common course that represented a pragmatic middle way between the Europe-wide approach favoured by Heydrich and the 'stop-gap solutions' pursued by Himmler. Immediately after Heydrich's visit to Bratislava, whole families began to be deported from Slovakia. As it was no longer just younger Jews of both sexes 'fit for work' who were being deported, the original arrangements for deportations had to be altered. There is evidence that seven transports arrived at Auschwitz between 13 April and 20 June, the majority of the deportees being assigned as forced labour,[315] while a further thirty-four transports during the same period terminated in the ghettos of the Lublin district.[316]

The systematic mass murder of Polish Jews classified as 'unfit for work' began at precisely the point when the transports from the Reich and Slovakia were arriving in the Lublin district. The SS and Police Leader (SSPF) Odilo Globocnik had been preparing for this since the previous autumn by constructing the Belzec extermination camp. Concrete preparations for deportations to Belzec from the ghettos in the Lublin district can be shown to have started in January 1942.[317] The 'violent clearance' of the Lublin ghetto began on 16 March when the relatively small facility containing a hut with three gas chambers had been completed[318] and two days after Himmler had met the responsible SSPF, Globocnik, on 14 March.[319] It lasted until 20 April. Many people were shot on the spot, a few thousand were kept to work in the ghetto, and around 30,000 were deported to Belzec and murdered there. Deportations from further ghettos in the district began on 24 March. By the middle of April some 14,000 Jews from these smaller ghettos had been deported to Belzec. The extermination camp was then closed temporarily so that it could be extended and murder even more people.[320]

By 27 March it is clear from his diary that the Propaganda Minister Goebbels was informed about the murders: 'Beginning with Lublin the Jews from the General Government are now being deported to the east. A fairly barbaric procedure is being used, not to be described in any detail, and not much is left of the Jews themselves'; 60 per cent of the Jews would 'have to be liquidated, while only 40 per cent can be used as labour'. The ghettos being 'evacuated' in the General Government, Goebbels continued, were 'now being filled with Jews deported from the Reich. After a certain time the process will begin again'.[321]

That the first objective was to murder Jews 'unfit for work' was confirmed by evidence given by Eichmann in Jerusalem, who stated that after the mass murders had got underway Globocnik had asked Heydrich for permission to kill a further 150,000 and probably 250,000 people.[322] The testimony of Josef Oberhauser, adjutant to the camp commandant at Belzec, Christian Wirth, supports this: at first only 'Jews unfit for work from various ghettos were to be liquidated', and it was not until April or May that Globocnik received via Brack the order 'to exterminate the Jews systematically'.[323]

Beginning on 13 March and immediately before the clearance of the ghettos, the deportation trains carrying Jews from the Reich arrived in the Lublin district, followed two weeks later by those from Slovakia.[324] With each trainload the Polish Jews, under the codeword 'Jewish exchange',[325] were then deported to Belzec and deportees from the Reich and Slovakia moved into their living quarters,[326] many of them dying in the following months as a result of the appalling living conditions.

A new wave of mass murders also began in mid-March in the neighbouring district of Galicia as well as the first deportations directly to extermination camps. In the space of about three weeks and frequently after bloody massacres on the spot, tens of thousands of people classified as 'unfit for work' from Lemberg (Lviv) and from various ghettos in the district were deported to Belzec and murdered there.[327] These deportations were also managed by Globocnik's staff.

Heydrich's announcement on 10 April in Bratislava of an extensive programme of deportations was preceded by concrete preparations with regard to France (those relating to Belgium and the Netherlands would not begin until a few months later). In view of the French Resistance's persistent attacks, the military administration in France, while continuing to shoot hostages, had decided at the end of 1941 to deport 1,000 Jewish men to the east as a 'reprisal'.[328]

On 1 March 1942 Eichmann approved the deportation of these 1,000 Jews, who were already under arrest.[329] On 4 March he adopted the suggestion made by Theodor Dannecker, the desk officer for 'Jewish matters' in Paris, who urged the French government to deport 'around 5000 Jews to the east', who 'in the first instance' should be 'Jewish men, fit for work, and not older than 55'.[330] The deportation of Jewish 'hostages' 'to the east', originally very much a Wehrmacht initiative, was therefore exploited by the RSHA to involve France in the Europe-wide deportation programme it was planning.

The first 'hostage transport', 1,112 people in total, roughly half of them French and the other half Jews of other nationalities, did in fact arrive at Auschwitz on 30 March; all were registered at the camp.[331] In March responsibility for all police matters and in particular for all 'reprisal measures' had been transferred to the newly created post of Higher SS and Police Leader (HSSPF) in France, a post to which Karl Oberg, hitherto SSPF in the Radom district, was appointed.[332]

As a response to repeated attacks by the French Resistance, by the end of May a further 471 people, Jews and communists, had been shot in occupied France. In addition, the military administration had ear-marked so many people for deportation in response to individual assassination attempts that the quota of 5,000 Jews for deportation set in the RSHA's March plans had already been filled.[333]

At the start of May during a visit to Paris Heydrich is claimed to have announced that 'more extensive, more appropriate, and more numerically far-reaching' solutions were in preparation to kill the European Jews[334] and at the same time to have opposed further shoot-ings of hostages in France on the grounds that they would only provoke the Resistance to further actions.[335] The first of the next five transports with 1,000 people in each was to leave Compiègne on 5 June for Auschwitz, while the last of the trains arrived at Auschwitz on 8 July. All the deportees in these transports were registered at the camp.[336]

Thus from the end of 1941 onwards the murder of Jews had been extended beyond the occupied Soviet territories to specific regions in Poland. The victims were Polish Jews classified as 'unfit for work' in the Warthegau, in annexed Upper Silesia, and in the districts of Lublin and Galicia in the General Government. Jews from the Reich, from Slovakia, and from France who had been deported to 'the east' had in general not yet been systematically and comprehensively murdered (though the death rate in the ghettos and camps was high), even if they had been classified as 'unfit for work'. There was, however, one import-ant exception: in the Riga area there were already large-scale selections and killings among the Jews who had been deported there, for example on 5 February in the Riga ghetto and again in the second half of March in the ghetto and in the Jungfernhof camp.[337]

The escalation of 'Jewish policy' in May/June 1942

In May and June 1942 the SS dramatically changed its modus operandi. During this period the policy of extermination was intensified and amounted to a decision to murder indiscriminately all European Jews within its reach as quickly as possible and certainly before the end of the war. The Jews in the occupied Soviet territories (including those annexed by the Soviet Union up to 1940) were to be murdered in situ and the rest primarily in extermination camps on Polish soil. Only

those Jews still 'fit for work' were to be allowed to survive for a relatively short time, exploited to the point of total exhaustion, and then
also murdered. This meant that the original plan for the 'final solution'
that Heydrich had presented at the Wannsee Conference had been
changed in three crucial respects. Originally Heydrich had focused primarily on the post-war period and his idea had been that the 'final
solution' should take place in the occupied Soviet territories and consist of a combination of forced labour involving physical exertion
beyond human endurance and planned killings (he had not specified
the method to be used for these murders). Even at the Wannsee
Conference, however, it had become clear that, as a result of the development of the war, the fact that deportations had already begun, and
that in the regions affected by them mass murders and/or preparations
for mass murders had already been initiated, Heydrich's plan had already
been superseded. After a transitional period of a few months the new
procedure, pursued in particular by Himmler, was taking shape. What at
the Wannsee Conference were still being referred to as measures 'anticipating' the 'impending final solution', or as 'stop-gap solutions', were
now to be the basis for the actual campaign of murder.

The decision-making process that led to the implementation of this
new plan in May and June 1942 is obscure. We have, however, already
seen that by early April Himmler and Heydrich had reached agreement that a total of half a million Jews were to be deported from the
Reich, Slovakia, and western Europe. What is striking is that in a
period of only a week between the end of April and the beginning of
May Himmler and Heydrich met a total of seven times in three different locations (Berlin, Munich, and Prague). This exceptionally inten-
sive series of meetings was book-ended by two lengthy meetings
Himmler had with Hitler on 23 April and 3 May 1942.[338] We do not
know what was discussed at these meetings, but the fact that immediately afterwards 'Jewish policy' escalated in an overwhelmingly uniform manner in very diverse settings suggests that in late April/early
May Hitler, Himmler, and Heydrich reached agreement on a Europe-
wide 'final solution'. The subsequent escalation, which is described in
outline in the remainder of this chapter, affected in particular Jews
from Reich territory and Slovakia, Polish Jews, western European Jews,
and Jews from the Soviet Union.

While the third wave of deportations from the Reich begun in
March was still in progress, the Gestapo initiated a fourth series directed

towards the occupied eastern territories: the transports to Minsk, which had been suspended in November 1941, were resumed. From May to September 1942 some 16,000 people were deported there in at least seventeen transports,[339] which were interrupted only by a temporary transport block from mid-June to mid-July arising from the military situation. By contrast with the previous winter, the Jews from the German Reich were no longer confined in a ghetto but instead the trains proceeded to a stop near to the Maly Trostinez estate, a few kilometres from Minsk. From 11 May onwards almost all of those deported there were either shot immediately or suffocated in gas vans.[340] In April 1942 Heydrich was reported to have visited Minsk and personally announced the resumption of the deportations and the imminent murders.[341]

Meanwhile, from mid-June onwards the last transports from the third wave of deportations from the Reich were being directed to the extermination camp of Sobibor, which by then was completed and resembled Belzec in structure and mode of operation.[342] Once there, deportees who had not been removed from the trains at stops in Lublin to be deployed as forced labour were murdered in the gas chambers. There is reliable evidence for this procedure being applied to a transport from Theresienstadt, to one from Berlin, and to one from Vienna that arrived in Sobibor between 15 and 19 June. It is possible that two further transports from Theresienstadt that reached Lublin on 15 and 16 June were dealt with in the same way.[343] As early as 18 May half of the roughly 800 people who had been deported a few days before from Theresienstadt to Siedliszcze had been taken to Sobibor along with Polish Jews and murdered.[344]

In June the deportation began and continued up to October 1942 of some 45,000 German and Austrian Jews to Theresienstadt, which took on its second function of being an 'old people's ghetto' in addition to being a transit camp for Czech Jews.[345] Now the elderly and infirm and also those who enjoyed particular 'privileges'[346] were held there in order to lend plausibility to the claim that the rest of the Jews in the east were being put to work and thus to obscure the plan of mass murder that was the real intention.

From the beginning of June onwards, deportees from a total of ten Slovakian transports who had not been classed as 'fit for work' at the selection at Lublin—in other words, predominantly women and children—and were confined in the camp at Majdanek were not taken

to a ghetto but were instead deported directly to Sobibor and murdered. The last of these transports to Sobibor left Slovakia on 14 June,
a day before deportations from Reich territory to the Lublin district
were halted.[347]

Thus the deportations to Minsk in May and the transports in mid-
June to Sobibor marked the start of a new phase in the policy of extermination. Those deported were no longer housed temporarily in
ghettos or forced labour camps, where most perished miserably within
a short time: the vast majority of deportees were now being shot or
murdered by gassing immediately on reaching their destination. The
pattern that had prevailed up to that point of deporting local Jews to
the extermination camps in order to 'make room' for Jews arriving
from the Reich had thus been abandoned.

The same escalation in 'Jewish policy', the systematic murder
of Jews from the Reich, can also be shown for the same period in the
Warthegau. In this territory the mass murders of local Jews begun in
December 1941 had continued in the first months of 1942.[348] Between
4 and 13 May 10,914 Reich Jews deported the previous year to the
ghetto were transferred to Chelmno and murdered there; of the original 20,000 people, more than 3,000 had died in the meantime. The
victims of the May operation were those who were not employed in
the ghetto.[349] It is thus clear that the ban Himmler had put in November
1941 on the systematic murder of deported German Jews was lifted
sometime around April 1942; it is probably no coincidence that on
16 and 17 April Himmler was in the Warthegau and had meetings with
Greiser and Koppe.[350]

There is a further indication that Himmler had already ordered the
murder of older Jews in mid-May. On 18 May Müller, the Gestapo
chief, informed Rudolf Jäger, head of the Security Police in Lithuania,
that as a result of a 'general instruction from the Reichsführer SS and
Chief of the German Police', 'Jews and Jewesses aged between 16 and
32 and fit for work' were 'to be exempted from special measures until
further notice. These Jews are to be taken to join prisoners in work
units in concentration camps or work camps'. This exemption apply-
ing to younger Jewish men and women 'fit for work' thus implies that
at this point an order was in force subjecting older Jews and those
'unfit for work', whether men or women, to 'special measures'—in
other words, to being murdered. There is, however, no documentary
evidence for this order.[351]

In mid-May the mass murder began of Jews in those Polish territories that had been annexed by the Reich in 1939 as Eastern Upper
Silesia. On 12 May 1942 Heydrich abolished the police border that up
until then had separated the western strip of Eastern Upper Silesia
(territory with a relatively large German population that had been
ceded after the First World War) from the eastern part (where the
population was overwhelmingly Polish). This border had ensured that
Jews who had been compulsorily 'resettled' from the west to the east
were not able to return. Now the provisional arrangement of a 'deportation zone' for Jews in the east of the province had ceased.[352] The very
same day,[353] thousands of Jews deemed 'unfit for work' from Sosnowitz
(Sosnowiec) and Bendzin (Będzin), as well as from a number of other
places, were deported to Auschwitz and murdered in a gas chamber
temporarily installed in a former farmhouse.[354] During the period
from May to August 1942 a total of some 38,000 Jews were deported
from the 'eastern strip', approximately 20,000 to Auschwitz and the
remainder to the work camps of the 'Schmelt Organization'.[355]

Far more significant, however, was the fact that at the same time the
Nazi regime began the systematic murder of Jews from the General
Government, who, numbering more than 1.7 million, represented the
greatest concentration of Jews in Nazi-controlled territory. The 'final
solution' had thereby moved to a new level, for mass murder on this
unprecedented scale was bound to have repercussions for the further
radicalization of 'Jewish policy' throughout the territory under Nazi
domination.

The Lublin district, which SSPF Globocnik regarded as the model
for a radical population policy for the entire General Government, was
once again at the forefront of operations. From early May onwards the
Jewish population was systematically removed from rural areas, regardless of whether Jews were arriving from other countries and before the
civil administration was able to begin the process of classifying all Jews
'fit for work'. Apart from some 2,000 forced workers who were moved
to Majdanek, the victims were deported to Sobibor, the second extermination camp in the General Government and now completed.
More than 55,000 people fell victim to this wave of deportations.[356]

On 10 June 1942, however, these deportations were suspended and
on 19 June a general ban was imposed on transport use on account of
the Wehrmacht's summer offensive, thereby interrupting the deportations to extermination camps. Those planning the 'final solution' in

occupied Poland made use of this interval to extend the policy of systematic murder to all districts of the General Government.

The precondition for this fateful decision was the fact that in May Himmler had succeeded in significantly strengthening the position of his SS within the General Government. The Governor General, Frank, whose position had been weakened by a serious corruption affair, had been forced at the beginning of May to assent to the appointment of HSSPF Krüger as state secretary for security matters and, significantly, also as Himmler's representative in all questions concerning German settlement in his territory.[357] In particular, in a decree of 3 June Krüger was given responsibility for dealing with 'all Jewish matters'.[358] As in the occupied Soviet territories the previous year, the fact that here again powers over police and ethnic settlement issues were combined in Himmler's hands was a crucial precondition for the further escalation of the policy of systematic murder within the General Government.

The period between the end of May and the beginning of June was especially critical for this escalation. On 27 May Czech Resistance fighters attempted to assassinate Heydrich and on 4 June he died from his injuries. The fact that in Heydrich a key figure in the plan to exterminate the Jews had been killed gave the SS a welcome excuse to exact 'revenge'. As a result of their perverted logic, however, this revenge could only be directed at the group of people who had been identified as the real enemies in this war: in other words, the Jews. Thus Himmler in his address to the SSPFs after Heydrich's funeral in Berlin on 9 June announced: 'We are sure to have finished Jewish migration within a year; no Jews will be migrating after that'.[359] On 10 June 1942 1,000 Jews were deported from Prague to Majdanek as 'retribution' for Heydrich's death.[360]

Revenge was not, however, the sole reason why during the weeks following Heydrich's death Himmler pursued the murder policy with increased intensity, so that it developed into a Europe-wide programme of extermination. For it was not until after his death that Heydrich's idea of a European 'final solution', a comprehensive plan to be executed essentially after the end of the war, subject to Göring's approval, finally became obsolete. As is evident from developments between autumn 1941 and spring 1942, Himmler had already persuaded Heydrich in large measure to adopt his approach, but now the Reichsführer SS, who, significantly, now took over as head of the RSHA, had a completely free hand. The waves of deportations he in particular had set in motion in

various countries had been described by Heydrich as 'stop-gap solutions' anticipating the 'impending final solution'. Now Himmler could
expand them into a Europe-wide programme of mass murder without
needing to take Heydrich's views into consideration at all. In particular,
as Himmler took instructions directly from Hitler, he had no need of
authorization from Reich Marshal Göring.

The biggest undertaking within the European 'final solution' was
the murder of the Jews throughout the General Government, which
was largely prepared for during the month of May. Like the mass murders in the districts of Lublin and Galicia, it was to be organized by
Globocnik's staff. The entire operation was entitled 'Action Reinhardt'
(sometimes 'Reinhard'), as a posthumous homage to Heydrich, who
did in fact use both spellings of his name.[361] 'Action Reinhardt' encom-
passed the murder of the Jews of the General Government and of the
Bialystok district in the extermination camps of Belzec, Sobibor, and
Treblinka, which was built in May,[362] as well as in Majdanek. It also
included the murder of other Jews in these camps, as well as the
exploitation of the belongings and assets of the victims and the use
of Jews as forced labour.[363]

Alongside the extension of systematic mass murder to the whole of
the General Government, from June onwards Himmler's organization
took over total control of Jewish forced labour. Hitherto this had been the
only thing standing in the way of the Jewish population's complete
annihilation. During the months that followed, the use of Jews as a
source of labour was subject to growing restrictions and by this means
forced labour as administered by the SS, which amounted to 'extermination through work', now became an integral component of the
murder programme in the General Government also.[364]

When the ban on transport was lifted on 7 July, the Warsaw district
became the first focus for deportations within the General Government.
By 12 September more than 250,000 people had been deported from
the Warsaw ghetto to Treblinka and murdered. Deportations from the
Crakow district to Belzec, which had commenced at the end of May
and in the meantime been suspended, were also resumed. From late
summer 1942 and into the autumn, the machinery of deportation and
murder was operating in the Lublin, Galicia, and Radom districts.[365]

In addition, on Himmler's express orders considerable efforts were
made during the transport ban in June to accelerate deportations from
western Europe. The decision to increase drastically the deportations

from France, the Netherlands, and Belgium also came only a few days after Heydrich's death and may thus be interpreted as part of this escalation triggered by his assassination.

At a meeting on 11 June in the RSHA deportation quotas were agreed: 15,000 Dutch, 10,000 Belgian, and 100,000 French Jews, including Jews from the unoccupied territory, were to be deported. 'From 13 July onwards around three transports per week will set off'.[366] As it was impossible just then to clarify how deportations from unoccupied France could be carried out, these quotas were changed again shortly after. Now, from the middle of July or the beginning of August, daily transports with up to 1,000 people in each would deport 'approximately 40,000 Jews from occupied France, 40,000 from the Netherlands, and 10,000 from Belgium to the camp at Auschwitz for deployment as labour'.[367]

Shortly after this, Himmler was again pressing for deportations of French Jews to be accelerated.[368] Consequently, a further ten transports totalling about 10,000 people left for Auschwitz between 19 July and 7 August. These were 'stateless Jews' who had been rounded up in Paris on 16 and 17 July during a large-scale raid.[369] After this the SS extended deportations to include the unoccupied zone of France.

Deportations to Auschwitz from the Netherlands began on 15 July[370] and from Belgium to the same destination on 4 August 1942.[371] Meanwhile, additional makeshift gas chambers had been created at Auschwitz in a second farmhouse, the so-called White House or Bunker II. On 4 July 1942 628 people selected from a transport arriving from Slovakia were murdered there. From that day onwards it became regular practice in Auschwitz to separate out those Jews 'unfit for work' from the transports arriving from the various European countries (children and their mothers were the primary targets) and then murder them in the gas chambers.[372]

As early as July the German authorities (the RSHA and/or the Foreign Ministry) approached Germany's allies Romania,[373] Croatia,[374] and Finland (in the latter case Himmler took the initiative personally)[375] in an attempt to persuade them to deliver up their Jews. In September there was an approach to Bulgaria.[376] At this point, however, only the Croats were prepared to hand over their Jews to the Germans.

Hence by summer 1942 the extermination machine was operating at full capacity both in the extermination camps of 'Action Reinhardt' and in the combined concentration and extermination camp at Auschwitz.

Here too Himmler's key role in coordinating and driving things forward is evident. On 9 July he had discussions with Krüger and Globocnik about plans concerning the 'Jewish question' and the future of the 'ethnic German nation' that had been on the table since the beginning of June.[377] After several meetings with Hitler on 11, 12, and 14 July, Himmler used his chief of staff Karl Wolff to press the Transport Ministry to allow an increase in capacity for transports to the extermination camps.[378] On 17 and 18 July he inspected Auschwitz and requested a demonstration of how people were murdered in a gas chamber.[379] Comments he made on the evening of 17 July at a social gathering organized by the Gauleiter of Upper Silesia suggested to at least one of those present that the Nazi leadership had now decided to murder all European Jews. This information was sent on to Switzerland and from there it reached the west.[380] After his stay at Auschwitz Himmler visited Globocnik in Lublin on 18 and 19 July, and on 19 July he issued the crucial order to Krüger, the HSSPF, that the 'resettlement of the entire Jewish population of the General Government' was to be 'carried out and completed by 31 December 1942'. After this date there were to be no more Jews living in the General Government apart from those in four 'internment camps'.[381]

Alongside the events described above taking place in Poland and in Central and western Europe, during the period from May to July 1942 there was also a marked escalation in the policy of extermination in the Soviet Union. From May 1942 onwards the civilian administration and the SS set in motion a second wave of murders in the occupied eastern territories. It affected above all the General Commissariat of White Ruthenia and the Reich Commissariat of the Ukraine and culminated in summer 1942 in a policy of total annihilation. District by district, ghetto by ghetto, the entire Jewish population of these territories was now systematically murdered, the only exceptions being a small number of specialist workers and those who managed to flee and survive in the forests.[382] Here too we have clear evidence of Himmler's central role as supreme enforcer of Hitler's murderous policy. On 28 July he wrote to Gottlob Berger, head of the SS Head Office, that it was completely out of the question for him to formulate a decree defining the term 'Jew' in the occupied eastern territories. 'All these stupid definitions are simply tying our own hands. The occupied eastern territories will be made free of Jews. The Führer has burdened me with carrying out this very grave order'.[383]

Conclusion

The Wannsee Conference
in historical context

M ost participants in the Wannsee Conference who could be questioned after the war claimed they could hardly remember it or denied being there. This was the line taken by State Secretary Dr Bühler of the Office of the Governor General when testifying at the main trial for war crimes at Nuremberg (in other words, before the prosecuting authorities had discovered the conference minutes). He assured the court that he had come away from a one to one meeting with Heydrich before the conference 'firmly persuaded that the resettlement of the Jews, though not undertaken for the benefit of the latter, would for the sake of the German nation's reputation and standing be carried out in a humane fashion'.[384]

Conference participants made further witness statements to Robert Kempner, the prosecutor in the so-called Wilhelmstrasse trial of high-ranking officials. According to his own testimony, State Secretary Neumann had quite simply had 'nothing to do with it in my official role'.[385] State Secretary Stuckart declared: 'I didn't take part . . . I'm not quite sure of that now'. In the end he admitted he was present but challenged the claim that he had proposed sterilizing the so-called 'Mischlinge'. Given that the minutes proved that he had in fact made that proposal, he then proceeded to present sterilization as an alternative to more extreme measures, though he was unwilling to admit that in claiming this he had implicitly accepted the murder of all other Jews.[386] State Secretary Klopfer from the Party Chancellery claimed not to remember 'whether I was there until the end'. Whether he was or not, discussions were, he said, restricted to the 'resettlement' of the Jews.[387] Leibbrandt, who had been representing the Ministry for the

East, said that it 'was the usual kind of meeting where you're not quite clear what is going on and then someone writes a set of minutes'. He claimed he had heard nothing about a 'final solution' but then made strenuous efforts to assert that he had tried to distance himself from this 'madness'.[388] Only Ministerialdirigent Kritzinger spoke relatively candidly about the regime's 'Jewish policy', saying he had considered it shameful. Nevertheless, he told Kempner, he had not quit his post but had 'simply carried on and waited for the end'.[389]

The emptiness of these excuses and the brazenness of the lies that were told are evident not only from the minutes themselves but also from the background to the conference. As we have seen, Stuckart, Klopfer, and the others represented key institutions working with the Reich Security Head Office (RSHA) throughout 1941 to create the necessary administrative preconditions for the deportation of the Jews. On the basis of the information available at the end of 1941 they had to assume that deportation meant death. The idea that in January 1942 they were unaware of the meaning of Heydrich's remarks about the 'final solution' or that they had been completely steamrollered ignores the fact that the murder of the European Jews depended on a division of labour and cooperation between the SS and the administration. The overwhelmingly positive response of the representatives of the 'central authorities' to Heydrich's plans for the 'final solution' on 20 January 1942 is comprehensible only against the background of this close cooperation. The significance of the Wannsee Conference lies secondly above all in the fact that it reflects a radical revision in the thinking of the German leadership about the future direction of 'Jewish policy' and about what the 'final solution' involved. Heydrich's main focus was on exploiting the war, which he assumed would soon be won, to achieve a radical 'solution to the Jewish question'. From his perspective German dominance of the continent of Europe and the conquest of living space in the east provided the preconditions for a further variation on the 'territorial solution'—one with unequivocally lethal consequences. After Germany's victory all European Jews were to be deported to 'the east', where they would perish through a mixture of forced labour, unbearable living conditions, and mass murder. Early in 1941 Heydrich had agreed this with Hitler and the purpose of the Wannsee Conference as far as he was concerned was to force the other authorities to accept once and for all that he was 'in charge'. He would then develop a deportation plan that had to be approved by

Göring and would therefore be regarded as having Hitler's authorization. In the meantime, however, Himmler had set about undermining Heydrich's plan and—a crucial factor—in doing so he was acting in constant and direct consultation with Hitler.

Since summer 1941 Himmler's aim had been to make the 'final solution' serve the interests of the war. This is the crucial difference between him and Heydrich. Himmler pursued this policy first of all in the occupied territories of the Soviet Union. By turning his killing squads' campaign of terror, initially focused on the Soviet Union's alleged Jewish-Bolshevist elite, into an out-and-out genocide, he intended to establish irreversible facts on the ground, in order to set about creating a racially based, radical new order in the living space conquered by Germany. He was acting in close consultation with Hitler, who always authorized every important measure concerned with 'Jewish policy'. This aim of making the 'final solution' serve the interests of the war also dictated Himmler's actions in autumn 1941, again in close contact with Hitler. Both were now bent on using the Jews of Central and western Europe as hostages. The deportation of the German and then the European Jews, which was planned in the first instance as an 'appropriate' response to Stalin's announcement of the forced resettlement of the Volga Germans, was rapidly repurposed. The deportation of Jews to the east was intended to make their 'racial comrades' in the United States exert the necessary pressure on the government there to prevent the United States from entering the war. When this strategy failed, however, Himmler focused his efforts on speeding up the deportation project and expanding it into a programme to murder all European Jews while the war was still in progress, with Hitler setting the guidelines and authorizing Himmler's actions.

Although Himmler was not present at the Wannsee Conference and Heydrich had evidently done all he could to prevent anyone close to Himmler from attending, the effects of Himmler's accelerated actions to implement 'Jewish policy' left a clear mark on the conference. Heydrich was visibly at pains to integrate the deportations that were already underway into his overarching plan, calling them 'stop-gap solutions' or experiments; yet Bühler's clear references to concrete preparations for the 'final solution' on General Government territory called into question Heydrich's plan of forcing the European Jews to 'migrate eastwards'. Although at first Himmler also pursued the idea of exploiting Jews deported to concentration camps for his own 'eastern programme', in the space of a few months his plan for a 'final solution' culminated in an idea of total war of the most radical kind conceivable and one that was in tune with Hitler's own ideas. Heydrich's unexpected death then gave Himmler the opportunity to realize his plan quickly and completely. The enormity of murder on a scale of millions was designed to give the war as a whole the character of a racially motivated war of annihilation. Occupied and allied states were to be drawn into this programme to create a 'new order' and by participating in an unprecedented atrocity were to be bound, come what may, to Germany and its regime. By treating this plan as an 'open secret' Himmler was also sending a message to the German people that they had long since burnt their bridges and were now faced with the alternatives of victory or annihilation by the 'Jewish world enemy'. The murder of the Jews thus became the linchpin of German war, occupation, and alliance policy.

Thus what were originally means and end had been reversed. War was no longer being waged in order to create the conditions for the 'final solution', but rather the 'final solution' was being placed in the service of the war. It was above all the Wannsee Conference, convened by Heydrich on 20 January 1942, that set the course for this reversal.

Acknowledgements

I should like to express my sincere thanks to the staff of the House of the Wannsee Conference for giving me the opportunity to present key ideas developed in this book and to discuss them with other participants at a symposium on 20 and 21 January 2012 to mark the seventieth anniversary of the conference. I am deeply indebted to Dr Gerhard Keiper of the Foreign Ministry's Political Archive, both for permission to reproduce the conference minutes and for essential information. Finally, I should like to thank Pantheon Verlag and in particular Annette C. Anton and Jens Dehning for overseeing the publication of this book, and also my editor Stefan Mayr and historian Daniela Lilli for their meticulous and expert work on the manuscript.

Appendix: Original minutes

166

30 Ausfertigungen
16. Ausfertigung

Besprechungsprotokoll.

I.   An der am 20.1.1942 in Berlin, Am Großen
Wannsee Nr. 56/58, stattgefundenen Besprechung über
die Endlösung der Judenfrage nahmen teil:

Gauleiter Dr. Meyer und Reichsamtsleiter Dr. Leibbrandt	Reichsministerium für die besetzten Ostgebiete
Staatssekretär Dr. Stuckart	Reichsministerium des Innern
Staatssekretär Neumann	Beauftragter für den Vierjahresplan
Staatssekretär Dr. Freisler	Reichsjustizministerium
Staatssekretär Dr. Bühler	Amt des Generalgouverneurs
Unterstaatssekretär Luther	Auswärtiges Amt
SS-Oberführer Klopfer	Partei-Kanzlei
Ministerialdirektor Kritzinger	Reichskanzlei

K210400

372024

2. II. 29. 3. R.

167

– 2 –

⚡-Gruppenführer Hofmann	Rasse- und Siedlungs-hauptamt
⚡-Gruppenführer Müller ⚡-Obersturmbannführer Eichmann	Reichssicherheits-hauptamt
⚡-Oberführer Dr. Schöngarth Befehlshaber der Sicherheits-polizei und des SD im General-gouvernement	Sicherheitspolizei und SD
⚡-Sturmbannführer Dr. Lange Kommandeur der Sicherheitspoli-zei und des SD für den General-bezirk Lettland, als Vertreter des Befehlshabers der Sicher-heitspolizei und des SD für das Reichskommissariat Ostland.	Sicherheitspolizei und SD

II.   Chef der Sicherheitspolizei und des SD,
⚡-Obergruppenführer H e y d r i c h , teilte
eingangs seine Bestellung zum Beauftragten für die
Vorbereitung der Endlösung der europäischen Judenfrage durch den Reichsmarschall mit und wies darauf hin, daß zu dieser Besprechung geladen wurde,
um Klarheit in grundsätzlichen Fragen zu schaffen.
Der Wunsch des Reichsmarschalls, ihm einen Ent-
wurf über die organisatorischen, sachlichen und
materiellen Belange im Hinblick auf die Endlösung
der europäischen Judenfrage zu übersenden, erfor-
dert die vorherige gemeinsame Behandlung aller
an diesen Fragen unmittelbar beteiligten Zentral-
instanzen im Hinblick auf die Parallelisierung
der Linienführung.

K210401

372025

168

- 3 -

Die Federführung bei der Bearbeitung der
Endlösung der Judenfrage liege ohne Rücksicht auf
geographische Grenzen zentral beim Reichsführer-ℋ
und Chef der Deutschen Polizei (Chef der Sicherheitspolizei und des SD).

Der Chef der Sicherheitspolizei und des
SD gab sodann einen kurzen Rückblick über den bisher geführten Kampf gegen diesen Gegner. Die we-
sentlichsten Momente bilden

  a/ die Zurückdrängung der Juden aus den
     einzelnen Lebensgebieten des deut-
     schen Volkes,

  b/ die Zurückdrängung der Juden aus dem
     Lebensraum des deutschen Volkes.

Im Vollzug dieser Bestrebungen wurde als
einzige vorläufige Lösungsmöglichkeit die Beschleu-
nigung der Auswanderung der Juden aus dem Reichsgebiet verstärkt und planmäßig in Angriff genommen.

Auf Anordnung des Reichsmarschalls wurde
im Januar 1939 eine Reichszentrale für jüdische Auswanderung errichtet, mit deren Leitung der Chef der
Sicherheitspolizei und des SD betraut wurde. Sie
hatte insbesondere die Aufgabe

  a/ alle Maßnahmen zur Vorbereitung einer
     verstärkten Auswanderung der Juden zu
     treffen,

  b/ den Auswanderungsstrom zu lenken,

  c/ die Durchführung der Auswanderung im
     Einzelfall zu beschleunigen.

Das Aufgabenziel war, auf legale Weise
den deutschen Lebensraum von Juden zu säubern.

169

- 4 -

Über die Nachteile, die eine solche Aus-
wanderungsforcierung mit sich brachte, waren sich
alle Stellen im klaren. Sie mußten jedoch ange-
sichts des Fehlens anderer Lösungsmöglichkeiten
vorerst in Kauf genommen werden.

Die Auswanderungsarbeiten waren in der
Folgezeit nicht nur ein deutsches Problem, sondern auch ein Problem, mit dem sich die Behörden
der Ziel- bzw. Einwandererländer zu befassen hat-
ten. Die finanziellen Schwierigkeiten, wie Erhö-
hung der Vorzeige- und Landungsgelder seitens
der verschiedenen ausländischen Regierungen, feh-
lende Schiffsplätze, laufend verschärfte Einwan-
derungsbeschränkungen oder -sperren, erschwerten
die Auswanderungsbestrebungen außerordentlich.
Trotz dieser Schwierigkeiten wurden seit der
Machtübernahme bis zum Stichtag 31.10.1941 insgesamt rund 537.000 Juden zur Auswanderung ge-
bracht. Davon

vom 30.1.1933 aus dem Altreich   rd. 360.000
vom 15.3.1938 aus der Ostmark   rd. 147.000
vom 15.3.1939 aus dem Protektorat
              Böhmen und Mähren   rd. 30.000.

Die Finanzierung der Auswanderung erfolg-
te durch die Juden bzw. jüdisch-politischen Organisationen selbst. Um den Verbleib der verproleta-
risierten Juden zu vermeiden, wurde nach dem Grund-
satz verfahren, daß die vermögenden Juden die Abwanderung der vermögenslosen Juden zu finanzieren
haben; hier wurde, je nach Vermögen gestaffelt,
eine entsprechende Umlage bzw. Auswandererabgabe
vorgeschrieben, die zur Bestreitung der finanziellen Obliegenheiten im Zuge der Abwanderung vermö-
gensloser Juden verwandt wurde.

K210403   372027

- 5 -

Neben dem Reichsmark-Aufkommen sind De-
visen für Vorzeige- und Landungsgelder erforderlich gewesen. Um den deutschen Devisenschatz zu
schonen, wurden die jüdischen Finanzinstitutionen
des Auslandes durch die jüdischen Organisationen
des Inlandes verhalten, für die Beitreibung entsprechender Devisenaufkommen Sorge zu tragen.
Hier wurden durch diese ausländischen Juden im
Schenkungswege bis zum 30.10.1941 insgesamt rund
9.500.000 Dollar zur Verfügung gestellt.

Inzwischen hat der Reichsführer-ﬆ und
Chef der Deutschen Polizei im Hinblick auf die
Gefahren einer Auswanderung im Kriege und im Hinblick auf die Möglichkeiten des Ostens die Auswanderung von Juden verboten.

III.   Anstelle der Auswanderung ist nunmehr
als weitere Lösungsmöglichkeit nach entsprechender vorheriger Genehmigung durch den Führer die
Evakuierung der Juden nach dem Osten getreten.

Diese Aktionen sind jedoch lediglich
als Ausweichmöglichkeiten anzusprechen, doch
werden hier bereits jene praktischen Erfahrun-
gen gesammelt, die im Hinblick auf die kommende
Endlösung der Judenfrage von wichtiger Bedeutung
sind.

Im Zuge dieser Endlösung der europäischen Judenfrage kommen rund 11 Millionen Juden in Betracht, die sich wie folgt auf die einzelnen Länder verteilen:

K210404

171

– 6 –

L a n d	Zahl
A. Altreich	131.800
Ostmark	43.700
Ostgebiete	420.000
Generalgouvernement	2.284.000
Bialystok	400.000
Protektorat Böhmen und Mähren	74.200
Estland – judenfrei –	
Lettland	3.500
Litauen	34.000
Belgien	43.000
Dänemark	5.600
Frankreich / Besetztes Gebiet	165.000
Unbesetztes Gebiet	700.000
Griechenland	69.600
Niederlande	160.800
Norwegen	1.300
B. Bulgarien	48.000
England	330.000
Finnland	2.300
Irland	4.000
Italien einschl. Sardinien	58.000
Albanien	200
Kroatien	40.000
Portugal	3.000
Rumänien einschl. Bessarabien	342.000
Schweden	8.000
Schweiz	18.000
Serbien	10.000
Slowakei	88.000
Spanien	6.000
Türkei (europ. Teil)	55.500
Ungarn	742.800
UdSSR	5.000.000
Ukraine 2.994.684	
Weißrußland aus-	
schl. Bialystok 446.484	
Zusammen: über	11.000.000

K210405   372029

172

- 7 -

Bei den angegebenen Judenzahlen der verschiedenen ausländischen Staaten handelt es sich
jedoch nur um Glaubensjuden, da die Begriffsbe-
stimmungen der Juden nach rassischen Grundsätzen
teilweise dort noch fehlen. Die Behandlung des
Problems in den einzelnen Ländern wird im Hinblick
auf die allgemeine Haltung und Auffassung auf gewisse Schwierigkeiten stoßen, besonders in Ungarn
und Rumänien. So kann sich z.B. heute noch in Rumänien der Jude gegen Geld entsprechende Dokumente, die ihm eine fremde Staatsangehörigkeit amt-
lich bescheinigen, beschaffen.

Der Einfluß der Juden auf alle Gebiete
in der UdSSR ist bekannt. Im europäischen Gebiet
leben etwa 5 Millionen, im asiatischen Raum knapp
1/4 Million Juden.

Die berufsständische Aufgliederung der
im europäischen Gebiet der UdSSR ansässigen Juden
war etwa folgende:

In der Landwirtschaft	9,1 %
als städtische Arbeiter	14,8 %
im Handel	20,0 %
als Staatsarbeiter angestellt	23,4 %
in den privaten Berufen - Heilkunde, Presse, Theater, usw.	32,7 %.

Unter entsprechender Leitung sollen nun
im Zuge der Endlösung die Juden in geeigneter Weise im Osten zum Arbeitseinsatz kommen. In großen
Arbeitskolonnen, unter Trennung der Geschlechter,
werden die arbeitsfähigen Juden straßenbauend in
diese Gebiete geführt, wobei zweifellos ein Groß-
teil durch natürliche Verminderung ausfallen wird

Der allfällig endlich verbleibende Rest-
bestand wird, da es sich bei diesem zweifellos um
den widerstandsfähigsten Teil handelt, entsprechend
behandelt werden müssen, da dieser, eine natürliche
Auslese darstellend, bei Freilassung als Keimzelle
eines neuen jüdischen Aufbaues anzusprechen ist.
(Siehe die Erfahrung der Geschichte.)

Im Zuge der praktischen Durchführung der
Endlösung wird Europa vom Westen nach Osten durch-
gekämmt. Das Reichsgebiet einschließlich Protektorat Böhmen und Mähren wird, allein schon aus Grün-
den der Wohnungsfrage und sonstigen sozial-politi-
schen Notwendigkeiten, vorweggenommen werden müssen.

Die evakuierten Juden werden zunächst Zug
um Zug in sogenannte Durchgangsghettos verbracht,
um von dort aus weiter nach dem Osten transportiert
zu werden.

Wichtige Voraussetzung, so führte ͱ-Ober-
gruppenführer H e y d r i c h weiter aus, für die
Durchführung der Evakuierung überhaupt, ist die ge-
naue Festlegung des in Betracht kommenden Personen-
kreises.

Es ist beabsichtigt, Juden im Alter von
über 65 Jahren nicht zu evakuieren, sondern sie einem Altersghetto - vorgesehen ist Theresienstadt -
zu überstellen.

Neben diesen Altersklassen - von den am
31.10.1941 sich im Altreich und der Ostmark befind-
lichen etwa 280.000 Juden sind etwa 30 % über 65 Jahre alt - finden in den jüdischen Altersghettos weiterhin die schwerkriegsbeschädigten Juden und Juden
mit Kriegsauszeichnungen (EK I) Aufnahme. Mit dieser

174

- 9 -

zweckmäßigen Lösung werden mit einem Schlag die
vielen Interventionen ausgeschaltet.

Der Beginn der einzelnen größeren Evakuierungsaktionen wird weitgehend von der militäri-
schen Entwicklung abhängig sein. Bezüglich der Behandlung der Endlösung in den von uns besetzten und
beeinflußten europäischen Gebieten wurde vorgeschla-
gen, daß die in Betracht kommenden Sachbearbeiter
des Auswärtigen Amtes sich mit dem zuständigen Re-
ferenten der Sicherheitspolizei und des SD bespre-
chen.

In der Slowakei und Kroatien ist die Angelegenheit nicht mehr allzu schwer, da die wesentlich-
sten Kernfragen in dieser Hinsicht dort bereits einer Lösung zugeführt wurden. In Rumänien hat die Regierung inzwischen ebenfalls einen Judenbeauftragten
eingesetzt. Zur Regelung der Frage in Ungarn ist es
erforderlich, in Zeitkürze einen Berater für Juden-
fragen der Ungarischen Regierung aufzuoktroyieren.

Hinsichtlich der Aufnahme der Vorbereitun-
gen zur Regelung des Problems in Italien hält //-Ober-
gruppenführer H e y d r i c h eine Verbindung z.
Polizei-Chef in diesen Belangen für angebracht.

Im besetzten und unbesetzten Frankreich
wird die Erfassung der Juden zur Evakuierung aller
Wahrscheinlichkeit nach ohne große Schwierigkeiten
vor sich gehen können.

Unterstaatssekretär L u t h e r teilte
hierzu mit, daß bei tiefgehender Behandlung dieses
Problems in einigen Ländern, so in den nordischen
Staaten, Schwierigkeiten auftauchen werden, und es
sich daher empfiehlt, diese Länder vorerst noch zu-

K210408

372032

175

rückzustellen. In Anbetracht der hier in Frage kommenden geringen Judenzahlen bildet diese Zurückstellung ohnedies keine wesentliche Einschränkung.

Dafür sieht das Auswärtige Amt für den Südosten und Westen Europas keine großen Schwierigkeiten.

SS-Gruppenführer H o f m a n n beabsichtigt, einen Sachbearbeiter des Rasse- und Siedlungshauptamtes zur allgemeinen Orientierung dann nach Ungarn mitsenden zu wollen, wenn seitens des Chefs der Sicherheitspolizei und des SD die Angelegenheit dort in Angriff genommen wird. Es wurde festgelegt, diesen Sachbearbeiter des Rasse- und Siedlungshauptamtes, der nicht aktiv werden soll, vorübergehend offiziell als Gehilfen zum Polizei-Attaché abzustellen.

IV.   Im Zuge der Endlösungsvorhaben sollen die Nürnberger Gesetze gewissermaßen die Grundlage bilden, wobei Voraussetzung für die restlose Bereinigung des Problems auch die Lösung der Mischehen- und Mischlingsfragen ist.

Chef der Sicherheitspolizei und des SD erörtert im Hinblick auf ein Schreiben des Chefs der Reichskanzlei zunächst theoretisch die nachstehenden Punkte:

1) Behandlung der Mischlinge 1. Grades.

Mischlinge 1. Grades sind im Hinblick auf die Endlösung der Judenfrage den Juden gleichgestellt.

K210409

372033

176

- 11 -

Von dieser Behandlung werden ausgenommen:

a) Mischlinge 1. Grades verheiratet mit
Deutschblütigen, aus deren Ehe Kinder
(Mischlinge 2. Grades) hervorgegangen
sind. Diese Mischlinge 2. Grades sind
im wesentlichen den Deutschen gleichgestellt.

b) Mischlinge 1. Grades, für die von den
höchsten Instanzen der Partei und des
Staates bisher auf irgendwelchen Le-
bensgebieten Ausnahmegenehmigungen er-
teilt worden sind.
Jeder Einzelfall muß überprüft werden,
wobei nicht ausgeschlossen wird, daß
die Entscheidung nochmals zu Ungunsten
des Mischlings ausfällt.

Voraussetzungen einer Ausnahmebewilligung
müssen stets grundsätzliche Verdienste des in
Frage stehenden Mischlings selbst sein. (Nicht
Verdienste des deutschblütigen Eltern- oder Ehe-
teiles.)

Der von der Evakuierung auszunehmende
Mischling 1. Grades wird - um jede Nachkommen-
schaft zu verhindern und das Mischlingsproblem
endgültig zu bereinigen - sterilisiert. Die
Sterilisierung erfolgt freiwillig. Sie ist aber
Voraussetzung des Verbleibens im Reich. Der ste-
rilisierte "Mischling" ist in der Folgezeit von
allen einengenden Bestimmungen, denen er bislang
unterworfen ist, befreit.

2) Behandlung der Mischlinge 2. Grades.

Die Mischlinge 2. Grades werden grund-
sätzlich den Deutschblütigen zugeschlagen, mit
Ausnahme folgender Fälle, in denen die Mischlinge 2. Grades den Juden gleichgestellt werden:

K210410   372034

177

- 12 -

a) Herkunft des Mischlings 2. Grades
   aus einer Bastardehe (beide Teile
   Mischlinge).

b) Rassisch besonders ungünstiges Er-
   scheinungsbild des Mischlings 2.
   Grades, das ihn schon äußerlich
   zu den Juden rechnet.

c) Besonders schlechte polizeiliche
   und politische Beurteilung des
   Mischlings 2. Grades, die erken-
   nen läßt, daß er sich wie ein Jude fühlt und benimmt.

   Auch in diesen Fällen sollen aber dann
Ausnahmen nicht gemacht werden, wenn der Mischling 2. Grades deutschblütig verheiratet ist.

3) Ehen zwischen Volljuden und Deutschblütigen.

   Von Einzelfall zu Einzelfall muß hier
entschieden werden, ob der jüdische Teil evakuiert wird, oder ob er unter Berücksichtigung
auf die Auswirkungen einer solchen Maßnahme
auf die deutschen Verwandten dieser Mischehe
einem Altersghetto überstellt wird.

4) Ehen zwischen Mischlingen 1. Grades und
   Deutschblütigen.

   a) Ohne Kinder.

   Sind aus der Ehe keine Kinder hervorgegangen, wird der Mischling 1. Grades
   evakuiert bzw. einem Altersghetto überstellt. (Gleiche Behandlung wie bei Ehen
   zwischen Volljuden und Deutschblütigen,
   Punkt 3.)

K210411

372035

- 13 -

b) Mit Kindern.

Sind Kinder aus der Ehe hervorgegangen
(Mischlinge 2. Grades), werden sie,
wenn sie den Juden gleichgestellt werden, zusammen mit dem Mischling 1. Grades evakuiert bzw. einem Ghetto überstellt. Soweit diese Kinder Deutschen
gleichgestellt werden (Regelfälle),
sind sie von der Evakuierung auszuneh-
men und damit auch der Mischling 1. Grades.

5) Ehen zwischen Mischlingen 1. Grades und Mischlingen 1. Grades oder Juden.

Bei diesen Ehen (einschließlich der Kinder) werden alle Teile wie Juden behandelt und
daher evakuiert bzw. einem Altersghetto überstellt.

6) Ehen zwischen Mischlingen 1. Grades und Mischlingen 2. Grades.

Beide Eheteile werden ohne Rücksicht darauf, ob Kinder vorhanden sind oder nicht, evakuiert bzw. einem Altersghetto überstellt, da et-
waige Kinder rassenmäßig in der Regel einen stär-
keren jüdischen Bluteinschlag aufweisen, als die
jüdischen Mischlinge 2. Grade)

ᛋᛋ-Gruppenführer H o f m a n n steht auf
dem Standpunkt, daß von der Sterilisierung weitgehend Gebrauch gemacht werden muß; zumal der Misch-

K210412   372036

179

- 14 -

ling, vor die Wahl gestellt, ob er evakuiert oder
sterilisiert werden soll, sich lieber der Sterilisierung unterziehen würde.

Staatssekretär Dr. S t u c k a r t
stellt fest, daß die praktische Durchführung der
eben mitgeteilten Lösungsmöglichkeiten zur Bereinigung der Mischehen- und Mischlingsfragen in dieser Form eine unendliche Verwaltungsarbeit mit
sich bringen würde. Um zum anderen auf alle Fälle
auch den biologischen Tatsachen Rechnung zu tragen,
schlug Staatssekretär Dr. S t u c k a r t vor,
zur Zwangssterilisierung zu schreiten.

Zur Vereinfachung des Mischehenproblems
müßten ferner Möglichkeiten überlegt werden mit
dem Ziel, daß der Gesetzgeber etwa sagt: "Diese
Ehen sind geschieden".

Bezüglich der Frage der Auswirkung der
Judenevakuierung auf das Wirtschaftsleben erklär-
te Staatssekretär N e u m a n n , daß die in
kriegswichtigen Betrieben im Arbeitseinsatz stehenden Juden derzeit, solange noch kein Ersatz zur
Verfügung steht, nicht evakuiert werden könnten.

ɬ-Obergruppenführer H e y d r i c h
wies darauf hin, daß diese Juden nach den von ihm
genehmigten Richtlinien zur Durchführung der derzeit laufenden Evakuierungsaktionen ohnedies nicht
evakuiert würden.

Staatssekretär Dr. B ü h l e r stellte
fest, daß das Generalgouvernement es begrüßen würde, wenn mit der Endlösung dieser Frage im Generalgouvernement begonnen würde, weil einmal hier das
Transportproblem keine übergeordnete Rolle spielt

K210413   372037

- 15 -   180

und arbeitseinsatzmäßige Gründe den Lauf dieser
Aktion nicht behindern würden. Juden müßten so
schnell wie möglich aus dem Gebiet des Generalgouvernements entfernt werden, weil gerade hier
der Jude als Seuchenträger eine eminente Gefahr
bedeutet und er zum anderen durch fortgesetzten
Schleichhandel die wirtschaftliche Struktur des
Landes dauernd in Unordnung bringt. Von den in
Frage kommenden etwa 2 1/2 Millionen Juden sei
überdies die Mehrzahl der Fälle arbeitsunfähig.

Staatssekretär Dr. B ü h l e r stellt
weiterhin fest, daß die Lösung der Judenfrage im
Generalgouvernement federführend beim Chef der
Sicherheitspolizei und des SD liegt und seine Arbeiten durch die Behörden des Generalgouvernements
unterstützt würden. Er hätte nur eine Bitte, die
Judenfrage in diesem Gebiet so schnell wie möglich
zu lösen.

Abschließend wurden die verschiedenen Ar-
ten der Lösungsmöglichkeiten besprochen, wobei so-
wohl seitens des Gauleiters Dr. M e y e r als auch
seitens des Staatssekretärs Dr. B ü h l e r der
Standpunkt vertreten wurde, gewisse vorbereitende
Arbeiten im Zuge der Endlösung gleich in den be-
treffenden Gebieten selbst durchzuführen, wobei
jedoch eine Beunruhigung der Bevölkerung vermieden
werden müsse.

Mit der Bitte des Chefs der Sicherheitspolizei und des SD an die Besprechungsteilnehmer,
ihm bei der Durchführung der Lösungsarbeiten entsprechende Unterstützung zu gewähren, wurde die
Besprechung geschlossen.

K210414   372038

Credits

Notes

1. In the minutes of the Wannsee Conference Alfred Meyer, Georg Leibbrandt, Wilhelm Stuckart, Roland Freisler, Josef Bühler, Eberhard Schöngarth, and Rudolf Lange are listed as 'Dr.', whereas in the case of Gerhard Klopfer, who was awarded a doctorate in 1929, this title is omitted.

2. Wolfgang Scheffler, 'Die Wannsee-Konferenz und ihre historische Bedeutung', in Gedenkstätte Haus der Wannsee-Konferenz (ed.), *Erinnern für die Zukunft. Ansprachen und Vorträge zur Eröffnung der Gedenkstätte* (Berlin, 1992), pp. 17–34 (p. 30).

3. In an essay for the symposium to mark the seventieth anniversary of the conference ('"Wannsee" als Herausforderung. Die Historiker und die Konferenz', in Norbert Kampe and Peter Klein (eds), *Die Wannsee-Konferenz am 20. Januar 1942. Dokumente, Forschungsstand, Kontroversen* (Cologne, Weimar, and Vienna, 2013), pp. 401–14) Mark Roseman refers to the fact that the mistaken belief that the decision to proceed with a 'final solution' was taken there is still very much alive in the public perception of the conference.

4. Helmut Krausnick assumed that there was a direct connection between Hitler's decision and the decision to carry out a genocide of the European Jews in spring 1941 (see 'Judenverfolgung', in Hans Buchheim and others, *Anatomie des SS-Staates*, vol. 2, 2nd edn (Munich, 1979), pp. 235–366, esp. pp. 297 and 305f.). Hermann Graml took a similar view, assuming that in the first half of June 1941 Himmler and Heydrich had learnt of Hitler's intention to murder the European Jews (*Reichskristallnacht. Antisemitismus und Judenverfolgung im Dritten Reich* (Munich, 1988), pp. 222f.). Wolfgang Benz (*Der Holocaust* (Munich, 1995), pp. 50ff.) sees the 'genesis of the final solution' in the context of the Madagascar Plan (see note 40). Richard Breitman (*Heinrich Himmler. Der Architekt der 'Endlösung'. Himmler und die Vernichtung der europäischen Juden* (Paderborn and Munich, 1996)) assumes that Hitler and Himmler made the decision in early 1941. Saul Friedländer ('Vom Antisemitismus zur Ausrottung', in Eberhard Jäckel and Jürgen Rohwer (eds), *Der Mord an den Juden im Zweiten Weltkrieg. Entschlußbildung und Verwirklichung* (Stuttgart, 1985), pp. 18–60 (p. 47)) and Raul Hilberg ('Die Aktion Reinhard', in *Der Mord an den Juden im Zweiten Weltkrieg*, pp. 125–36) put the date as summer 1941.

5. Tobias Jersak, 'Entscheidungen', in particular pp. 299ff. See also Jersak, 'Interaktion'.

6. Uwe Adam (*Judenpolitik im Dritten Reich* (Düsseldorf, 1972), p. 312) placed
   the decision between September and November 1941, seeing it as an 'escape
   route' from 'total deadlock', for on the one hand the German leadership had
   begun deporting the Jews from Germany, but on the other the war situation
   stymied the original intention of 'consigning the deportees to the occupied
   Russian territories'. Phillipe Burrin places the decision between mid-
   September and October, emphasizing the connection between it and the
   developing military crisis (*Hitler und die Juden. Die Entscheidung für den
   Völkermord* (Frankfurt a. M., 1993), pp. 154ff.). Christopher Browning also
   places the decision to murder the European Jews in this period, though by
   contrast with Burrin he considers it crucial that the Germans believed victory over the Russians was imminent. Browning has always emphasized the
   close link with the decision in July 1941 to murder all the Soviet Jews, as he
   did in his extensive study *Die Entfesselung der 'Endlösung'. Nationalsozialistische
   Judenpolitik 1939–1942* (Munich, 2003), especially p. 455, in which he added
   further nuance to his analysis: in mid-September, he states, with the start of
   deportations, Hitler had given his approval in principle for the murder of
   deportees. By the end of October the crucial decisions had been taken to
   set the course for this (ibid., pp. 532ff.). Götz Aly has also settled on the first
   half of October as the critical period in which an 'official decision, if there
   was one', would have been taken (*Endlösung. Völkerverschiebung und der Mord
   an den europäischen Juden* (Frankfurt a. M., 1995), p. 358).
7. Christian Gerlach, 'Die Wannsee-Konferenz, das Schicksal der deutschen
   Juden und Hitlers politische Grundsatzentscheidung, alle Juden Europas
   zu ermorden', in *WerkstattGeschichte* 18 (1997), 7–44. Leendert Johan
   Hartog had already put forward a similar view. See *Der Befehl zum
   Judenmord. Hitler, Amerika und die Juden* (Bodenheim, 1997).
8. Andrej Angrick discusses the Wannsee Conference as a 'stage-managed
   self-authorization' in his essay 'Die inszenierte Selbstermächtigung?
   Motive und Strategie Heydrichs für die Wannsee-Konferenz', *Die
   Wannsee-Konferenz*, pp. 241–58.
9. See note 151.
10. Martin Broszat, in 'Hitler und die Genesis der "Endlösung". Aus Anlaß
    der Thesen von David Irving', in *VfZ* 25/4 (1977), 739–75, especially
    p. 752, develops the hypothesis that the extermination of the Jews emerged
    'not only from a pre-existing desire to destroy but also as an "escape route"
    out of a cul-de-sac [the Nazis] had got themselves into': 'Once under way
    and institutionalized, however, the practice of liquidation became an over-
    whelming force and finally led to a comprehensive "programme" becom-
    ing a reality'. Hans Mommsen puts forward a similar argument in his
    apodictic statement that we can 'fundamentally rule out the idea that
    Hitler set the policy of genocide in motion by issuing a direct "Führer
    command"' ('Die Realisierung des Utopischen: Die "Endlösung der
    Judenfrage" im "Dritten Reich"', in *GG* 9/3 (1983), 381–420, p. 417).

Arguing against intentionalist interpretations as a discussant in *Der Mord an den Juden im Zweiten Weltkreig. Entschlußbildung und Verwirklichung* (Stuttgart, 1985), p. 66, Mommsen takes the view 'that Hitler more or less hid behind the extermination process that was already in motion'.

11. I am basing my arguments above all on my 1998 book *Politik der Vernichtung* (*Politik der Vernichtung. Die Verfolgung und Ermordung der europäischen Juden 1933–1945* (Munich and Zurich, 1998)), a revised and extended edition of which appeared in English in 2010 (*Holocaust: The Nazi Persecution and Murder of the Jews* (Oxford, 2010)). For a summary see also my survey *Der ungeschriebene Befehl. Hitler und der Weg zur 'Endlösung'* (Munich and elsewhere, 2001), which is the revised version of a report I provided as an expert witness in the *Irving v. Lipstadt* trial in 2000.

12. Norbert Kampe (ed.), *Villenkolonien in Wannsee 1870–1945. Großbürgerliche Lebenswelt und Ort der Wannsee-Konferenz* (Berlin, 2000), pp. 24ff.

13. On Minoux see Johannes Tuchel, *Am Großen Wannsee 56–58. Von der Villa Minoux zum Haus der Wannsee-Konferenz* (Berlin, 1992), pp. 17ff.

14. Ibid., pp. 99ff.

15. Ibid., pp. 105f.

16. Ibid.

17. TNA, FO 371/30899, Press Reading Bureau at Stockholm, report of 14 April 1942.

18. Michael Haupt, *Das Haus der Wannsee-Konferenz. Von der Industriellenvilla zur Gedenkstätte* (Paderborn, 2009), p. 105f.

19. Facsimiles are printed in Kampe, 'Dokumente zur Wannsee-Konferenz', in Kampe and Peter Klein (eds), *Die Wannsee-Konferenz*, pp. 17–115, p. 30 onwards.

20. Tuchel, p. 111.

21. A facsimile is printed in Kampe, 'Dokumente', p. 30 onwards.

22. See Eichmann's minute of 1 December 1941 in Kampe, 'Dokumente', p. 25.

23. For the invitation issued subsequently to Bühler on 1 December 1941 see Peter Klein, *Die Wannsee-Konferenz vom 20. Januar 1942. Analyse und Dokumentation* (booklet) (Berlin, 1996), p. 29f.

24. Letter of 1 December 1941 from Heydrich to Krüger omitting the personal invitation (Klein, *Die Wannsee-Konferenz*, p. 30). See also Angrick's comments on this in 'Die inszenierte Selbstermächtigung? Motive und Strategie Heydrichs für die Wannsee-Konferenz', in Norbert Kampe and Peter Klein (eds), *Die Wannsee-Konferenz*, pp. 241–58, p. 245f.

25. On the persecution of the Jews before the Second World War see in particular Saul Friedländer, *Das Dritte Reich und die Juden. Die Jahre der Verfolgung 1933–1939* (Munich, 1997); Uwe Dietrich Adam, *Judenpolitik im Dritten Reich* (Düsseldorf, 1972); Peter Longerich, *Politik der Vernichtung. Die Verfolgung und Ermordung der europäischen Juden 1933–1945* (Munich and Zurich, 1998).

26. Michael Wildt (ed.), *Die Judenpolitik des SD 1935 bis 1938. Eine Dokumentation* (Munich, 1995).

27. BAB, R 58/486, Bürkel's circular of 20 August 1938. The same file contains further material relating to the creation of the Central Office. On the background to and setting up of the Central Office see Hans Safrian, *Die Eichmann-Männer* (Vienna, 1993), pp. 23ff. and Herbert Rosenkranz, *Verfolgung und Selbstbehauptung. Die Juden in Österreich 1938–1945* (Vienna, 1978), pp. 120ff.

28. OA, 500-1-506, undated note ('Top Secret! Jews') by the Jewish department.

29. BAB, R 58/276.

30. Report on the first meeting of the Committee of the Reich Office for Jewish Emigration on 11 February 1939 (*ADAP* D 5, no. 665).

31. This is evident from Göring's statements at the meetings of 12 November 1938 (*IMT 28*, 1816-PS, pp. 499ff.) and 6 December 1938 (see Götz Aly and Susanne Heim, *Vordenker der Vernichtung. Auschwitz und die deutschen Pläne für eine neue europäische Ordnung* (Frankfurt a. M., 1991)).

32. BAB, R 58/23a. The appointment dates from 7 July 1936.

33. Herbert A. Strauss, 'Jewish Emigration from Germany: Nazi Policies and Jewish Responses', in *The Leo Baeck Institute Year Book*, 25 (1980), 313–61 (I), p. 326.

34. Ino Arndt and Heinz Boberach, 'Deutsches Reich', in Wolfgang Benz (ed.), *Dimension des Völkermords. Die Zahl der jüdischen Opfer des National-sozialismus* (Munich, 1991), pp. 23–66, pp. 34ff. According to Strauss ('Jewish Emigration', p. 326) in 1940 and the first months of 1941 23,000 Jews managed to emigrate from the 'Altreich'.

35. Bogdan Musial, *Deutsche Zivilverwaltung und Judenverfolgung im General-gouvernement. Eine Fallstudie zum Distrikt Lublin 1939–1944* (Wiesbaden, 1999), pp. 123ff.

36. Adam, pp. 263ff.

37. Longerich, *Politik der Vernichtung*, pp. 251ff.

38. Miroslav Kárný, 'Nisko in der Geschichte der Endlösung', in *Judaica Bohemiae*, 23 (1987), 69–84; Jonny Moser, *Nisko. Die ersten Judendeportationen*, ed. by Joseph W. and James R. Moser (Vienna, 2012); Hans Günter Adler, *Der verwaltete Mensch. Studien zur Deportation der Juden aus Deutschland* (Tübingen, 1974), pp. 125ff.; Christopher Browning, 'Nazi Resettlement Policy, and the Search for a Solution to the Jewish Question, 1939–1941', in *German Studies Review* 9/3 (1986), 497–519; Safrian, pp. 68ff.; Ludmila Nesládowská (ed.), *The Case of Nisko in the History of the Final Solution of the Jewish Problem in Commemoration of the 55th Anniversary of the First Deportation of Jews in Europe 1944* (Ostrava, 1995).

39. The German requests have disappeared, but the negative statement of 9 February 1940 on the part of the resettlement administration at the Council of People's Commissars of the USSR, which was prepared for the

Soviet foreign minister Vyacheslav M. Molotov, is available. On this see Pavel Polian, 'Hätte der Holocaust beinahe nicht stattgefunden? Überlegungen zu einem Schriftwechsel im Wert von zwei Millionen Menschenleben', in Johannes Hürter and Jürgen Zarusky (eds), *Besatzung, Kollaboration, Holocaust. Neue Studien zur Verfolgung und Ermordung der europäischen Juden* (Munich, 2008), pp. 1–20.

40. Magnus Brechtken, *Madagaskar für die Juden. Antisemitische Idee und politische Praxis 1885–1945* (Munich, 1997); Browning, 'Nazi Resettlement Policy'; Hans Jansen, *Der Madagaskar-Plan. Die beabsichtigte Deportation der europäischen Juden nach Madagaskar* (Munich, 1997); Leni Yahil, 'Madagascar: Phantom of a Solution for the Jewish Question', in George L. Mosse and Bela Vago (eds), *Jews and Non-Jews in Eastern Europe, 1918–1945* (New York and elsewhere, 1974), pp. 315–34.

41. PAAA, R 100857, Plan for solving the Jewish problem, 2 July 1940.

42. Note from Dannecker for Adolf Eichmann, 21 January 1941, CDJC, V-59, printed in Serge Klarsfeld, *Vichy-Auschwitz. Die Zusammenarbeit der deutschen und französischen Behörden bei der "Endlösung der Judenfrage" in Frankreich* (Nördlingen, 1989), pp. 361ff. The second document is a note from the Nazi Party propaganda headquarters concerning a statement by Eichmann at a meeting on 20 March 1941 in the Propaganda Ministry (printed in Adler, *Der verwaltete Mensch*, p. 152).

43. Heydrich at a meeting on 8 January 1941 in the RSHA, according to Krüger's report; see *Das Diensttagebuch des deutschen Generalgouverneurs in Polen 1939–1945*, ed. by Werner Präg and Wolfgang Jacobmeyer (Stuttgart, 1975). On 11 January Frank had stated clearly to Krüger that Hitler had described it as essential for the General Government to accept 800,000 Jews and Poles (*Diensttagebuch*, 11 January 1941).

44. Up to that point some 20,000 people from the Warthegau (among them over 2,000 Jews) and 5,000 Jews from Vienna had been deported. For further detail see Aly, *Endlösung*, p. 219. On the deportations from Vienna see Safrian, p. 97f.; Adler, *Der verwaltete Mensch*, pp. 147ff; Alfred Gottwald and Diana Schulle, *Die 'Judendeportationen'*, pp. 46ff.

45. This is evident from Heydrich's note of 26 March 1941 about an interview with Göring (see Aly, *Endlösung*, p. 270, who cites as his source OA, 5000-3-795). He notes that he has shown Göring a plan for the 'solution to the Jewish question', which the latter has approved, 'subject to a change regarding Rosenberg's responsibilities, and asked to see again'.

46. Rosenberg was appointed 'Commissioner for the central administration dealing with issues concerning the eastern European territories' on 20 April 1941; this followed on from Hitler's giving Rosenberg the assignment orally on 7 April, which Rosenberg was expecting (Ernst Piper, *Alfred Rosenberg. Hitlers Chefideologe* (Munich, 2005), pp. 509ff.).

47. *IMT* 26, 710-PS, p. 11f.

48. IfZ, NO 203, Brack to Himmler, 28 March 1941. According to a statement made by Brack in May 1947, Himmler gave him this task in January 1941 because he feared any intermingling of Polish and western European Jews (*TWC*, vol. 1, p. 732).

49. *Diensttagebuch*, 17 July 1941. The entry for 20 June 1942 in *Die Tagebücher von Joseph Goebbels*, 2 Parts, 9 and 15 vols, commissioned by the Institut für Zeitgeschichte with support from the Russian State Archive and ed. by Elke Fröhlich (Munich, 1993–2006) *Tagebücher von Josef Goebbels* is another source indicating Hitler's assurance to Frank.

50. On the invasion of the Soviet Union see Boog and others, *Der Angriff auf die Sowjetunion* (Stuttgart, 1983); Peter Jahn (ed.), *Erobern und Vernichten. Der Krieg gegen die Sowjetunion 1941–1945* (Berlin, 1991); Andreas Hillgruber, *Hitlers Strategie. Politik und Kriegführung 1940/41* (Frankfurt a. M., 1965); Gerd Ueberschär and Wolfgang Wette (eds), 'Unternehmen Barbarossa'. Der deutsche Überfall auf die Sowjetunion 1941. Berichte, Analysen, Dokumente* (Paderborn, 1984); *Verbrechen der Wehrmacht. Dimensionen des Vernichtungskrieges 1941–1944* (exhibition catalogue), ed. by Hamburg Institut für Sozialforschung (Hamburg, 2002); Bernd Wegner (ed.), *Zwei Wege nach Moskau. Vom Hitler-Stalin-Pakt bis zum 'Unternehmen Barbarossa'* (Munich, 1991).

51. Christian Gerlach, *Kalkulierte Morde. Die deutsche Wirtschafts- und Vernichtungspolitik in Weißrußland, 1941 bis 1944* (Hamburg, 1999), pp. 66ff. On food policy planning see also Gerlach, 'Deutsche Wirtschaftsinteressen. Besatzungspolitik und der Mord an den Juden in Weißrußland, 1941–1943', in Ulrich Herbert (ed.), *Nationalsozialistische Vernichtungspolitik 1939–1945. Neue Forschungen und Kontroversen* (Frankfurt a. M., 1998), pp. 263–91; Aly and Heim (eds), *Vordenker der Vernichtung*, pp. 366ff.; Rolf-Dieter Müller, 'Von der Wirtschaftsallianz zum kolonialen Ausbeutungskrieg', in Horst Boog and others, *Der Angriff auf die Sowjetunion* (Stuttgart, 1983), pp. 184ff.

52. Müller, 'Wirtschaftsallianz'; on the economic aspects of the war see also in particular Gerlach, *Kalkulierte Morde. Die deutsche Wirtschafts- und Vernichtungspolitik in Weißrußland, 1941 bis 1944* (Hamburg, 1999), pp. 59ff.; Andreas Hillgruber, 'Der Ostkrieg und die Judenvernichtung', in Ueberschär and Wette (eds), 'Unternehmen Barbarossa', pp. 219–36.

53. BAF, RH 22/12. The tenor is similar in the instructions prepared by the department for Wehrmacht propaganda on how to treat propaganda relating to Operation Barbarossa (BAF, RW 4/v. 578) and in the June edition of the publication *Mitteilungen für die Truppe* (Information for Troops). On the use of propaganda to engender the necessary attitudes, see Jürgen Förster, 'Das Unternehmen "Barbarossa" als Eroberungs- und Vernichtungskrieg', in Horst Boog and others (eds), *Der Angriff auf die Sowjetunion* (Stuttgart, 1983), pp. 525ff.

54. Quoted from 'Richtlinien auf Sondergebieten zur Weisung Barbarossa', 13 March 1941; on cooperation with the Wehrmacht see the order from the Army High Command/Quartermaster General, 26 March 1941 (both

printed in Longerich, *Die Ermordung der europäischen Juden. Eine umfassende Dokumentation des Holocaust 1941–1945* (Munich, 1989), nos 26 and 27). On the Einsatzgruppen see Helmut Krausnick and Hans-Heinrich Wilhelm, *Die Truppe des Weltanschauungskrieges. Die Einsatzgruppen der Sicherheitspolizei und des SD 1938–1942* (Stuttgart, 1981); Klaus-Michael Mallmann and others (eds), *Die 'Ereignismeldungen UdSSR' 1941. Dokumente der Einsatzgruppen in der Sowjetunion* (Darmstadt, 2011); Peter Klein (ed.), *Die Einsatzgruppen in der besetzten Sowjetunion 1941/42. Die Tätigkeits- und Lageberichte des Chefs der Sicherheitspolizei und des SD* (Berlin, 1997). On the Order Police see Christopher Browning, *Ordinary Men: Reserve Police Battalion 101 and the Final Solution in Poland* (New York, 1992); Daniel Goldhagen, *Hitler's Willing Executioners: Ordinary Germans and the Holocaust* (New York, 1996); Jürgen Matthäus, 'What about the "Ordinary Men"? The German Order Police and the Holocaust in the Occupied Soviet Union', in *HGS*, 10/2 (1996), 134–50; Klaus-Michael Mallmann, 'Vom Fußvolk der Endlösung. Ordnungspolizei, Ostkrieg und Judenmord', in Dan Diner, *Deutschlandbilder* (Gerlingen, 1997), pp. 355–92; Arico Massimo, *Ordnungspolizei: Ideological War and Genocide in the East 1941–42* (Stockholm, 2012). On the SS Death's Head Brigades see Martin Cüppers, *Wegbereiter der Shoah. Die Waffen-SS, der Kommandostab Reichsführer-SS und die Judenvernichtung 1939–1945* (Darmstadt, 2005). These were made up of two motorized infantry brigades and two cavalry regiments that were combined at the beginning of August into one cavalry brigade.

55. BAB, R 70 SU/31, printed in Longerich, *Die Ermordung der europäischen Juden*, pp. 116ff.
56. Longerich, *Politik der Vernichtung*, pp. 321ff.
57. Ibid., pp. 352ff.
58. Ibid., pp. 533ff.
59. Longerich, *Heinrich Himmler. Biographie*, 3rd edn (Munich, 2008), pp. 449ff.
60. Führer decree concerning the police security of the newly occupied eastern territories (IfZ, NG 1688, printed in *'Führer-Erlasse' 1939–1945. Edition sämtlicher überlieferter, nicht im Reichsgesetzblatt abgedruckter, von Hitler während des Zweiten Weltkrieges schriftlich erteilter Direktiven aus den Bereichen Staat, Partei, Wirtschaft, Besatzungspolitik und Militärverwaltung*, compiled and with an introduction by Martin Moll (Stuttgart, 1997), no. 99); on this, see Longerich, *Himmler*, pp. 545ff.
61. *IMT* 26, 686-PS, p. 255f.
62. Longerich, *Himmler*, pp. 545ff.
63. Lösener's minute for Frick, printed in Bernhard Lösener, 'Als Rassereferent im Reichsministerium des Innern', ed. by Walter Strauss, in *VfZ* 9/3 (1961), 262–313, p. 303, according to which on 15 August 1941 Eichmann announced at a meeting in the Propaganda Ministry that Hitler had rejected a proposal from Obergruppenführer Heydrich to proceed with evacuations during the war. Heydrich was now working on a plan aimed at 'partial evacuation of the larger cities'.

64. *Die Tagebücher von Joseph Goebbels*, entries for 19 and 20 August 1941. Hitler's words clearly contradict Wolf Gruner's suggestion that the decision in favour of partial deportations had already been taken in August. See 'Von der Kollektivausweisung zur Deportation der Juden aus Deutschland (1938–1945). Neue Perspektiven und Dokumente', in Birthe Kundrus and Beate Meyer (eds), *Die Deportation der Juden aus Deutschland. Pläne—Praxis—Reaktionen 1938–1945* (Göttingen, 2004), pp. 21–62, pp. 46ff.

65. Max Domarus, *Hitler. Reden und Proklamationen 1932–1945*, vol. 2 (Munich, 1965), p. 1057. See also Daniel Terner, *Prophet und Prophezeihung*, p. 17f.; Longerich, *Holocaust*, p. 124f.

66. *Der Dienstkalender Heinrich Himmlers 1941/42*, commissioned by the Forschungsstelle für Zeitgeschichte in Hamburg, ed. with a commentary and introduction by Peter Witte and others (Hamburg, 1999), entries for 2 and 4 September. According to the editors' comments on the 4 September entry, Koppe's letter of 10 September has been lost but the passage concerning his acceptance of 60,000 Jews into the Lodz ghetto can be reconstructed from his staff's records of correspondence.

67. Decree issued on 28 August 1941 by the Supreme Soviet and printed in Alfred Eisfeld, *Deportation, Sondersiedlung, Arbeitsarmee. Deutsche in der Sowjetunion 1941 bis 1956* (Cologne, 1996), p. 54f.

68. *Die Tagebücher von Joseph Goebbels*, entry for 9 September 1941; Alfred Rosenberg, *Die Tagebücher von 1934 bis 1944* (ed. and with a commentary by Jürgen Matthäus and Frank Bajohr (Frankfurt a. M., 2015)), entry for 12 September 1941, indicates that he must have received the information after 7 September (see the preceding entry).

69. Rosenberg, *Tagebücher*, entry for 11 September 1941.

70. The paper was presented by Otto Bräutigam, Rosenberg's representative at the Army High Command; see Bräutigam, 'Das Kriegstagebuch des Diplomaten Otto Bräutigam', with an introduction and commentary by Hans-Dieter Heilmann, in Götz Aly and others (eds), *Biedermann und Schreibtischtäter. Materialien zur deutschen Täter-Biographie* (Berlin, 1989), pp. 123–87, entries for 14 and 15 September 1941; BAB, R 6/109, Guidelines for radio propaganda concerning the exiling of ethnic Germans to Siberia, with correspondence from Leibbrandt to Bräutigam from 13 September 1941.

71. *Dienstkalender*, entry for 16 September 1941. On 22 August the legation councillor Carl-Theo Zeitschel presented Abetz with a proposal to this effect. Zeitschel reported in a letter of 8 October that Abetz had gained Himmler's consent that 'Jews in concentration camps in the occupied [French] territory [could] be deported to the east as soon as transport [was] available'. Both of Zeitschel's letters are reproduced in Klarsfeld, *Vichy-Auschwitz*, pp. 23ff.

72. *Dienstkalender*, entry for 17 September 1941.

73. BAB, NS 19/2655, printed in Longerich, *Die Ermordung der europäischen Juden*, no. 54.
74. Werner Koeppen, *Herbst 1941 im 'Führerhauptquartier'. Berichte Werner Koeppens an seinen Minister Alfred Rosenberg*, ed. and with a commentary by Martin Vogt (Koblenz, 2002), 21 September 1941 (concerning the previous day). The idea of a 'reprisal' targeting the Jews in Germany can be traced elsewhere around this time. Already on 5 September Karl Hübner, head of Office IV of the NSDAP's Foreign Organization (AO), had proposed to Ernst Wilhelm Bohle, head of the AO, that, in view of measures taken by the United States and/or South American states against Germans, 'Germany should focus on Jews living within its sphere of influence as a reprisal for the injustice done to its citizens' and should emphasize in propaganda 'the fate awaiting those Jews who are under our control'. The head of the Political Department made negative comments on this proposal on 28 September 1941 (see the sequence of documents in PAAA, R 105015).
75. On this see David Reynolds, *The Creation of the Anglo-American Alliance, 1937–1941: A Study in Competitive Co-operation* (Chapel Hill, NC, 1981), pp. 167ff.
76. For more details see Longerich, *Davon haben wir nichts gewusst! Die Deutschen und die Judenverfolgung 1933–1945* (Munich, 2006), p. 183f.
77. Erwin Klink, 'Heer und Kriegsmarine', in Horst Boog and others, *Der Angriff auf die Sowjetunion*, pp. 451–651, esp. pp. 595ff.
78. Longerich, *Davon haben wir nichts gewusst!*, p. 183f.
79. For Berlin see Susanne Willems, *Der entsiedelte Jude. Albert Speers Wohnungsmarktpolitik für den Berliner Hauptstadtbau* (Berlin, 2002); for Hanover see Marlis Buchholz, *Die Hannoverschen Judenhäuser: Zur Situation der Juden in der Zeit der Ghettoisierung und Verfolgung, 1941 bis 1945* (Hildesheim, 1987); for Breslau see Willy Cohn, *Als Jude in Breslau 1941. Aus den Tagebüchern von Studienrat a. D. Dr. Willy Israel Cohn*, ed. by Joseph Walk (Gerlingen, 1984), 8, 9, 15, 23 August and 11 September 1941; for Hamburg see Angela Schwarz, 'Von den Wohnstiften zu den "Judenhäusern"', in Angelika Ebbinghaus and Karsten Linne (eds), *Kein abgeschlossenes Kapitel: Hamburg im 'Dritten Reich'* (Hamburg, 1997), pp. 232–47; for Bochum see Hubert Schneider, *Die 'Entjudung' des Wohnraums – 'Judenhäuser' in Bochum. Die Geschichte der Gebäude und ihrer Bewohner* (Münster, 2010).
80. On the auctions see Frank Bajohr, *'Arisierung' in Hamburg. Die Verdrägung der jüdischen Unternehmer 1933–45* (Hamburg, 1997), pp. 331ff.; Andreas Nachama (ed.), *Vor aller Augen. Die Deportation der Juden und die Versteigerung ihres Eigentums. Fotografien aus Lörrach 1940* (Berlin, 2011).
81. For Hamburg see Peter Witte, 'Two Decisions Concerning the "Final Solution to the Jewish Question", Deportations to Łódź and Mass Murder in Chełmno', in *HGS*, 9/3 (1995), 318–45, p. 323f.; for Cologne see

Browning, *Die Entfesselung der 'Endlösung'. Nationalsozialistische Judenpolitik 1939–1942* (Munich, 2003), p. 468.

82. Walter Manoschek, *'Serbien ist judenfrei'. Militärische Besatzungspolitik und Judenvernichtung in Serbien 1941/42* (Munich, 1993), pp. 43ff.

83. Ahlrich Meyer,' "…daß französische Verhältnisse anders sind als polnische". Die Bekämpfung des Widerstands durch die deutsche Militärverwaltung in Frankreich 1941', in Guus Meershoek and others, *Repression und Kriegsverbrechen. Die Bekämpfung von Widerstands- und Partisanenbewegungen gegen die deutsche Besatzung in West- und Südosteuropa* (Berlin, 1997), pp. 43–92; Wolfram Weber, *Die Innere Sicherheit im besetzten Belgien und Nordfrankreich 1940–1944. Ein Beitrag zur Geschichte der Besatzungsverwaltungen* (Düsseldorf, 1978), pp. 59ff.; Fritz Petrick (ed.), *Die Okkupationspolitik des deutschen Faschismus in Dänemark und Norwegen (1940–1945)* (Berlin and Heidelberg, 1992), p. 33.

84. Detlef Brandes, *Die Tschechen unter deutschem Protektorat. Besatzungspolitik, Kollaboration und Widerstand im Protektorat Böhmen und Mähren bis Heydrichs Tod (1939–1942)*, vol. 1 (Munich, 1969), pp. 270ff.

85. Klein refers to this in 'Die Rolle der Vernichtungslager Kulmhof (Chełmno), Belzec (Bełżec) und Auschwitz-Birkenau in den frühen Deportationsvorbereitungen', in Dittmar Dahlmann and Gerhard Hirschfeld (eds), *Lager, Zwangsarbeit, Vertreibung und Deportation. Dimensionen der Massenverbrechen in der Sowjetunion und in Deutschland 1933 bis 1945* (Essen, 1999), pp. 459–84, p. 473. He has studied 'an extensive SD file' on the subject in the Osobyi Archive in Moscow. (OA, 500-4-146).

86. On 28 September Wilhelm Keitel modified the order to the effect that hostages from nationalist and democratic and bourgeois backgrounds could in certain circumstances be shot; see Bräutigam, *Kriegstagebuch*, vol. 1, no. 101, entry for 16 September 1941: *IMT* 27, 1590-PS, p. 373f.

87. *Die Tagebücher von Joseph Goebbels*, entry for 24 September 1941.

88. Koeppen, *Herbst 1941*.

89. Miroslav Kárný and others, *Deutsche Politik im Protektorat 'Böhmen und Mähren' unter Reinhard Heydrich 1941–1942. Eine Dokumentation* (Berlin, 1997), doc. 29.

90. The objection was raised by Georg Thomas, head of the War Economy and Armaments Office (11 October 1941, with Himmler's refusal dated 22 October 1941) and by the governor of Kalisz-Lodz, Friedrich Uebelhoer (Uebelhoer to Himmler, 4 October 1941, insisting on Lodz as a 'work ghetto', and 9 October 1941; Heydrich to Himmler, 8 October 1941; Himmler to Uebelhoer and Greiser, 10 and 11 October 1941; all documents in BAB, NS 19/2655).

91. Ian Kershaw, 'Improvised Genocide? The Emergence of the "Final Solution" in the "Warthegau"', in *Transactions of the Royal Historical Society*, 2 (1992), 51–78, pp. 70ff.; Michael Alberti, *Die Verfolgung und Vernichtung der Juden im Reichsgau Wartheland 1939–1945* (Wiesbaden, 2006), p. 404.

The reconstruction of this compromise is based on Greiser's letter of 1 May 1942 to Himmler in which he announced that the 'special treatment of around 100,000 Jews in my Gau' would be 'completed in the next 2–3 months' (BAB, NS 19/1585).

92. These were the terms used by Rolf-Heinz Höppner, head of the SD section for Posen, in a letter dated 16 July to Eichmann (printed in Longerich, *Die Ermordung der europäischen Juden*, no. 12); for a detailed recent discussion see Klein, *Die 'Ghettoverwaltung Litzmannstadt' 1940–1944. Eine Dienstelle im Spannungsfeld von Kommunalbürokratie und staatlicher Verfolgungspolitik* (Hamburg, 2009), pp. 353ff.

93. BAB, NS 19/2655, Heydrich to Himmler, 8 October 1941.

94. Alfred Gottwaldt and Diana Schulle, *Die 'Judendeportationen' aus dem Deutschen Reich 1941–1945. Eine kommentierte Chronologie* (Wiesbaden, 2005), pp. 52ff.; Alberti, *Die Verfolgung*, pp. 373ff.; Klein, *Die 'Ghettoverwaltung Litzmannstadt'*, pp. 336ff.

95. Gottwaldt and Schulle, *Die 'Judendeportationen'*, pp. 84ff.; Safrian, *Eichmann-Männer*, pp. 150ff.; important sources for Minsk are Karl Löwenstein's account, *Minsk. Im Lager der deutschen Juden* (Bonn, 1961) and Heinz Rosenberg's memoir, *Jahre des Schreckens... und ich blieb übrig, dass ich Dir's ansage* (Göttingen, 1993).

96. Gottwaldt and Schulle, *Die 'Judendeportationen'*, pp. 110ff.

97. *Die Tagebücher von Joseph Goebbels*, entry for 18 November 1941.

98. StA Shitomir, P 1151-1-137. I am very grateful to Wendy Lower for giving me a copy of this document.

99. See note 71.

100. CDJC, I-28, printed in Klarsfeld, *Vichy-Auschwitz*, p. 369f.

101. BAB, NS 19/1734; this statement was linked to Heydrich's demand that there should be no experts in Jewish matters working in the Ministry for the East.

102. PAAA, R 103195, Luther's speech note for Ribbentrop, 17 October 1941; see also Browning, *'Die Entfesselung der Endlösung'*, p. 90f.

103. Ulrich Herbert, 'Die deutsche Militärverwaltung in Paris und die Deportation der französischen Juden', in Christian Jansen, Lutz Niethammer, and Bernd Weisbrod (eds), *Von der Aufgabe der Freiheit: Politische Verantwortung und bürgerliche Gesellschaft im 19. und 20. Jahrhundert. Festschrift für Hans Mommsen zum 5. November 1995* (Berlin, 1995), pp. 427–50, pp. 437ff.

104. *ADAP* D 8, no. 425.

105. Himmler's *Dienstkalender*, entry for 20 October 1941. The editors quote from a declaration by Mach of 26 March 1942 to the Slovakian State Council, which provides evidence of the German offer.

106. IfZ, ED 53, Major Gerhard Engel's handwritten accounts from after the war, known as the Engel diary, 2 November 1941 (incorrectly dated 2 October 1941 in Engel, *Heeresadjutant bei Hitler, 1938–1943. Aufzeichnungen*

des Majors Engel, ed. and with a commentary by Hildegard von Kotze (Munich, 1974), p. 111). Himmler's *Dienstkalender* confirms a meeting between Himmler and Hitler on 2 November 1941. On the assassinations in Saloniki see Klein, 'Die Rolle der Vernichtungslager', p. 473.

107. This event was reconstructed on the basis of witness statements. See Mathias Beer, 'Die Entwicklung der Gaswagen beim Mord an den Juden', in *VfZ*, 35/3 (1987), 403–17, p. 407; StA München, Staatsanwaltschaften, 34865/4, Staatsanwaltschaft München, indictment of Karl Wolff, 19 April 1963, pp. 140ff.; Himmler's *Dienstkalender*, entry for 15 August 1941.

108. Beer, 'Die Entwicklung der Gaswagen', p. 408; Angelika Ebbinghaus and Gerd Preissler, 'Die Ermordung psychisch kranker Menschen in der Sowjetunion. Dokumentation', in Götz Aly, *Aussonderung und Tod. Die klinische Hinrichtung der Unbrauchbaren* (Berlin, 1985), pp. 75–107, pp. 88ff.; statement by Widmann, 11 January 1960, ZStL, 202 AR-Z 152/159, pp. 33ff. In addition, see statements by Georg Frentzel, 27 August 1970 and Alexander N. Stepanow (at the time chief medical officer at the psychiatric clinic in Mogilew), 20 July 1944, both in StAnw München, Zentraler Untersuchungsvorgang 9 (Ermittlungsakten des Ministeriums für Staatssicherheit der DDR).

109. Beer, 'Die Entwicklung der Gaswagen', pp. 409ff.

110. Ibid., p. 411.

111. Before Christmas 1941 two vehicles were driven from Berlin to Riga to Einsatzgruppe A (see Beer, 'Die Entwicklung der Gaswagen', p. 413). On SK 4a (Einsatzgruppe C) see ibid., p. 412. For EK 8 (Einsatzgruppe B) see the statement by Otto Matonoga on 8/9 June 1945 to the Soviet investigating authorities (StAnw München, Zentraler Untersuchungsvorgang 9). Einsatzgruppe D used a gas van at the end of 1941; see Beer, 'Die Entwicklung der Gaswagen', p. 413; StA Staatsanwaltschaften, 35280/35, Landgericht München, 119c Js 1/69, judgment of 15 November 1974, pp. 32ff.; statement by Jeckel, 21 December 1945, printed in Hans-Heinrich Wilhelm, 'Die Einsatzgruppe A der Sicherheitspolizei und des SD 1941/42. Eine exemplarische Studie', in Helmut Krausnick and Wilhelm, *Die Truppe des Weltanschauungskrieges. Die Einsatzgruppen der Sicherheitspolizei und des SD 1938–1942* (Stuttgart, 1981), pp. 281–636, p. 548.

112. Alberti, *Die Verfolgung*, pp. 422ff.

113. Patricia Heberer, 'Eine Kontinuität der Tötungsoperationen. T4-Täter und die Aktion Reinhard', in Bogdan Musił (ed.), *Aktion Reinhardt*, pp. 285–308, p. 295. Himmler's *Dienstkalender* for 14 December 1941 records a meeting between him and Brack, against which the word 'euthanasia' appears. On Brack's provision of staff see in particular Brack's letter to Himmler of 23 June 1942 (BAB, NS 19/1583).

114. Judgment of the Landgericht Stuttgart of 15 August 1950, printed in *Justiz und NS-Verbrechen. Sammlung (west-)deutscher Strafurteile wegen*

nationalsozialistischer Tötungsverbrechen, 1945–2012, ed. by Christiaan F. Rüter and Dick W. de Mildt (Amsterdam and Munich, 1978), vol. 7, no. 231a.

115. Lucjan Dobroszycki (ed.), *The Chronicle of the Łódź Ghetto 1941–1944* (New Haven, CT and London, 1984), p. 96f. and 124f.

116. Letter from Lange to Stahlecker, 1 October 1941, OA 504-2-8. On the deportations to Riga, the conditions in which the deportees lived, and the murders committed in Riga see Scheffler's survey in 'Das Schicksal der in die baltischen Staaten deportierten deutschen, österreichischen und tschechoslowakischen Juden 1941–1945', in *Buch der Erinnerung. Die ins Baltikum deportierten deutschen, österreichischen und tschechoslowaskischen Juden*, ed. by Wolfgang Scheffler and Diana Schulle, vol. 1 (Munich, 2003), pp. 1–78; Andrej Angrick and Peter Klein, *Die 'Endlösung in Riga. Ausbeutung und Vernichtung 1941–1944* (Darmstadt, 2006), pp. 199ff.

117. YIVO, Occ E 3–29, Aktennotiz Generalkommissar Drechsler, 20 October 1941.

118. IfZ, NO 365. Only a draft of the letter has survived, but the date (25 October) matches an appointment Lohse had in the Ministry for the East. The letter was preceded by correspondence that has been lost; see Angrick and Klein, *Die 'Endlösung' in Riga*, p. 200.

119. Ibid., p. 42f.

120. IfZ, Fb 101/29, Riflemen's report. On this see Scheffler, 'Massenmord in Kowno', in *Buch der Erinnerung*, pp. 83–7; Gottwaldt and Schulle, *Die 'Judendeportationen'*, pp. 98ff.

121. Printed in *Dienstkalender*. The time was 13.30.

122. Gerald Fleming, *Hitler and the Final Solution* (Berkeley, Los Angeles, CA, and London, 1984), pp. 87ff.; incident report 151 of 5 January 1942, printed in Mallmann and others, *Die 'Ereignismeldungen UdSSR'*.

123. *Dienstkalender*, 30 November and 4 December 1942; TNA, HW 16/32, Himmler's telegrams to Jeckeln, 1 and 4 December 1941.

124. Angrick and Klein, *Die 'Endlösung' in Riga*, pp. 212ff.; Gottwaldt and Schulle, *Die 'Judendeportationen'*, pp. 110ff.; on the individual transports see *Buch der Erinnerung*.

125. Jean-Claude Pressac, *Die Krematorien von Auschwitz. Die Technik des Massenmordes*, 2nd edn (Munich, 1995), pp. 38ff.

126. Christian Gerlach, 'Failure of Plans for an SS Extermination Camp in Mogilev, Belorussia', in *HGS*, 11/1 (1997), 60–78.

127. Dieter Pohl, *Nationalsozialistische Judenverfolgung in Ostgalizien 1941–1944. Organisation und Durchführung eines staatlichen Massenverbrechens* (Munich, 1996), pp. 67ff. and 110ff. On these early murders see also Thomas Sandkühler, *'Endlösung' in Galizien. Der Judenmord in Ostpolen und die Rettungsinitiativen von Berthold Beitz 1941–1944* (Bonn, 1996), pp. 114ff.

128. Pohl, *Nationalsozialistische Judenverfolgung*, pp. 138ff.; Sandkühler, *'Endlösung' in Galizien*, pp. 148ff.

129. See *Dienstkalender*.

130. BAB, BDC-Akte Globocnik, letter to Himmler of 1 October 1941 in which the proposals were only hinted at. See also Pohl, *Von der 'Judenpolitik' zum Judenmord. Der Distrikt Lublin des Generalgouvernements, 1934–1944* (Frankfurt a. M., 1993), p. 101.

131. This is also the view of the editors of the *Dienstkalender* (p. 233, note 35).

132. See Longerich, *Politik der Vernichtung*, p. 426f.

133. *Diensttagebuch*, entry for 14 October 1941.

134. Longerich, *Politik der Vernichtung*, especially p. 427f. The Third Decree concerning Limits on Sojourns in the General Government was finally backdated to 15 October 1941; see the Jewish Historical Institute Warsaw (ed.), *Faschismus—Getto—Massenmord* (Frankfurt a. M., 1962), p. 128f. The meetings took place between 14 and 21 October in Warsaw, Lublin, Radom, Krakow, and Lemberg (IfZ, MA 120, abridged in *Diensttagebuch*, pp. 413ff.).

135. ZStL, 208 AR-Z 252/59, 6, p. 1179, statement by Stanislaw Kozak, beginning of construction work on 1 November, printed in *Nationalsozialistische Massentötungen durch Giftgas. Eine Dokumentation*, ed. by Hermann Langbein, Adalbert Rückerl, Eugen Kogon, and others (Frankfurt a. M., 1983), p. 152f. This date is confirmed by Michael Tregenza ('Belzec Death Camp', in *Wiener Library Bulletin*, 30 (1977/8), 8–25).

136. Pohl, *Von der 'Judenpolitik' zum Judenmord. Der Distrikt Lublin des Generalgouvernements, 1934–1944* (Frankfurt a. M., 1993), pp. 101 and 105f.

137. Bogdan Musial's thesis that there was a direct link between the decision to build Belzec and plans to settle ethnic Germans is speculative, as is his claim that from the outset Belzec's purpose was to murder the Jews from the whole of the General Government in the space of about two years. See *Deutsche Zivilverwaltung*, pp. 201ff. and 207f.

138. Sybille Steinbacher, *'Musterstadt' Auschwitz. Germanisierungspolitik und Judenmord in Oberschlesien* (Munich, 2000), pp. 135ff.

139. Ibid., pp. 138ff.

140. Ibid., pp. 273ff. The author leaves the method of killing open.

141. Dwork and van Pelt, *Auschwitz*, p. 205, quoted after Pery Broad, 'Erinnerungen', in Jadwiga Bezwińska and Danuta Czech (eds), *KL Auschwitz in den Augen der SS*, 3rd edn (Katowice, 1981), pp. 133–45, pp. 174ff.

142. The fact that the murder of these prisoners took place at the beginning of September 1941 can be regarded as certain as a result of Stanisław Kłodziński's study based on interviews with about 200 former prisoners. According to Franciszek Piper (*Die Zahl der Opfer von Auschwitz. Aufgrund der Quellen und der Erträge der Forschung, 1945 bis 1990* (Oświęcim, 1993), p. 23), this mass murder was preceded by experiments with poison gas in August 1941. See also Danuta Czech, *Kalendarium der Ereignisse im Konzentrationslager Auschwitz-Birkenau 1939–1945* (Reinbek bei Hamburg, 1989), pp. 115ff., Jerzy Brandhuber, 'Die sowjetischen Kriegsgefangenen

im Konzentrationslager Auschwitz', in *Hefte von Auschwitz*, 4 (1961), 5–62, and Wojciech Barcz, 'Die erste Vergasung', in Hans Günther Adler, Hermann Langbein, and Ella Lingens-Reiner (eds), *Auschwitz. Zeugnisse und Berichte*, 2nd edn (Cologne and Frankfurt a. M., 1979), pp. 17–18, p. 17f.

143. OA, 502-1-312, Firma Topf & Söhne an Bauleitung Auschwitz, 31 October 1941. See also Jean-Claude, Pressac, *Die Krematorien von Auschwitz*, pp. 31ff.

144. Michael Thad Allen ('The Devil in the Details: The Gas Chambers of Birkenau, October 1941', in *HGS* 16/2 (2002), 189–216) has suggested October 1941 as the date and used this as the basis for drawing the resulting conclusion with regard to a 'Führer decision'; in doing so he disagrees strongly with Dwork and van Pelt (*Auschwitz*, pp. 355ff.); Browning agrees with Allen's dating (*Die Entfesselung der 'Endlösung'*, p. 514).

145. See pp. 86ff.

146. Hitler, *Monologe im Führerhauptquartier*, 25 October 1941.

147. *Dienstkalender*, 15 November 1941; BAB, R 43 II/684a, Brandt to Lammers, sending Himmler's note for the file on the discussion, 25 November 1941.

148. Outline of the speech quoted by Wilhelm, *Rassenpolitik und Kriegsführung. Sicherheitspolizei und Wehrmacht in Polen und in der Sowjetunion 1939–1942* (Passau, 1991), p. 131f., after PAAA, Pol XIII, 25, VAA-Berichte; see also the notes by a press correspondent on the speech that was actually made, printed in Jürgen Hagemann, *Die Presselenkung im Dritten Reich* (Bonn, 1970), p. 146.

149. *ADAP* D 8, no. 515, notes of the meeting on 28 November 1941 and 30 November 1941 between Hitler and the Grand Mufti in the presence of the Reich Foreign Minister.

150. PAAA, R 100857, letter from Heydrich to Luther.

151. Heydrich's foregrounding of the 'European' dimension casts doubt on Gerlach's thesis in 'Die Wannsee-Konferenz' that the original intention was first and foremost to establish a definition of German Jews with regard to the 'final solution'.

152. PAAA, R 100857, minute on the invitation of 29 November 1941.

153. *Die Tagebücher von Joseph Goebbels*, entry for 13 December 1941.

154. This is Gerlach's argument in 'Die Wannsee-Konferenz'.

155. See *Dienstkalender*.

156. According to Gerlach ('Die Wannsee-Konferenz', pp. 22 and 27), the meaning of the expression 'partisan' has to be understood in the light of Hitler's succumbing, in the face of an impending war on two fronts, to a 'kind of continental Europe fortress mentality' and regarding the European Jews quite simply as dangerous enemies in his own backyard. The term 'partisan' to characterize European Jews does not, however, occur in Hitler's otherwise altogether stereotypical anti-Semitic tirades.

On the other hand, the idea that Jews in the occupied Soviet territories were in general partisans or supported partisans and therefore had to be eliminated was so prevalent among Germans by the end of 1941 that Hitler's comment seems unambiguous.

157. Rosenberg, *Tagebücher*, no. 14 (this minute refers to a meeting that took place when Rosenberg showed Hitler a Sportpalast speech he had written): 'On the Jewish question I said that the comments on the New York Jews might have to be modified after this decision. I took the view that we should not talk of exterminating the Jews. The Führer agreed with this and said they had foisted the war on us and brought destruction; it was no wonder that they felt the consequences first'. The word 'decision' does not, however, refer to a 'fundamental decision' by Hitler to exterminate the Jews, as Gerlach claims ('Die Wannsee-Konferenz', p. 24), but clearly means Germany's declaration of war on the United States.

158. Domarus, *Hitler*, vol. 2, p. 1821.

159. See notes 280 and 281.

160. According to his *Diensttagebuch*, Frank was in Berlin from 10 to 13 December 1941, taking part in the Reichstag session on 11 December.

161. *Diensttagebuch*, p. 457f.

162. Musial, *Deutsche Zivilverwaltung*, p. 219.

163. There is a facsimile in Kampe, 'Dokumente zur Wannsee-Konferenz', p. 38.

164. As only the invitations to Luther and Hofmann survive, we know about the changes to the list of invitees from the minutes of the conference: Lange is mentioned as representing Stahlecker (who must therefore have also received an invitation), whereas Schöngarth is not listed as representing Krüger. The second invitation was therefore most likely sent directly to Schöngarth and not to Krüger.

165. On discussions among the population about the deportations of German Jews and the speculations arising from them see Longerich, *'Davon haben wir nichts gewusst!'*, pp. 194ff. On the circulation of information about the murder of Jews, in particular in the Soviet Union, see ibid., pp. 222ff.

166. Jacobsen, *Nationalsozialistische Außenpolitik 1933–1938* (Frankfurt a. M. and Berlin, 1968), pp. 279ff. and 303ff.; Browning, 'Unterstaatssekretär Martin Luther and the Ribbentrop Foreign Office', in *Journal of Contemporary History*, 12/2 (1977), 313–44.

167. For details see Longerich, *Propagandisten im Krieg. Die Presseabteilung des Auswärtigen Amtes unter Ribbentrop* (Munich, 1987), pp. 54ff.

168. On the Foreign Ministry's involvement in the 'Jewish question' in Serbia, see Browning, *'Die Endlösung' und das Auswärtige Amt. Das Referat D III der Abteilung Deutschland 1940–1943* (Darmstadt, 2010), pp. 78ff. The impetus for this came from a proposal made by the Foreign Ministry's representative in Belgrade, Felix Benzler, on 14 August 1941 to deport the Jews further down the Danube or to the General Government (PAAA,

R 9943). Subsequent discussion of this proposal can be found in file PAAA, R 100874; Eichmann's suggestion is recorded in a marginal note made by Rademacher on 13 September 1941.

169. PAAA, R 100874, ministerial office to Luther, 2 October 1941.
170. Rademacher's note, 25 October 1941, *ADAP* D 8, no. 425.
171. Manoschek, *'Serbien ist judenfrei'*, pp. 55ff.
172. Rademacher, 25 October 1941, *ADAP* D 8, no. 425.
173. PAAA, R 1000853, Luther to RSHA, 10 January 1942; the file contains the relevant correspondence with the German embassies in these countries. The RSHA's telephone enquiry referred only to Slovakia and Croatia; see Browning, *'Die Endlösung' und das Auswärtige Amt*, p. 92f.
174. Browning, *'Die Endlösung' und das Auswärtige Amt*, pp. 98ff.; PAAA, R 101122, Müller to Ribbentrop, 30 October, on sending the first five reports from the Einsatzgruppen to the Foreign Ministry; ibid., 25 November, sixth report sent by Heydrich. On 10 December 1941 Department D III wrote a summary of the activities and state of play contained in the Einsatzgruppe reports one to five, while Luther summarized the sixth report on the same day. Ribbentrop received both via Ernst von Weizsäcker. These documents conveyed details about the mass murders of Jews, including precise statistics. The reports and summaries had a relatively wide circulation within the Foreign Ministry; on this see Browning, *'Die Endlösung' und das Auswärtige Amt*, p. 101.
175. For what follows see PAAA, R 100857, 8 December 1941, unsigned.
176. Luther was evidently indicating that after the approaches to the governments of Romania, Croatia, and Slovakia, he intended to approach Hungary also to allow the deportation of Hungarian Jews from Germany. In August 1941 Hungary had already deported some 16,000 'stateless' Jews from their own country to the occupied Soviet territories, where they were murdered by German SS and police units in the so-called Kamenez-Podolsk massacre.
177. IfZ, NG 1111, Lammers's letter of 20 July 1941.
178. Hans-Christian Jasch, *Staatssekretär Wilhelm Stuckart und die Judenpolitik. Der Mythos von der sauberen Verwaltung* (Munich, 2012), pp. 17ff.
179. Beate Meyer, *'Jüdische Mischlinge'. Rassenpolitik und Verfolgungserfahrung 1933–1945* (Hamburg, 1999), p. 102.
180. Jasch, *Staatssekretär Wilhelm Stuckart*, pp. 197ff.; Jasch, 'Zur Rolle der Innenverwaltung im Dritten Reich bei der Vorbereitung und Organisation des Genozids an den Europäischen Juden: der Fall des Dr. Wilhelm Stuckart (1902–1953)', in *Die Verwaltung*, 43/2 (2010), 217–71; Cornelia Essner, *Die 'Nürnberger Gesetze' oder die Verwaltung des Rassenwahns 1933–1945* (Paderborn and Munich, 2002), pp. 113ff.
181. Wilhelm Stuckart and Hans Globke, *Kommentare zur deutschen Rassengesetzgebung* (Munich, 1936).
182. Meyer, *'Jüdische Mischlinge'*, p. 162.

183. For examples see Jasch, 'Zur Rolle der Innenverwaltung', pp. 290ff. and in more detail in *Staatssekretär Wilhelm Stuckart*, pp. 290ff.
184. Markus Heckmann, *NS-Täter und Bürger der Bundesrepublik* (Münster, 2010); Armin Nolzen, 'Gerhard Klopfer, die Abteilung III in der Partei-Kanzlei und deren "Judenpolitik"', in Norbert Kampe and Peter Klein (eds), *Die Wannsee-Konferenz*, pp. 303–22.
185. For details see Longerich, *Hitlers Stellvertreter. Führung der Partei und Kontrolle des Staatsapparates durch den Stab Heß und die Partei-Kanzlei Bormann* (Munich and elsewhere, 1992), pp. 211f., 214ff., and 64ff.
186. IfZ, F 71, minute by Feldscher on the outcome of the meeting in the headquarters of the Security Police about the solution to the European 'Jewish question', according to which the RSHA, Party Chancellery, and Four-Year Plan Office took the same line on this matter.
187. *Akten der Reichskanzlei*, electronic version at www.bundesarchiv.de with a biography in tabular form.
188. Heydrich's appointment, mentioned earlier, as head of the 'Currency Investigation Office' in July 1936 was designed to facilitate the seizure of Jewish property. Various measures arising from Göring's Four-Year Plan for Aryanization continued the policy of expropriation, which reached its zenith in the anti-Jewish economic legislation following the November pogrom; for details see Longerich, *Politik der Vernichtung*, pp. 1124ff.
189. OA, 700-1-6. See also Longerich, *Politik der Vernichtung*, p. 722.
190. On this see Lösener's recollections. In particular, he repeats his minute for Frick of 18 August 1941 on this meeting ('Als Rassereferent im Reichsministerium des Innern', pp. 302ff.). At a meeting in the Propaganda Ministry on 20 March 1941 attended also by Eichmann, Gutterer had demanded the deportation of the Berlin Jews (see note 42).
191. Helmut Ortner, *Der Hinrichter Roland Freisler—Mörder im Dienste Hitlers* (Frankfurt a. M., 2014); BAB, R 3001/56247 and 56248 (personal file).
192. *Akten der Partei-Kanzlei der NSDAP*, ed. by the Institut für Zeitgeschichte, part 1 ed. by Helmut Heiber, part 2 ed. by Peter Longerich (Munich and elsewhere, 1983/1992), part 2, items 34325, 34352f., and 34369.
193. See note 389.
194. IfZ, NG 2610, minute for Lammers, 13 December 1940.
195. On the development of the 11th decree regulating the Reich Citizenship Law see Essner, *Die 'Nürnberger Gesetze'*, pp. 292ff.
196. IfZ, NG 2610, Stuckart's letter of 11 December 1940. Ibid., note by Lammers, 20 December 1940, and the Reich Chancellery to the Interior Ministry, 27 December 1940.
197. IfZ, NG 300. Transcript of the meeting of 15 January 1942 and the Reich Chancellery's summarizing minute of 30 January 1941.
198. Details in Essner, *Die 'Nürnberger Gesetze'*, pp. 298ff.
199. IfZ, NG 1123, Lammers to the Interior Ministry, 7 June 1941.

200. Ibid., Lammers to Bormann, 7 June 1941.

201. RGBl. 1941, I, pp. 722ff.

202. On the 13 August meeting see IfZ, F 71/3, minute by Feldscher (Interior Ministry) from 13 August 1941 and by Lösener from 14 August 1941.

203. (Lost) letter from the Reich Chancellery of 16 August to the head of the Racial Policy Office of the NSDAP, Walter Groß, who at a conference in Frankfurt in March 1941 had demanded that 'Jewish Mischlinge' be treated as Jews and was now being told by Lammers that Hitler did not share this view. A copy was sent to the Interior Ministry and is referred to in a draft letter that Lösener composed for Frick (quoted in Lösener, 'Als Rassereferent', p. 304). It would seem to be the same letter that Heydrich later specifically referred to at the Wannsee Conference (see pp. 75ff.; Essner, Die 'Nürnberger Gesetze', pp. 330ff.). According to the same source (Lösener), the RSHA and Party Chancellery advanced the opposing view at the 'working party's' meeting on 21 August.

204. See Lösener ('Als Rassereferent', p. 297f.) on the meeting on 21 August of the interministerial 'working party' created on 13 August to clarify the issue of the definition of Jewishness to be applied in Europe under German domination. (Lösener also mentions here a further meeting.)

205. IfZ, NG 978, notes by Groß from 13 October on a discussion with Lammers on 2 October containing an account of the results of the 'working party' from his perspective.

206. IfZ, F 71/3, minute by Lösener of 14 August on the 13 August meeting; Essner, Die 'Nürnberger Gesetze', p. 336.

207. Lösener ('Als Rassereferent', pp. 302ff.) on the meeting in the Propaganda Ministry on 15 August, the purpose of which was clearly to create the necessary 'atmosphere' among the state and Party departments for the introduction of a distinguishing mark for Jews; Essner, 'Nürnberger Gesetze', pp. 337ff.

208. Heinz-Jürgen Priamus, Meyer. Zwischen Kaisertreue und NS-Täterschaft: Biographische Konturen eines deutschen Bürgers (Essen, 2011), in particular pp. 35ff.

209. Jacobsen, Nationalsozialistische Außenpolitik, p. 60f.

210. On the role of the civil administration see Gerlach, Kalkulierte Morde, pp. 655ff; Andreas Zellhuber, 'Unsere Verwaltung treibt einer Katastrophe zu...': Das Reichsministerium für die besetzten Ostgebiete und die deutsche Besatzungsherrschaft in der Sowjetunion 1941–1945 (Munich, 2006), pp. 217ff.; Ministry for the East's guidelines for the civil administration in the occupied eastern territories from September 1941 ('Brown Folder'), printed in IMT 26, 347-EC, pp. 344ff.

211. IfZ, NO 1020, written report on the meeting of 4 October 1941.

212. BAB, R6/9, minute by Rosenberg, 19 November 1941 (printed in Rosenberg, Tagebücher, no. 12); ibid., NS 19/3885, Himmler's note from 15 November 1941.

213. *Dienstkalender*, 15 November 1941 (with substantial commentary by the editors). The outcome of the meeting was put in writing in a joint instruction of 19 November from Himmler and Rosenberg (BAB, R 6/9).

214. In a minute written early in 1942 Rosenberg complained about the police in the eastern territories being a 'law unto themselves': BAB, R 6/9 (printed in Rosenberg, *Tagebücher*, no. 15). On 8 July 1942, in a face-to-face meeting with Lammers present, Rosenberg and Himmler made repeated efforts to clarify the issue of responsibilities in the occupied eastern territories (see BAB, R 6/9, Lammers's notes).

215. YIVO, Occ E 3–28; see also *IMT* 32, 3363-PS, p. 436.

216. YIVO, OCC E 3–28, Ministry for the East (Bräutigam), 18 December 1941. Rosenberg's minute from early 1942 (see note 214) also states that considerations concerning the war economy 'must be taken into account for the time being'.

217. Pohl, *Von der 'Judenpolitik' zum Judenmord*, pp. 60ff.; Robert Seidel, *Deutsche Besatzungspolitik in Polen. Der Distrikt Radom 1939–1945* (Paderborn and Munich, 2006), pp. 223ff.; Musial, *Deutsche Zivilverwaltung*, pp. 110ff.

218. See note 134.

219. Pohl, *Von der 'Judenpolitik' zum Judenmord*, p. 94.

220. Musial, *Deutsche Zivilverwaltung*, pp. 219ff. The decree did not, however, come into force because it was overtaken by events.

221. Robert Gerwarth, *Reinhard Heydrich. Biographie* (Munich, 2011).

222. Isabel Heinemann, 'Otto Hofmann und das Rasse- und Siedlungshauptamt. Die "Lösung der Judenfrage" als Element der rassenpolitischen Neuordnung Europas', in Norbert Kampe and Peter Klein (eds), *Die Wannsee-Konferenz*, pp. 323–40, pp. 328ff.; IfZ, ZS 797–65; BAB, BDC, SS-O Hofmann.

223. David Cesarani, *Adolf Eichmann. Bürokrat und Massenmörder* (Berlin, 2004); Safrian, *Eichmann-Männer*.

224. Scheffler, 'Die Wannsee-Konferenz', p. 17.

225. Andreas Seeger, *'Gestapo-Müller'. Die Karriere eines Schreibtischtäters* (Berlin, 1996); Joachim Bornschein, *Gestapochef Heinrich Müller. Technokrat des Terrors* (Leipzig, 2004).

226. *VEJ* 4, Doc. 18, instruction of 6 October 1939; see also *VEJ* 4, Doc. 40, Müller's letter of 21 December 1939, suspending deportations temporarily.

227. These expulsions were organized by the RSHA (Pohl, *Von der 'Judenpolitik' zum Judenmord*, p. 51). The order of 15 March 1941 to cease deportations to the General Government also bore Müller's signature (*VEJ* 4, p. 38).

228. Hilberg, *Die Vernichtung der europäischen Juden* (Frankfurt a. M., 1999), p. 299.

229. Christian Streit, *Keine Kameraden. Die Wehrmacht und die sowjetischen Kriegsgefangenen 1941–1945* (Stuttgart, 1978), pp. 186f., 210, 255, and 257;

Reinhard Otto, *Wehrmacht, Gestapo und soujetische Kriegsgefangene im deutschen Reichsgebiet 1941/42* (Munich, 1998), in particular pp. 51, 70, 74f., 219, and 236ff.

230. *VEJ* 3, Doc. 71; *VEJ* 5, Doc. 286.

231. *ToE*, no. 1089, printed in Pätzold and Schwarz, *Tagesordnung: Judenmord*, no. 29.

232. Bornschein, *Gestapochef Heinrich Müller*, pp. 110ff.

233. IfZ, NO 2522, Müller's letter to the Gestapo control centres, 5 November 1942.

234. BAB, BDC, SS-O Schöngarth; Pohl, *Von der 'Judenpolitik' zum Judenmord*, p. 94.

235. See p. 51.

236. Wilhelm, 'Die Einsatzgruppe A'.

237. Peter Klein, 'Dr. Rudolf Lange als Kommandeur der Sicherheitspolizei und des SD in Lettland', in Wolf Kaiser (ed.), *Täter im Vernichtungskrieg. Der Überfall auf die Sowjetunion und der Völkermord an den Juden* (Berlin and Munich, 2002), pp. 125–36.

238. This epithet, which Andrej Angrick and Peter Klein use for him in *Die 'Endlösung' in Riga*, will be examined in more detail here.

239. *The Trial of Adolf Eichmann: Record of Proceedings in the District Court of Jerusalem*, 9 vols (Jerusalem, 1992–5), vol. 4, testimony by Eichmann, p. 1826f.

240. Angrick and Klein, *Die 'Endlösung' in Riga*, p. 274f.

241. Angrick and Klein evaluate the 1975 testimony of a former Latvian auxiliary policeman as evidence of about 900 people being removed from a transport from Brünn and Prague at Skirotava station on 19 January. In his testimony he speaks of 800 to 900 people being shot on 13 January 1942; the small number and the age group of the survivors clearly also suggest that all the older deportees were murdered. That does not, however, provide indisputable evidence for the murder of some 900 Czech Jews on 19 January (*Die 'Endlösung' in Riga*, pp. 239ff.). What the authors present here in the form of a cautious attempt at reconstruction appears in an essay on the prehistory of the Wannsee Conference as an incontrovertible fact (Klein, 'Die Wannsee-Konferenz als Echo auf die gefallene Entscheidung zur Ermordung der europäischen Juden', in Norbert Kampe and Klein (eds), *Die Wannsee-Konferenz*, pp. 182–201, p. 197) designed to support the thesis that the conference should be interpreted as an 'echo of the decision that had already been made to murder the European (!) Jews'.

242. Gottwaldt and Schulle, *Die Judendeportationen*, pp. 121ff.; *Buch der Erinnerung*. The Latvian former auxiliary policeman mentioned above tells in his statement of a second massacre with 500 victims that Angrick and Klein link to the arrival on 30/31 January 1942 of a fourth transport from Berlin. The accuracy of this reconstruction is similarly by no means certain (*Die 'Endlösung' in Riga*, p. 242f.).

243. Ibid., pp. 226ff. (Jungfernhof) and 265ff. (Salaspils).

244. Extensive evidence for selections such as these exists only after the Wannsee Conference: in early February in the Riga ghetto and in mid-March in the so-called 'Dünamünde-Aktion' with an estimated 4,800 victims; see Angrick and Klein, *Die 'Endlösung' in Riga*, pp. 243ff. and 338ff.

245. On this Angrick and Klein (*Die 'Endlösung' in Riga*, p. 275) quote an undated progress report by Lange entitled 'Jewry' from Riga State Archive. Shortened versions of the passages quoted were also used in Einsatzgruppe A's similarly undated report. Part III ('Jews') is printed as Document 2273-PS in *IMT* 30, pp. 71ff.

246. Report dated 2 February 1942; quoted after Klein, 'Die Rolle der Vernichtungslager', p. 246f. (original in Riga State Archive).

247. On this see Angrick, 'Die inszenierte Selbstermächtigung?', pp. 249ff.

248. *Die Tagebücher von Joseph Goebbels*, 7 March 1942.

249. It can be found there in File R 100857 (originally it was catalogued under Inland II g 177). It is reproduced here by kind consent of the Foreign Ministry's Political Archive PAAA. On the repeated claims of forgery, for which there is no evidence, see Christian Mentel, 'Das Protokoll der Wannsee-Konferenz. Überlieferung, Veröffentlichung und revisionistische Infragestellung', in Norbert Kampe and Peter Klein (eds), *Die Wannsee-Konferenz*, pp. 116–38.

250. *The Trial of Adolf Eichmann*, vol. 7, Eichmann's testimony, pp. 877ff. and ibid., vol. 4, pp. 1422ff.

251. Kampe, 'Ermächtigung und Wannsee-Protokoll. Zu den Randbemerkungen und Stempeln. Überlieferungsgeschichte und Fälschungsvorwurf gegen die zentralen Dokumente', published at www.ghwk.de. According to the PAAA in August 2016, there is no more reliable information regarding the marks. This book contains a black-and-white reproduction of the minutes. On the homepage of the Wannsee Conference Museum, www.ghwk.de, it is possible to view the document with its various markings.

252. Whereas nowadays 'final solution' is the generally accepted term to denote the systematic murder of the European Jews, in early 1942, when the plans for the mass murder were still incomplete, its meaning was not yet absolutely plain. While the term had still been used in 1939/40 for the deportation of Jews to a 'Jewish reservation', when these deportation plans came to nothing the use of the term indicated a still more radical procedure, though it only gradually took on a precise shape. The Wannsee Conference itself was part of this process. On the use of the term see Longerich, *Der ungeschriebene Befehl. Hitler und der Weg zur 'Endlösung'* (Munich and elsewhere, 2001), pp. 22ff.

253. See p. 50f.

254. The figure of 537,000 Jews probably included the statistical mortality surplus. In place of the figure of 360,000 given by Heydrich, the Reich Union of Jews in Germany established a total of 352,294 emigrations for the Altreich in the years 1933–41 (*VEJ* 3, Doc. 233).

255. In August 1941 the Reich Union of Jews in Germany had responded to a request from the Central Office for Jewish Emigration by using reference works to compile extensive material on the number of Jews in the individual states; these figures were evidently adjusted by Eichmann's office on the basis of the knowledge it had of the demographic changes consequent in the intervening period on the increasing radicalization of Jewish persecution in 1941. On this see Kampe, 'Dokumente', p. 20, no. 1.1, and *The Trial of Adolf Eichmann*, vol. 7, Eichmann's testimony, p. 850f.

256. On this see Dan Michman, 'Waren die Juden Nordafrikas im Visier der Planer der "Endlösung"? Die "Schoah" und die Zahl 700 000 in Eichmanns Tabelle am 20. Januar 1942', in Norbert Kampe and Peter Klein (eds), *Die Wannsee-Konferenz*, pp. 379–400.

257. Klaus-Michael Mallmann and Martin Cüppers, *Halbmond und Hakenkreuz. Das Dritte Reich, die Araber und Palästina* (Darmstadt, 2006).

258. Taken from *Der Große Brockhaus*, vol. 9 (Statistics on 'Jews').

259. Gerald Reitlinger (*Die Endlösung. Hitlers Versuch der Ausrottung der Juden Europas 1939–1945* (Berlin, 1956), p. 108) interprets this passage as synonymous with 'the work camps in Poland and Auschwitz'; Krausnick ('Judenverfolgung', p. 323) assumed that concealed 'behind this obfuscating language' was the idea of conducting 'experiments by means of rapid and discreet technical means' with a view to subsequent 'extermination'; Breitman (*Himmler*, p. 331) assumes that after the Wannsee Conference Heydrich was 'still' putting forward the plan of 'immediately killing all Jews deported to the extermination camps'.

260. In autumn the previous year the SSPF of the Galicia district, Friedrich Katzmann, had begun constructing this important supply road by using local Jewish forced labour. Now construction was to continue in the Ukraine. To this end Himmler gave a number of SSPFs responsibility for building further sections. On 7 February he made Hans-Adolf Prützmann, HSSPF for Ukraine and Russia South, overall director of the project (*Dienstkalender*, 7 February 1942). On 19 February he ordered a road linking Uman, Dnjepropetrovsk, and Mariopol to be built by the Todt Organization, the Reichsführer SS providing the 'guards for the population who would be engaged in the work'. See Willi A. Boelcke (ed.), *Deutschlands Rüstung im Zweiten Weltkrieg. Hitlers Konferenzen mit Albert Speer, 1942–1945* (Frankfurt a. M., 1969), p. 64. In 1942 a total of some 50,000 Ukrainian forced workers, the same number of POWs, and some 10,000 Jews were put to work to build DG IV. There is proof of about thirty camps for Jewish workers in the Galician section and approximately twenty more on the Ukrainian part of the road. Among those prisoners newly arrived in the camps, all those 'unfit for work' (the elderly, children, the sick) were removed and murdered. Thereafter, inmates were constantly being shot for inadequate work or for other reasons. On DG IV see Hermann Kaienburg, 'Jüdische Arbeitslager an

der "Straße der SS" ', in *1999. Zeitschrift für Sozialgeschichte des 20. und 21. Jahrhunderts*, 11/1 (1996), 13–39. On the Galician section of the project see Thomas Sandkühler, *'Endlösung' in Galizien. Der Judenmord in Ostpolen und die Rettungsinitiativen von Berthold Beitz 1941–1944* (Bonn, 1996), pp. 141ff.; Pohl, *Nationalsozialistische Judenverfolgung in Ostgalizien 1941–1944*, pp. 167ff and 338ff.

261. See note 98.

262. As far as we can see, this took place at a big meeting Himmler had with almost all the chiefs of SS head offices on 14/15 January 1942 (*Dienstkalender*). For details of the creation of the Business and Administration Head Office see note 284.

263. In the next chapter I go into detail about these wide-ranging organizational measures to exploit Jewish prisoners in particular.

264. Miroslav Kárný and others (eds), *Deutsche Politik im Protektorat 'Böhmen und Mähren' unter Reinhard Heydrich 1941–1942. Eine Dokumentation* (Berlin, 1997), no. 77.

265. See note 291.

266. See p. 21.

267. Adler, *Theresienstadt. 1941–1945. Das Antlitz einer Zwangsgemeinschaft. Geschichte Soziologie Psychologie* (Göttingen, 2005).

268. Luther claimed later that he had demanded at the meeting 'that all matters concerning foreign countries' should be 'agreed in advance with the Foreign Ministry'. 'Gruppenführer Heydrich agreed to this and has stuck to it' (note of 21 August 1942, printed in Pätzold and Schwarz, *Tagesordnung: Judenmord*, p. 127f.).

269. Browning, *Die Entfesselung der 'Endlösung'*, p. 150.

270. On Lecca and his German connections see Hildrun Glass, *Deutschland und die Verfolgung der Juden im rumänischen Machtbereich 1940–1944* (Munich, 2014), pp. 78ff. Lecca was appointed at the end of October 1941.

271. In December 1941 Luther had mentioned to Ribbentrop the Italian government's lack of interest in solving the 'Jewish question'. See Meir Michaelis, *Mussolini and the Jews: German-Italian Relations and the Jewish Question in Italy, 1922–1945* (Oxford, 1978), p. 304.

272. Beate Meyer, *'Jüdische Mischlinge'. Rassenpolitik und Verfolgungserfahrung 1933–1945* (Hamburg, 1999), part 1. Privileged status might also be granted if the wife was Jewish *and* there were no children.

273. This was still Stuckart's position at the meeting in the Ministry for the East on 29 January, even though he was visibly in retreat (BAB, R 6/74; one of the two notes is printed in Wolfgang Benz, Konrad Kwiet, and Jürgen Matthäus (eds), *Einsatz im 'Reichskommissariat Ostland'. Dokumente zum Völkermord im Baltikum und in Weißrußland 1941–1944* (Berlin, 1998), no. 21).

274. BAB, R 6/74, minute by Labs; Essner, *Die 'Nürnberger Gesetze'*, p. 367.

275. See p. 46.

276. Heydrich is alluding to the First Regulation of the Reich Citizenship Law enabling Hitler as an act of mercy and in consultation with the Interior Minister to grant exemptions from the classification laid down by the Nuremberg Laws. By the time this procedure was suspended in autumn 1942 a total of 991 cases received a positive decision. Requests from National Socialists from Jewish backgrounds were presented to Hitler via the Party Chancellery; on this see Meyer, *'Jüdische Mischlinge'*, pp. 152ff.; Essner, *Die 'Nürnberger Gesetze'*, pp. 201ff.

277. On Stuckart's role at the Wannsee Conference see Jasch, *Staatssekretär Wilhelm Stuckart*, pp. 316ff.

278. *Dienstkalender*, 21 January 1942, phone call at 15.30: 'Jewish question, meeting in Berlin'.

279. All the letters can be seen in photocopy on the homepage of the Wannsee Conference Museum, www.ghwk.de (originals in StA Riga and BAB, BDC, SS-O Heydrich).

280. Domarus, *Hitler*, vol. 2, p. 1828f.

281. Ibid., p. 1844.

282. Himmler's order on the occasion of his tour of inspection in Lublin, 30 July 1941, printed in Czeslawa Madajczyka (ed.), *Zamojszczyzna— Sonderlaboratorium der SS. Zbiór dokumentów polskich i niemieckich z okresu okupacji hitlerowskiej*, vol. 1 (Warsaw, 1977), pp. 26ff.

283. Jan Erik Schulte, *Zwangsarbeit und Vernichtung. Das Wirtschaftsimperium der SS. Oswald Pohl und das SS-Wirtschafts-Verwaltungshauptamt, 1933–1945* (Paderborn and elsewhere, 2001), pp. 334ff.

284. Hitler's decision to combine these areas was presumably taken on 15 January 1942 (*Dienstkalender*); the corresponding order from Pohl was issued on 19 January 1942 (IfZ, NO 495); for additional detail see Schulte, *Zwangsarbeit*, p. 357.

285. Ibid., pp. 343ff.

286. Ibid., pp. 351ff. See also Streit, *Keine Kameraden*, p. 212f.

287. Jewish Historical Institute Warsaw (ed.), *Faschismus—Getto—Massenmord* (Frankfurt a. M., 1962), p. 268. On this decision and its effects see in particular Allen, *The Business of Genocide*, pp. 148ff., and Schulte, *Zwangsarbeit*, p. 361. The previous day Himmler had telephoned Heydrich and given him responsibility for putting 'Jews in the concentration camps'. He also telephoned Pohl to tell him about 'new business tasks' that he discussed with him on 28 February (*Dienstkalender*). On Himmler's mid-January decision and Pohl's subsequent order to create the Business and Administrative Head Office see notes 262 and 284. On 17 January 1942 the Reich Ministry for the East sent a telex to Reich Commissar Lohse announcing a fundamental change regarding the preservation of Jewish workers: 'On the instructions of Business HQ for the East, Jewish craftsmen from industry and skilled trades whose exploitation as individuals is particularly important in the interests of the war economy

must be preserved for labour. Their preservation must be ensured by negotiation with local offices of the Reichsführer SS' (see BAB, R 92/1157; see also Scheffler, 'Das Schicksal', p. 6).

288. BAB, NS 19/2065; on this see also Karl Heinz Roth, '"Generalplan Ost" und der Mord an den Juden. Der "Fernplan der Umsiedlung in den Ostprovinzen" aus dem Reichssicherheitshauptamt vom November 1939', in *1999. Zeitschrift für Sozialgeschichte des 20. und 21. Jahrhunderts*, 12/2 (1997), 50–70.

289. *IMT* 38, 129-R, pp. 365ff., 30 April 1942.

290. See p. 91f.

291. *Dienstkalender*, 17 February 1942. Hitler seems to have responded more or less with indifference: 'Führer read it—my proposal, perhaps contact Eicke'.

292. Henry Picker, *Hitlers Tischgespräche im Führerhauptquartier. Entstehung, Struktur und Folgen des Nationalsozialismus* (Berlin, 1977; original edition Bonn, 1951), 5 April 1942. It is, however, unclear whether he was talking about Jewish prisoners.

293. This is mentioned in an express letter of 27 March from the Reich Labour Ministry printed in *IMT* 37, 061-L, p. 493.

294. Wolf Gruner, *Der Geschlossene Arbeitseinsatz deutscher Juden: Zur Zwangsarbeit als Element der Verfolgung 1938–1943* (Berlin, 1997), pp. 291ff.; Adler, *Der verwaltete Mensch*, pp. 216ff.

295. *Die Tagebücher von Joseph Goebbels*, 30 May 1942; see also Gruner, *Der Geschlossene Arbeitseinsatz*, pp. 298ff.

296. Rainer Fröbe in 'Der Arbeitseinstaz von KZ-Häftlingen und die Perspektive der Industrie 1943–1945', in Ulrich Herbert (ed.), *Europa und der 'Reichseinsatz'. Ausländische Zivilarbeiter, Kriegsgefangene und KZ-Häftlinge in Deutschland 1938–1945* (Essen, 1991), pp. 351–83, p. 34, points out that during the whole of 1942 concentration camp inmates were used almost exclusively in construction, in part for building industrial sites. They were not generally used in production.

297. St A Würzburg, Gestapo files, printed in Adler, *Der verwaltete Mensch*, p. 188f.

298. Gerlach ('Die Wannsee-Konferenz', p. 143) indicates that five days before the assassination attempt Lammers sent documents to Heydrich that he might 'take account of in his meeting with the Reich Marshal'.

299. *The Trial of Adolf Eichmann*, no. 119, minutes of a meeting on 9 March 1943, printed in Longerich, *Die Ermordung der europäischen Juden*, p. 167f.

300. See note 97.

301. IfZ, NG 1068.

302. PAAA, R 100857, meeting transcript, printed in Pätzold and Schwarz, *Tagesordnung: Judenmord*, no. 31; Essner, *Die 'Nürnberger Gesetze'*, p. 167f.

303. Discussed in detail by Essner, *Die 'Nürnberger Gesetze'*, pp. 419ff. In particular, there is Stuckart's letter of 16 March 1942, Schlegelberger's of 5 April 1942, and Meyer's from 16 July 1942; see also Luther's note of 21 August 1942 (all in PAAA, R 100957).

304. IfZ, NG 1068.

305. IfZ, NO 626.

306. Gottwaldt and Schulle, *Die 'Judendeportationen'*, pp. 182ff. A progress report from the officer for the Four-Year Plan in the Transport Group mentions thirty-seven special trains of Jews for the month of April. That would make sixteen more than can be documented (BAB, R 23 IV/v. 47; see also Gerlach, 'Die Wannsee-Konferenz', p. 40).

307. Gottwaldt and Schulle, *Die 'Judendeportationen'*, pp. 167ff.

308. On the splitting up of the deportees in Lublin see Reuter's minute, Department for Population and Welfare, 17 March 1942, about Höfle's communication the previous day, quoted from Adler, *Theresienstadt. 1941–1945. Das Antlitz einer Zwangsgemeinschaft. Geschichte Soziologie Psychologie* (Göttingen, 2005), p. 50f.

309. On this and on the implementation of the deportations see Ladislav Lipscher, *Die Juden im slowakischen Staat 1939–1945* (Munich and Vienna, 1980), pp. 99ff.; Browning, *'Die Endlösung' und das Auswärtige Amt*, p. 120f.; Yehoshua, Büchler, 'The Deportation of Slovakian Jews to the Lublin District of Poland in 1942', in *HGS*, 6/2 (1991), 151–66.

310. Lipscher, *Die Juden im slowakischen Staat*, pp. 102ff.

311. Büchler, 'The Deportation of Slovakian Jews', p. 152.

312. Ibid., p. 153.

313. *ADAP* E 2, pp. 161ff.

314. Minute from the office of the Slovakian Prime Minister Tuka, Moreshet Archive, Givat Haviva, Israel (copy in StA Prague), printed in *Tragédia slovenských Židov. Fotografie a Dokumenty* (Bratislava, 1949).

315. According to Franciszek Piper ('Vernichtung', in Wacław Długoborski and Franciszek Piper (eds), *Auschwitz 1940–1945. Studien zur Geschichte des Konzentrations- und Vernichtungslagers Auschwitz*, vol. 3 (Oświęcim, 1999), p. 166) and Czech (*Kalendarium*), 'selections' took place for the first time on 29 April and on 20 June. The transports in question were, according to Czech, one from Slovakia and a train from Sosnowitz.

316. Büchler, 'The Deportation of Slovakian Jews', pp. 152 and 166, and Czech, *Kalendarium*.

317. APL, Gouverneur Distrikt Lublin, Sygn. 270. On 20 January 1942 the Department for Population and Welfare in the General Government administration called on the corresponding offices at district level to send 'as soon as possible a list of ghettos created in their district' and also the number of people resident in them.

318. Yitzhak Arad, *Belzec, Sobibor, Treblinka. The Operation Reinhard Death Camps* (Bloomington and Indianapolis, IN, 1987), pp. 23ff. and 68ff.

319. BAB, NS 19/3959; see also Pohl, *Von der 'Judenpolitik' zum Judenmord*, p. 110.

320. Pohl, *Von der 'Judenpolitik' zum Judenmord*, pp. 113ff.; David Silberklang, 'Die Juden und die ersten Deportationen aus dem Distrikt Lublin', in Bogdan Musiał (ed.), *'Aktion Reinhardt'. Der Völkermord an den Juden im*

Generalgouvernement 1941–1944 (Osnabrück, 2004), pp. 141–64, pp. 145ff.; Musiał, *Deutsche Zivilverwaltung*, pp. 229ff.

321. *Die Tagebücher von Joseph Goebbels*, entry for 27 March 1942.

322. *The Trial of Adolf Eichmann*, vol. 7, p. 240.

323. StA Munich, Staatsanwaltschaften, 33033/15, Staatsanwaltschaft München I 110 Ks 3/64, testimony of 10 November 1964, pp. 2918ff.; see also Pohl, *Von der 'Judenpolitik' zum Judenmord*, p. 125f.

324. Gottwaldt and Schulle, *Die 'Judendeportationen'*, pp. 182ff.; Büchler, 'The Deportation of Slovakian Jews', pp. 153 and 166.

325. APL, Gouverneur Distrikt Lublin, Judenangelegenheiten, Sygn. 273, minutes from Lublin district administration, Subdepartment for Population and Welfare, 20 and 23 March 1942, with individual details of Central European Jews arriving and Polish Jews being deported; details in Longerich, *Politik der Vernichtung*, p. 487.

326. Adler, *Theresienstadt*, p. 50f. (with further details); Peter Witte, 'Letzte Nachrichten aus Siedliszcze. Der Transport AX aus Theresienstadt in den Distrikt Lublin', in *Theresienstädter Studien und Dokumente*, 3 (1996), 98–113, p. 100.

327. Pohl, *Nationalsozialistische Judenverfolgung in Ostgalizien*, pp. 179ff.

328. Klarsfeld, *Vichy-Auschwitz*, pp. 34ff.; Herbert, 'Die deutsche Militärverwaltung in Paris', p. 439; Ahlrich Meyer, 'Der Beginn der "Endlösung" in Frankreich—offene Fragen', *Sozial. Geschichte*, 18/3 (2003), 35–82.

329. Klarsfeld, *Vichy-Auschwitz*, p. 43.

330. CDJC, 1216-RF, minute by Dannecker, 10 March 1943, printed in Klarsfeld, *Vichy-Auschwitz*, p. 374f. Additional notes by Zeitschel, 11 March 1942 and also Eichmann's letter to the commander of the Security Police and SD for Belgium and France, Helmut Knochen, 12 March 1943, both printed in ibid., p. 375f.

331. Ibid., p. 376f.; Czech, *Kalendarium*, 30 March 1942.

332. Ruth Bettina Birn, *Die höheren SS- und Polizeiführer. Himmlers Vertreter im Reich und in den besetzten Gebieten* (Düsseldorf, 1986), p. 446f.

333. Herbert, 'Die deutsche Militärverwaltung in Paris', p. 440.

334. Reported by Walter Bargatzky, who worked as a lawyer in the war administration, on the basis of information from someone present. See his *Hotel Majestic. Ein Deutscher im besetzten Frankreich* (Freiburg im Breisgau, 1987), p. 103. See also Herbert, 'Die deutsche Militärverwaltung in Paris', p. 448.

335. Bargatzky, *Hotel Majestic*, p. 94. On this see also the information to the same effect given on 29 October 1949 by the former main judge attached to the military high command, quoted from Hans Luther, *Der französische Widerstand gegen die deutsche Besatzungsmacht und seine Bekämpfung* (Tübingen, 1957), p. 214; Herbert, *Best. Biographische Studien über Radikalismus, Weltanschauung und Vernunft, 1903–1989* (Bonn, 1996), p. 320.

336. Czech, *Kalendarium*.
337. Angrick and Klein, *Die 'Endlösung' in Riga*, pp. 243ff. and 338ff.
338. Himmler's notes do not reveal what was discussed at these meetings. The only exception is his presentation to Hitler on 3 May, after which Himmler recorded that matters concerning the Waffen-SS were discussed; additional non-military topics were, however, also discussed that Himmler did not record (*Dienstkalender*, p. 415, note 6).
339. Gottwaldt and Schulle, *Die 'Judendeportationen'*, pp. 237ff.
340. On this there are reports from one of the Sonderkommandos designated by the Waffen-SS battalion for special assignments. See *Unsere Ehre heißt Treue. Kriegstagebuch des Kommandostabes Reichsführer SS: Tätigkeitsberichte der 1. und 2. SS-Inf. Brigade, der 1. SS-Kavallerie-Brigade und von Sonderkommandos der SS*, ed. by Fritz Baade (Vienna, 1965), pp. 236ff.
341. *Justiz und NS-Verbrechen*, vol. 19, no. 552, judgment of 21 May 1963, p. 192.
342. On Sobibor see Jules Schelvis, *Vernichtungslager Sobibór* (Berlin, 1998).
343. Gottwaldt and Schulle, *Die 'Judendeportationen'*, pp. 211ff. The authors present a series of, albeit inconclusive, indications that from 3 June onwards the first deportation trains went directly to Sobibor or the passengers in them were taken to Sobibor after a break of only a few days en route.
344. Witte, 'Letzte Nachrichten aus Siedliszcze'.
345. Adler, *Der verwaltete Mensch*, pp. 193ff., also Jonney Moser, 'Österreich', in Wolfgang Benz (ed.), *Dimension des Völkermords*, pp. 67–94, p. 80f. For details of the process of deportation see Gottwaldt and Schulle, *Die 'Judendeportationen'*, pp. 260ff. During the following winter there were numerous smaller transports to Theresienstadt (ibid., pp. 337ff.). On Theresienstadt in general see Adler, *Theresienstadt*.
346. Such people included decorated war veterans with their wives and children under fourteen, as well as the Jewish partners from dissolved 'mixed marriages', who were not forced to wear the Jewish star, and unmarried 'Mischlinge', whom the Nuremberg Laws designated as Jews.
347. Büchler, 'The Deportation of Slovakian Jews', p. 166.
348. Dobroszycki (ed.), *The Chronicle of the Łódź Ghetto*, pp. 128, 131ff., 136ff., 140ff., 145, and 157.
349. Ibid., pp. 153f., 156f., 159ff., and 194.
350. See *Dienstkalender*.
351. ZStL, doc. UdSSR 401, printed in Klein (ed.), *Die Einsatzgruppen*, p. 410f. There is, however, an important indication of a document in which 'special measures' were explicitly ordered: Dieter Wisliceny, a close colleague of Eichmann's, claimed during questioning after the war that in summer 1942 he had seen a set of instructions from Himmler to Heydrich; in this letter the complete extermination of the Jews was ordered at Hitler's command and only Jews 'fit for work' were to be exempted from this extermination and sent to concentration camps (*The Trial of Adolf Eichmann*, no. 85, Wisliceny's testimony from 14 November 1945).

352. Steinbacher, 'Musterstadt' Auschwitz, p. 285f.

353. Scholars frequently assume that the deportations from Upper Silesia had already begun on 15 February (see, for example, Czech, Kalendarium, or Steinbacher, 'Musterstadt' Auschwitz, p. 277). This error stems from a reference made by Martin Broszat to a letter of 27 March 1958 sent to him by Arolsen, the international tracing organization. The letter, however, which is now accessible in the Institut für Zeitgeschichte in Munich, was misread. The deportation of the Jews from Bytom is in fact given as from '15.5.1942' onwards.

354. Czech (Kalendarium) proves that for 12 May 1942 1,500 Jewish men, women, and children from Sosnowitz were murdered in Bunker 1; in addition, on 20 June 1942 2,000 people from the same city were murdered, again in Bunker 1. This facility had already been used (Czech records it in the Kalendarium under 20 March 1942) to murder Upper Silesian Jews no longer 'fit for work' from the Schmelt forced labour camps. Such murders can be traced back to November 1941 (when they were still being carried out in the Schmelt camps) and took place in a different context from the murders that followed the deportations of the entire Jewish population from the 'eastern strip'; see Piper, 'Vernichtung,' p. 158f.; Dwork and van Pelt, Auschwitz, p. 20.

355. Steinbacher, 'Musterstadt' Auschwitz, p. 290.

356. Pohl, Von der 'Judenpolitik' zum Judenmord, pp. 120ff.

357. VOGG 1942, p. 263f., Führer decree of 7 May 1942 concerning the establishment of an office for the state secretary for security in the General Government; Gerhard Eisenblätter, Grundlinien der Politik des Reiches gegenüber dem Generalgouvernement, 1939–1945, unpublished doctoral dissertation (Frankfurt a. M., 1969), pp. 247ff. The basic decisions had been taken when Bormann, Himmler, and Lammers subjected Frank to an excruciating 'interrogation' on 5 March.

358. VOGG 1942, pp. 321ff., decree concerning the transfer of administrative matters to the state secretary for security; see also Pohl, Von der 'Judenpolitik' zum Judenmord, p. 125.

359. Himmler, Geheimreden 1933 bis 1945 und andere Ansprachen, ed. by Bradley F. Smith and Agnes Peterson (Frankfurt a. M., 1974), p. 159.

360. Gottwaldt and Schulle, Die 'Judendeportationen', p. 213.

361. Individual instances are provided by Peter Black, 'Die Trawniki-Männer und die Aktion Reinhard', in Bogdan Musiał (ed.), Aktion Reinhardt. Der Völkermord an den Juden im Generalgouvernement 1941–1944 (Osnabrück, 2004), pp. 309–52, p. 308f. The spelling 'Reinhart' is also found in the files.

362. On this see the survey by Jacek Andrzej Młynarczyk, 'Treblinka—ein Todeslager der "Aktion Reinhard"', in Bogdan Musiał (ed.), Aktion Reinhardt, pp. 257–84. On the construction phase see in addition Arad, Belzec, Sobibor, Treblinka.

363. On this see Globocnik's report of 5 January 1944 on the economic exploitation of 'Aktion Reinhardt', printed in IMT 34, 402-PS, pp. 70ff.

364. Pohl, *Nationalsozialistische Judenverfolgung*, p. 215 and Pohl, *Von der Judenpolitik zum Judenmord*, pp. 157ff.; Sandkühler, *'Endlösung' in Galizien*, pp. 181ff.

365. On Lublin see Pohl, *Von der Judenpolitik zum Judenmord*, pp. 132ff.; Arad, *Belzec, Sobibor, Treblinka*, p. 387; on Galicia see Pohl, *Nationalsozialistische Judenverfolgung*, pp. 216ff.; Arad, *Belzec, Sobibor, Treblinka*, pp. 384ff. On Radom see ibid., pp. 389 and 393ff; Młynarczyk, *Judenmord in Zentralpolen. Der Distrikt Radom im Generalgouvernement 1939–1945* (Darmstadt, 2007); Seidel, *Deutsche Besatzungspolitik*.

366. CDJC, 1217-RF, minute by Dannecker, 15 June 1942, printed in Klarsfeld, *Vichy-Auschwitz*, p. 379f. Dannecker's accompanying notes minute that an order from Himmler prompted this arrangement.

367. CDJC 1183-NG, printed in Klarsfeld, *Vichy-Auschwitz*, p. 384f. CDJC, XXVb-38, minute of 1 July on a telephone conversation with Novak, 18 June 1942, sheds light on the reasons for this change (printed in Klarsfeld, *Vichy-Auschwitz*, p. 383).

368. CDJC, 1123-RF, Dannecker's minute of 1 July 1942, printed in Klarsfeld, *Vichy-Auschwitz*, p. 390f.

369. Ibid., p. 122. On the raids and deportations of summer 1942 see also Renée Poznanski, *Jews in France during World War II* (Hanover, NH, 2001), pp. 251ff.

370. On the start and progress of the deportations see Jacques Presser, *Ashes in the Wind: The Destruction of the Dutch Jewry* (New York, 1968), pp. 146ff.; Bob Moore, *Victims and Survivors: The Nazi Persecution of the Jews in the Netherlands 1940–1945* (London, 1997), pp. 91ff.; Gerhard Hirschfeld, *Fremdherrschaft und Kollaboration: Die Niederlande unter deutscher Besatzung, 1940–1945* (Stuttgart, 1984), pp. 145ff.

371. Juliane Wetzel, 'Frankreich und Belgien', in Wolfgang Benz (ed.), *Dimension des Völkermords*, p. 129.

372. See note 354.

373. PAAA, R 100881, message from Killinger to the Foreign Ministry, 12 August 1942 and also to Himmler, 26 July 1942; Browning, *Die Entfesselung der 'Endlösung'*, pp. 162ff.

374. The German initiative was preceded by two requests from the Croatian government in October 1941 and May 1942 concerning the Jews resident in the country; see Jozo Tomasevich, *War and Revolution in Yugoslavia, 1941–1945: Occupation and Collaboration* (Stanford, CA, 2001), p. 595; Alexander Korb, *Im Schatten des Weltkriegs: Massengewalt der Ustaša gegen Serben, Juden und Roma in Kroatien 1941–1945* (Hamburg, 2013), pp. 417ff.; Holm Sundhausen, 'Jugoslawien', in Wolfgang Benz (ed.), *Dimension des Völkermords*, pp. 311–30, p. 323.

375. The only evidence of Himmler's approach is, however, a statement by the Finnish prime minister of the time, Rangell. He claims he immediately rejected this plan; see Hannu Rautkallio, *Finland and the Holocaust: The Rescue of Finland's Jews* (New York, 1987), pp. 163ff.; William B. Cohen and Jörgen Svennson, 'Finland and the Holocaust', in *HGS*, 9/1 (1995), 70–93, in particular p. 82f.

376. On preparations for these deportations see Frederick Barry Chary, *The History of Bulgaria* (Santa Barbara, CA, 2001), pp. 113ff.; Browning, *Die Entfesselung der 'Endlösung'*, pp. 172ff.; Hans-Joachim Hoppe, *Bulgarien, Hitlers eigenwilliger Verbündeter. Eine Fallstudie zur nationalsozialistischen Südosteuropapolitik* (Stuttgart, 1979), p. 285f.

377. BAB, NS 19/1755. The content of the plans can be seen only from the covering document. There is one folder titled 'State of Jewish project', in which 'problems and questions are set out that require an order', as well as one set of plans labelled 'Jews in the Lublin district'. Along with the third paper, which dealt with 'Ethnicity', these were forwarded by Himmler's staff to the head office of the Reich Commissar for German Ethnic Identity. On this and on what follows see also Pohl, *Von der 'Judenpolitik' zum Judenmord*, p. 127f.

378. BAB, NS 19/2655, 29 July 1941. Also contains Himmler's letter of thanks of 13 August 1941.

379. *Dienstkalender, Kommandant in Auschwitz. Autobiographische Aufzeichnungen von Rudolf Höß*, with an introduction and commentary by Martin Broszat (Stuttgart, 1958), pp. 157f. and 176ff.

380. Christopher Browning, 'The Decision Concerning the Final Solution', in Browning, *Fateful Months: Essays on the Emergence of the Final Solution* (New York, 1985), pp. 8–38; Walter Laqueur and Richard Breitman, *Der Mann, der das Schweigen brach. Wie die Welt vom Holocaust erfuhr* (Frankfurt a. M., 1986); *Kommandant in Auschwitz*, p. 178.

381. BAB, NS 19/1757, printed in Longerich, *Die Ermordung der europäischen Juden*, p. 201. See also Pohl, *Von der 'Judenpolitik' zum Judenmord*, p. 128.

382. On the reconstruction of these murders on the basis primarily of German interrogation files see Longerich, *Holocaust*, pp. 345ff. The most important studies of individual regions are Gerlach, *Kalkulierte Morde*, pp. 503ff.; Dieter Pohl, 'Schauplatz Ukraine. Der Massenmord an den Juden im Militärverwaltungsgebiet und im Reichskommissariat 1941–1943', in Christian Hartmann, Dieter Pohl, and others, *Der deutsche Krieg im Osten 1941–1944. Facetten einer Grenzüberschreitung* (Munich, 2009), pp. 155–98; Martin Dean, *Collaboration in the Holocaust: Crimes of the Local Police in Belorussia and Ukraine, 1941–44* (New York, 2000); Shmuel Spector, *The Holocaust of Volhynian Jews, 1941–1944* (Jerusalem, 1990); Wendy Lower, *Nazi Empire-Building and the Holocaust in Ukraine* (Chapel Hill, NC, 2005).

383. IfZ, NO 626.

384. *IMT* 20, pp. 78ff.

385. Robert M. W. Kempner, *Eichmann und Komplizen* (Zurich, Stuttgart, and Vienna, 1961), p. 159.

386. Ibid., pp. 151ff.

387. Ibid., p. 154.

388. Ibid., p. 156.

389. Kempner, *Ankläger einer Epoche. Lebenserinnerungen* (Frankfurt a. M. and elsewhere, 1983), p. 337f.

Bibliography

I. ARCHIVES

Archivum Panstwowe w Lublinie (APL)

Bundesarchiv, Abt. Berlin (BAB)
NS 19	Persönlicher Stab Reichsführer SS
R 6	Reichsministerium für die besezten Ostgebiete
R 26 IV	Beauftragter für den Vierjahresplan
R 43 II	Neue Reichskanzlei
R 58	Reichssicherheitshauptamt
R 70	Besetzte Gebiete
R 92	Generalkommissar in Riga
R 3001	Reichsjustizministerium

Bundesarchiv Militärarchiv, Abt. Freiburg (BAF)
RH 22	Befehlshaber rückwärtiger Heeresgebiete
RW 4	Wehrmachtführungsstab
RW 59	Personalverwaltende Stellen der Wehrmacht

Centre de documentation juive contemporaine, Paris (CDJC)

Institut für Zeitgeschichte, München (IfZ)
ED	Nachlässe
F	Manuskripte
Fb	Gerichtsakten
MA	Mikrofilme
Nürnberger	Dokumente aus den Serien NG, NO
ZS	Zeugenschrifttum

Osobyi Archiv, Moskau (OA; Sonderarchiv)

Politisches Archiv des Auswärtigen Amtes, Berlin (PAAA)

Staatsarchiv München (StA München)

Staatsarchiv Riga (StA Riga)

The National Archives, London (TNA)

YIVO Institute for Jewish Research (YIVO)

Zentrale Stelle Ludwigsburg (ZStL)

2. CONTEMPORARY PUBLICATIONS AND ALSO DOCUMENT COLLECTIONS, MEMOIRS, AND COLLECTIONS OF SOURCES PUBLISHED AFTER 1945

Akten der Partei-Kanzlei der NSDAP, ed. by the Institut für Zeitgeschichte, part 1 ed. by Helmut Heiber, part 2 ed. by Peter Longerich (Munich and elsewhere, 1983/1992).

Akten der Reichskanzlei. Weimarer Republik, electronic version at www.bundesarchiv.de.

Akten zur deutschen auswärtigen Politik 1918–1945. Aus dem Archiv des Auswärtigen Amtes, Series D: 1937–41; Series E: 1941–5 (Göttingen, 1950–81).

Aly, Götz and Susanne Heim, 'Staatliche Ordnung und organische Lösung. Die Rede Hermann Görings "über die Judenfrage" vom 6. Dezember 1939', in *Jahrbuch für Antisemitismusforschung* 2 (1993), pp. 378–404.

Barcz, Wojciech, 'Die erste Vergasung', in Hans Günther Adler, Hermann Langbein, and Ella Lingens-Reiner (eds), *Auschwitz. Zeugnisse und Berichte*, 2nd edn (Cologne and Frankfurt a. M., 1979), pp. 17–18.

Bargatzky, Walter, *Hotel Majestic. Ein Deutscher im besetzten Frankreich* (Freiburg im Breisgau, 1987).

Benz, Wolfgang, Konrad Kwiet, and Jürgen Matthäus (eds), *Einsatz im 'Reichskommissariat Ostland'. Dokumente zum Völkermord im Baltikum und in Weißrußland 1941–1944* (Berlin, 1998).

Boelcke, Willi A. (ed.), *Deutschlands Rüstung im Zweiten Weltkrieg. Hitlers Konferenzen mit Albert Speer, 1942–1945* (Frankfurt a. M., 1969).

Bräutigam, Otto, 'Das Kriegstagebuch des Diplomaten Otto Bräutigam', with an introduction and commentary by Hans-Dieter Heilmann, in Götz Aly and others (eds), *Biedermann und Schreibtischtäter. Materialien zur deutschen Täter-Biographie* (Berlin, 1989), pp. 123–87.

Broad, Pery, 'Erinnerungen', in Jadwiga Bezwińska and Danuta Czech (eds), *KL Auschwitz in den Augen der SS*, 3rd edn (Katowice, 1981), pp. 133–45.

Buch der Erinnerung. Die ins Baltikum deportierten deutschen, österreichischen und tschechoslowakischen Juden, ed. by Wolfgang Scheffler and Diana Schulle, vol. 1 (Munich, 2003).

Cohn, Willy, *Als Jude in Breslau 1941. Aus den Tagebüchern von Studienrat a. D. Dr. Willy Israel Cohn*, ed. by Joseph Walk (Gerlingen, 1984).

Czech, Danuta, *Kalendarium der Ereignisse im Konzentrationslager Auschwitz-Birkenau 1939–1945* (Reinbek bei Hamburg, 1989).

Das Diensttagebuch des deutschen Generalgouverneurs in Polen 1939–1945, ed. by Werner Präg and Wolfgang Jacobmeyer (Stuttgart, 1975).

Der Dienstkalender Heinrich Himmlers 1941/42, commissioned by the Forschungsstelle für Zeitgeschichte in Hamburg, ed. with a commentary and introduction by Peter Witte and others (Hamburg, 1999).

Der Große Brockhaus, vol. 9 (Leipzig, 1931).

Die Tagebücher von Joseph Goebbels, 2 parts, 9 and 15 vols, commissioned by the Institut für Zeitgeschichte with support from the Russian State Archive and ed. by Elke Fröhlich (Munich, 1993–2006).

Die Verfolgung und Ermordung der europäischen Juden durch das nationalsozialistische Deutschland 1933–1945, vol. 4, ed. by Klaus-Peter Friedrich (Munich, 2011).

Dobroszycki, Lucjan (ed.), *The Chronicle of the Łódź Ghetto 1941–1944* (New Haven, CT and London, 1984).

Domarus, Max, *Hitler. Reden und Proklamationen 1932–1945*, vol. 2 (Munich, 1965).

Engel, Gerhard, *Heeresadjutant bei Hitler, 1938–1943. Aufzeichnungen des Majors Engel*, ed. and with a commentary by Hildegard von Kotze (Munich, 1974).

Faschismus—Getto—Massenmord, ed. by Jüdisches Historisches Institut, Warsaw (Frankfurt a. M., 1962).

'Führer-Erlasse' 1939–1945. Edition sämtlicher überlieferter, nicht im Reichsgesetzblatt abgedruckter, von Hitler während des Zweiten Weltkrieges schriftlich erteilter Direktiven aus den Bereichen Staat, Partei, Wirtschaft, Besatzungspolitik und Militärverwaltung, compiled and with an introduction by Martin Moll (Stuttgart, 1997).

Himmler, Heinrich, *Geheimreden 1933 bis 1945 und andere Ansprachen*, ed. by Bradley F. Smith and Agnes Peterson (Frankfurt a. M., 1974).

Hitler, Adolf, *Monologe im Führerhauptquartier 1941–1944*, as recorded by Henrich Heim, ed. and with a commentary by Werner Jochmann (Hamburg, 1980).

International Military Tribunal: Der Prozess gegen die Hauptkriegsverbrecher vor dem Internationalen Militärgerichtshof, 14. Oktober 1945 bis 1. Oktober 1946, 42 vols (Nuremberg, 1947–9).

Justiz und NS-Verbrechen. Sammlung (west-)deutscher Strafurteile wegen nationalsozialistischer Tötungsverbrechen, 1945–2012, ed. by Christiaan F. Rüter and Dick W. de Mildt (Amsterdam and Munich, 1978).

Kampe, Norbert, 'Dokumente zur Wannsee-Konferenz', in Kampe and Peter Klein (eds), *Die Wannsee-Konferenz am 20. Januar 1942. Dokumente, Forschungsstand, Kontroversen* (Cologne, Weimar, Vienna, 2013), pp. 17–115.

Kárný, Miroslav and others (eds), *Deutsche Politik im Protektorat 'Böhmen und Mähren' unter Reinhard Heydrich 1941–1942. Eine Dokumentation* (Berlin, 1997).

Kempner, Robert M. W., *Ankläger einer Epoche. Lebenserinnerungen* (Frankfurt a. M. and elsewhere, 1983).

Klein, Peter (ed.), *Die Einsatzgruppen in der besetzten Sowjetunion 1941/42. Die Tätigkeits- und Lageberichte des Chefs der Sicherheitspolizei und des SD* (Berlin, 1997).

Koeppen, Werner, *Herbst 1941 im 'Führerhauptquartier'. Berichte Werner Koeppens an seinen Minister Alfred Rosenberg*, ed. and with a commentary by Martin Vogt (Koblenz, 2002).

Kommandant in Auschwitz. Autobiographische Aufzeichnungen von Rudolf Höß, with an introduction and commentary by Martin Broszat (Stuttgart, 1958).

Kriegstagebuch des Oberkommandos der Wehrmacht [Wehrmachtführungsstab], kept by Helmuth Greiner und Percy Ernst Schramm, ed. by Percy Ernst Schramm, 4 vols, vol. 1: 1 August 1940 to 31 December 1941 (Frankfurt a. M. 1961–5).

Loewenstein, Karl, *Minsk. Im Lager der deutschen Juden* (Bonn, 1961).

Longerich, Peter, *Die Ermordung der europäischen Juden. Eine umfassende Dokumentation des Holocaust 1941–1945* (Munich, 1989).

Lösener, Bernhard, 'Als Rassereferent im Reichsministerium des Innern', ed. by Walter Strauß, in *VfZ* 9/3 (1961), 262–313.

Mallmann, Klaus-Michael, and others (eds), *Die 'Ereignismeldungen UdSSR' 1941. Dokumente der Einsatzgruppen in der Sowjetunion* (Darmstadt, 2011).

Picker, Henry, *Hitlers Tischgespräche im Führerhauptquartier. Entstehung, Struktur und Folgen des Nationalsozialismus* (Berlin, 1977; Originalausgabe Bonn, 1951).

Rosenberg, Alfred, *Die Tagebücher von 1934 bis 1944,* ed. and with a commentary by Jürgen Matthäus and Frank Bajohr (Frankfurt a. M., 2015).

Stuckart, Wilhelm and Hans Globke, *Kommentare zur deutschen Rassengesetzgebung* (Munich, 1936).

The Trial of Adolf Eichmann. Record of Proceedings in the District Court of Jerusalem, 9 vols (Jerusalem, 1992–5).

Tragédia slovenských Židov. Fotografie a Dokumenty (Bratislava, 1949).

Trials of War Criminals before the Nuernberg Military Tribunals under Control Council Law No. 10, Nuernberg October 1946–April 1949, 15 vols (Washington, DC, 1949–53).

Unsere Ehre heißt Treue. Kriegstagebuch des Kommandostabes Reichsführer SS: Tätigkeitsberichte der 1. und 2. SS-Inf. Brigade, der 1. SS-Kavallerie-Brigade und von Sonderkommandos der SS, ed. by Fritz Baade (Vienna, 1965).

Verbrechen der Wehrmacht. Dimensionen des Vernichtungskrieges 1941–1944 (Ausstellungskatalog), hg. vom Hamburger Institut für Sozialforschung (Hamburg, 2002).

3. LITERATURE AFTER 1945

Adam, Uwe Dietrich, *Judenpolitik im Dritten Reich* (Düsseldorf, 1972).

Adler, Hans Günter, *Theresienstadt. 1941–1945. Das Antlitz einer Zwangsgemeinschaft. Geschichte Soziologie Psychologie* (Göttingen, 2005).

Adler, Hans Günter, *Der verwaltete Mensch. Studien zur Deportation der Juden aus Deutschland* (Tübingen, 1974).

Alberti, Michael, *Die Verfolgung und Vernichtung der Juden im Reichsgau Wartheland 1939–1945* (Wiesbaden, 2006).

Allen, Michael Thad, *The Business of Genocide: The SS, Slave Labor, and the Concentration Camps* (Chapel Hill, NC, 2002).

Allen, Michael Thad, 'The Devil in the Details: The Gas Chambers of Birkenau, October 1941', in *HGS* 16/2 (2002), 189–216.

Aly, Götz, 'Endlösung'. *Völkerverschiebung und der Mord an den europäischen Juden* (Frankfurt a. M., 1995).

Aly, Götz, and Susanne Heim, *Vordenker der Vernichtung. Auschwitz und die deutschen Pläne für eine neue europäische Ordnung* (Frankfurt a. M., 1991).

Angrick, Andrej, 'Die inszenierte Selbstermächtigung? Motive und Strategie Heydrichs für die Wannsee-Konferenz', in Norbert Kampe and Peter Klein (eds), *Die Wannsee-Konferenz am 20. Januar 1942. Dokumente, Forschungsstand, Kontroversen* (Cologne, Weimar, and Vienna, 2013), pp. 241–58.

Angrick, Andrej, and Peter Klein, *Die 'Endlösung' in Riga. Ausbeutung und Vernichtung 1941–1944* (Darmstadt, 2006).

Arad, Yitzhak, *Belzec, Sobibor, Treblinka: The Operation Reinhard Death Camps* (Bloomington and Indianapolis, IN, 1987).

Arndt, Ino, and Heinz Boberach, 'Deutsches Reich', in Wolfgang Benz, *Dimension des Völkermords. Die Zahl der jüdischen Opfer des Nationalsozialismus* (Munich, 1991), pp. 23–66.

Bajohr, Frank, *'Arisierung' in Hamburg. Die Verdrägung der jüdischen Unternehmer 1933–45* (Hamburg, 1997).

Beer, Mathias, 'Die Entwicklung der Gaswagen beim Mord an den Juden', in *VfZ* 35/3 (1987), 403–17.

Benz, Wolfgang, *Der Holocaust* (Munich, 1995).

Birn, Ruth Bettina, *Die höheren SS- und Polizeiführer. Himmlers Vertreter im Reich und in den besetzten Gebieten* (Düsseldorf, 1986).

Black, Peter, 'Die Trawniki-Männer und die Aktion Reinhard', in Bogdan Musiał (ed.), *Aktion Reinhardt. Der Völkermord an den Juden im Generalgouvernement 1941–1944* (Osnabrück, 2004), pp. 309–52.

Boog, Horst, and others, *Der Angriff auf die Sowjetunion* (Stuttgart, 1983).

Bornschein, Joachim, *Gestapochef Heinrich Müller. Technokrat des Terrors* (Leipzig, 2004).

Brandes, Detlef, *Die Tschechen unter deutschem Protektorat. Besatzungspolitik, Kollaboration und Widerstand im Protektorat Böhmen und Mähren bis Heydrichs Tod (1939–1942)*, vol. 1 (Munich, 1969).

Brandhuber, Jerzy, 'Die sowjetischen Kriegsgsefangenen im Konzentrationslager Auschwitz', in *Hefte von Auschwitz* 4 (1961), 5–62.

Brechtken, Magnus, *'Madagaskar für die Juden'. Antisemitische Idee und politische Praxis 1885–1945* (Munich, 1997).

Breitman, Richard, *Heinrich Himmler. Der Architekt der 'Endlösung'. Himmler und die Vernichtung der europäischen Juden* (Paderborn and Munich, 1996).

Broszat, Martin, 'Hitler und die Genesis der "Endlösung". Aus Anlaß der Thesen von David Irving', in *VfZ* 25/4 (1977), 739–75.

Browning, Christopher, *'Die Endlösung' und das Auswärtige Amt. Das Referat D III der Abteilung Deutschland 1940–1943* (Darmstadt, 2010).

Browning, Christopher, *Die Entfesselung der 'Endlösung'. Nationalsozialistische Judenpolitik 1939–1942* (Munich, 2003).

Browning, Christopher, *Ganz normale Männer. Das Reserve-Polizeibataillon 101 und die 'Endlösung' in Polen* (Reinbek bei Hamburg, 1993) (originally published in English as *Ordinary Men: Reserve Police Battalion 101 and the Final Solution in Poland* (New York, 1992).

Browning, Christopher, 'Nazi Resettlement Policy and the Search for a Solution to the Jewish Question, 1939–1941', in *German Studies Review* 9/3 (1986), 497–519.

Browning, Christopher, 'The Decision Concerning the Final Solution', in Browning, *Fateful Months: Essays on the Emergence of the Final Solution* (New York, 1985), pp. 8–38.

Browning, Christopher, 'Unterstaatssekretär Martin Luther and the Ribbentrop Foreign Office', in *Journal of Contemporary History* 12/2 (1977), 313–44.

Buchholz, Marlis, *Die hannoverschen Judenhäuser: Zur Situation der Juden in der Zeit der Ghettoisierung und Verfolgung, 1941 bis 1945* (Hildesheim, 1987).

Büchler, Yehoshua, 'The Deportation of Slovakian Jews to the Lublin District of Poland in 1942', in *HGS* 6/2 (1991), 151–66.

Burrin, Phillipe, *Hitler und die Juden. Die Entscheidung für den Völkermord* (Frankfurt a. M., 1993).

Cesarani, David, *Adolf Eichmann. Bürokrat und Massenmörder* (Berlin, 2004).

Chary, Frederick Barry, *The History of Bulgaria* (Santa Barbara, CA, 2001).

Cohen, William B., and Jörgen Svennson, 'Finland and the Holocaust', in *HGS* 9/1 (1995), 70–93.

Cüppers, Martin, *Wegbereiter der Shoah. Die Waffen-SS, der Kommandostab Reichsführer-SS und die Judenvernichtung 1939–1945* (Darmstadt, 2005).

Curilla, Wolfgang, *Die deutsche Ordnungspolizei und der Holocaust im Baltikum und in Weissrussland 1941–1944* (Paderborn, 2005).

Dean, Martin, *Collaboration in the Holocaust: Crimes of the Local Police in Belorussia and Ukraine, 1941–44* (New York, 2000).

Dwork, Debórah, and Robert-Jan van Pelt, *Auschwitz. Von 1270 bis heute* (Zurich and Munich, 1998).

Ebbinghaus, Angelika, and Gerd Preissler, 'Die Ermordung psychisch kranker Menschen in der Sowjetunion. Dokumentation', in Götz Aly, *Aussonderung und Tod. Die klinische Hinrichtung der Unbrauchbaren* (Berlin, 1985), pp. 75–107.

Eisenblätter, Gerhard, *Grundlinien der Politik des Reiches gegenüber dem Generalgouvernement, 1939–1945*, unpublished doctoral dissertation (Frankfurt a. M., 1969).

Eisfeld, Alfred, *Deportation, Sondersiedlung, Arbeitsarmee. Deutsche in der Sowjetunion 1941 bis 1956* (Cologne, 1996).

Essner, Cornelia, *Die 'Nürnberger Gesetze' oder die Verwaltung des Rassenwahns 1933–1945* (Paderborn and Munich, 2002).

Fleming, Gerald, *Hitler and the Final Solution* (Berkeley, Los Angeles, CA, and London, 1984).

Förster, Jürgen, 'Das Unternehmen "Barbarossa" als Eroberungs- und Vernichtungskrieg', in Horst Boog and others, *Der Angriff auf die Soujetunion* (Stuttgart, 1983).

Friedländer, Saul, *Das Dritte Reich und die Juden. Die Jahre der Verfolgung 1933–1939* (Munich, 1997).

Friedländer, Saul, 'Vom Antisemitismus zur Ausrottung', in Eberhard Jäckel and Jürgen Rohwer (eds), *Der Mord an den Juden im Zweiten Weltkrieg. Entschlußbildung und Verwirklichung* (Stuttgart, 1985), pp. 18–60.

Fröbe, Rainer 'Der Arbeitseinstaz von KZ-Häftlingen und die Perspektive der Industrie 1943–1945', in Ulrich Herbert (ed.), *Europa und der 'Reichseinsatz'. Ausländische Zivilarbeiter, Kriegsgefangene und KZ-Häftlinge in Deutschland 1938–1945* (Essen, 1991), pp. 351–83.

Gerlach, Christian, *Kalkulierte Morde. Die deutsche Wirtschafts- und Vernichtungspolitik in Weißrußland, 1941 bis 1944* (Hamburg, 1999).

Gerlach, Christian, 'Deutsche Wirtschaftsinteressen. Besatzungspolitik und der Mord an den Juden in Weißrußland, 1941–1943', in Ulrich Herbert (ed.), *Nationalsozialistische Vernichungspolitik 1939–1945. Neue Forschungen und Kontroversen* (Frankfurt a. M., 1998), pp. 263–91.

Gerlach, Christian, 'Failure of Plans for an SS Extermination Camp in Mogilev, Belorussia', in *HGS*, 11/1 (1997), 60–78.

Gerlach, Christian, 'Die Wannsee-Konferenz, das Schicksal der deutschen Juden und Hitlers politische Grundsatzentscheidung, alle Juden Europas zu ermorden', in *WerkstattGeschichte* 18 (1997), 7–44.

Gerwarth, Robert, *Reinhard Heydrich. Biographie* (Munich, 2011).

Glass, Hildrun, *Deutschland und die Verfolgung der Juden im rumänischen Machtbereich 1940–1944* (Munich, 2014).

Goldhagen, Daniel Jonah, *Hitlers willige Vollstrecker. Ganz gewöhnliche Deutsche und der Holocaust*, 3rd edn (Berlin, 1996) (originally published in English as *Hitler's Willing Executioners: Ordinary Germans and the Holocaust* (New York, 1996)).

Gottwaldt, Alfred, and Diana Schulle, *Die 'Judeneportationen' aus dem Deutschen Reich 1941–1945. Eine kommentierte Chronologie* (Wiesbaden, 2005).

Graml, Hermann, *Reichskristallnacht. Antisemitismus und Judenverfolgung im Dritten Reich* (Munich, 1988).

Gruner, Wolf, 'Von der Kollektivausweisung zur Deportation der Juden aus Deutschland (1938–1945). Neue Perspektiven und Dokumente', in Birthe Kundrus and Beate Meyer (eds), *Die Deportation der Juden aus Deutschland. Pläne—Praxis—Reaktionen 1938–1945* (Göttingen, 2004), pp. 21–62.

Gruner, Wolf, *Der Geschlossene Arbeitseinsatz deutscher Juden: Zur Zwangsarbeit als Element der Verfolgung 1938–1943* (Berlin, 1997).

Hagemann, Jürgen, *Die Presselenkung im Dritten Reich* (Bonn, 1970).

Hartog, Leendert Johan, *Der Befehl zum Judenmord. Hitler, Amerika und die Juden* (Bodenheim, 1997).

Haupt, Michael, *Das Haus der Wannsee-Konferenz. Von der Industriellenvilla zur Gedenkstätte* (Paderborn, 2009).

Heberer, Patricia, 'Eine Kontinuität der Tötungsoperationen. T4-Täter und die Aktion Reinhard', in Bogdan Musiał (ed.), *'Aktion Reinhardt'. Der Völkermord an den Juden im Generalgouvernement 1941–1944* (Osnabrück, 2004), pp. 285–308.

Heckmann, Markus, *NS-Täter und Bürger der Bundesrepublik* (Münster, 2010).

Heinemann, Isabel, 'Otto Hofmann und das Rasse- und Siedlungshauptamt. Die "Lösung der Judenfrage" als Element der rassenpolitischen Neuordnung Europas', in Norbert Kampe and Peter Klein (eds), *Die Wannsee-Konferenz am 20. Januar 1942. Dokumente, Forschungsstand, Kontroversen* (Cologne, Weimar, and Vienna, 2013), pp. 323–40.

Herbert, Ulrich, *Best. Biographische Studien über Radikalismus, Weltanschauung und Vernunft, 1903–1989* (Bonn, 1996).

Herbert, Ulrich, 'Die deutsche Militärverwaltung in Paris und die Deportation der französischen Juden', in Christian Jansen, Lutz Niethammer, and Bernd Weisbrod (eds), *Von der Aufgabe der Freiheit: Politische Verantwortung und bürgerliche Gesellschaft im 19. und 20. Jahrhundert. Festschrift für Hans Mommsen zum 5. November 1995* (Berlin, 1995), pp. 427–50.

Hilberg, Raul, *Die Vernichtung der europäischen Juden* (Frankfurt a. M., 1999).

Hilberg, Raul, 'Die Aktion Reinhard', in Eberhard Jäckel and Jürgen Rohwer (eds), *Der Mord an den Juden im Zweiten Weltkrieg. Entschlußbildung und Verwirklichung* (Stuttgart, 1985), pp. 125–36.

Hillgruber, Andreas, 'Der Ostkrieg und die Judenvernichtung', in Gerd R. Ueberschär and Wolfgang Wette (eds), *'Unternehmen Barbarossa'. Der deutsche Überfall auf die Swojetunion 1941. Berichte, Analysen, Dokumente* (Paderborn, 1984), pp. 219–36.

Hillgruber, Andreas, *Hitlers Strategie. Politik und Kriegführung 1940/1941* (Frankfurt a. M., 1965).

Hirschfeld, Gerhard, *Fremdherrschaft und Kollaboration: Die Niederlande unter deutscher Besatzung, 1940–1945* (Stuttgart, 1984).

Hoppe, Hans-Joachim, *Bulgarien, Hitlers eigenwilliger Verbündeter. Eine Fallstudie zur nationalsozialistischen Südosteuropapolitik* (Stuttgart, 1979).

Jacobsen, Hans-Adolf, *Nationalsozialistische Außenpolitik 1933–1938* (Frankfurt a. M. and Berlin, 1968).

Jahn, Peter (ed.), *Erobern und Vernichten. Der Krieg gegen die Sovjetunion 1941–1945* (Berlin, 1991).

Jansen, Hans, *Der Madagaskar-Plan. Die beabsichtigte Deportation der europäischen Juden nach Madagaskar* (Munich, 1997).

Jasch, Hans-Christian, *Staatssekretär Wilhelm Stuckart und die Judenpolitik. Der Mythos von der sauberen Verwaltung* (Munich, 2012).

Jasch, Hans-Christian, 'Zur Rolle der Innenverwaltung im Dritten Reich bei der Vorbereitung und Organisation des Genozids an den Europäischen Juden: der Fall des Dr. Wilhelm Stuckart (1902–1953)', in *Die Verwaltung* 43/2 (2010), 217–71.

Jersak, Tobias, 'Entscheidungen zu Mord und Lüge. Die deutsche Kriegsgesellschaft und der Holocaust', in Jörg Echternkamp (ed.), *Die deutsche Kriegsgselleschaft. 1939 bis 1945*. Vol. 1/2: *Politisierung, Vernichtun, Überleben (Das Deutsche Reich und der Zweite Weltkrieg*, vol. 9/1) (Munich, 2004), pp. 273–356.

Jersak, Tobias, 'Die Interaktion von Kriegsverlauf und Judenvernichtung. Ein Blick auf Hitlers Strategie im Spätsommer 1941', in *HZ* 268/2 (1999), 311–74.

Kaienburg, Hermann, 'Jüdische Arbeitslager an der "Straße der SS"', in *1999. Zeitschrift für Sozialgeschichte des 20. und 21. Jahrhunderts* 11/1 (1996), 13–39.

Kampe, Norbert (ed.), *Villenkolonien in Wannsee 1870–1945. Großbürgerliche Lebenswelt und Ort der Wannsee-Konferenz* (Berlin, 2000).

Kampe, Norbert, 'Ermächtigung und Wannsee-Protokoll. Zu den Randbemerkungen und Stempeln. Überlieferungsgeschichte und Fälschungsvorwurf gegen die zentralen Dokumente', published at www.ghwk.de (no year).

Kampe, Norbert, and Peter Klein (eds), *Die Wannsee-Konferenz am 20. Januar 1942. Dokumente, Forschungsstand, Kontroversen* (Cologne, Weimar, and Vienna, 2013).

Kárný, Miroslav, 'Nisko in der Geschichte der Endlösung', in *Judaica Bohemiae* 23 (1987), 69–84.

Kempner, Robert M. W., *Eichmann und Komplizen* (Zürich, Stuttgart, and Vienna, 1961).

Kershaw, Ian, 'Improvised Genocide? The Emergence of the "Final Solution" in the "Warthegau"', in *Transactions of the Royal Historical Society* 2 (1992), 51–78.

Klarsfeld, Serge, *Vichy-Auschwitz. Die Zusammenarbeit der deutschen und französischen Behörden bei der "Endlösung der Judenfrage" in Frankreich* (Nördlingen, 1989).

Klein, Peter, 'Die Wannsee-Konferenz als Echo auf die gefallene Entscheidung zur Ermordung der europäischen Juden', in Norbert Kampe and Klein (eds), *Die Wannsee-Konferenz am 20. Januar 1942. Dokumente, Forschungsstand, Kontroversen* (Cologne, Weimar, and Vienna, 2013), pp. 182–201.

Klein, Peter, *Die 'Ghettoverwaltung Litzmannstadt' 1940–1944. Eine Dienstelle im Spannungsfeld von Kommunalbürokratie und staatlicher Verfolgungspolitik* (Hamburg, 2009).

Klein, Peter, 'Dr. Rudolf Lange als Kommandeur der Sicherheitspolizei und des SD in Lettland', in Wolf Kaiser (ed.), *Täter im Vernichtungskrieg. Der Überfall auf die Sowjetunion und der Völkermord an den Juden* (Berlin and Munich, 2002), pp. 125–36.

Klein, Peter, 'Die Rolle der Vernichtungslager Kulmhof (Chełmno), Belzec (Bełzec) und Auschwitz-Birkenau in den frühen Deportationsvorbereitungen', in Dittmar Dahlmann and Gerhard Hirschfeld (eds), *Lager, Zwangsarbeit, Vertreibung und Deportation. Dimensionen der Massenverbrechen in der Sowjetunion und in Deutschland 1933 bis 1945* (Essen, 1999), pp. 459–84.

Klein, Peter, *Die Wannsee-Konferenz vom 20. Januar 1942. Analyse und Dokumentation* (booklet) (Berlin, 1996).

Klink, Ernst, 'Heer und Kriegsmarine', in Horst Boog and others, *Der Angriff auf die Sowjetunion* (Stuttgart, 1983), pp. 451–651.

Korb, Alexander, *Im Schatten des Weltkriegs: Massengewalt der Ustaša gegen Serben, Juden und Roma in Kroatien 1941–1945* (Hamburg, 2013).

Krausnick, Helmut, 'Judenverfolgung', in Hans Buchheim and others, *Anatomie des SS-Staates*, vol. 2, 2nd edn (Munich, 1979), pp. 235–366.

Krausnick, Helmut, and Hans-Heinrich Wilhelm, *Die Truppe des Weltanschauungskrieges. Die Einsatzgruppen der Sicherheitspolizei und des SD 1938–1942* (Stuttgart, 1981).

Laqueur, Walter, and Richard Breitman, *Der Mann, der das Schweigen brach. Wie die Welt vom Holocaust erfuhr* (Frankfurt a. M., 1986).

Lipscher, Ladislav, *Die Juden im slowakischen Staat 1939–1945* (Munich and Vienna, 1980).

Longerich, Peter, *Holocaust: The Nazi Persecution and Murder of the Jews* (Oxford, 2010).

Longerich, Peter, *Heinrich Himmler. Biographie*, 3rd edn (Munich, 2008).

Longerich, Peter, *'Davon haben wir nichts gewusst!' Die Deutschen und die Judenverfolgung 1933–1945* (Munich, 2006).

Longerich, Peter, *Der ungeschriebene Befehl. Hitler und der Weg zur 'Endlösung'* (Munich and elsewhere, 2001).

Longerich, Peter, *Politik der Vernichtung. Die Verfolgung und Ermordung der europäischen Juden 1933–1945* (München/Zürich, 1998).

Longerich, Peter, *Hitlers Stellvertreter. Führung der Partei und Kontrolle des Staatsapparates durch den Stab Heß und die Partei-Kanzlei Bormann* (Munich and elsewhere, 1992).

Longerich, Peter, *Propagandisten im Krieg. Die Presseabteilung des Auswärtigen Amtes unter Ribbentrop* (Munich, 1987).

Lower, Wendy, *Nazi Empire-Building and the Holocaust in Ukraine* (Chapel Hill, NC, 2005).

Luther, Hans, *Der französische Widerstand gegen die deutsche Besatzungsmacht und seine Bekämpfung* (Tübingen, 1957).

Madajczyka, Czeslawa (ed.), *Zamojszczyzna—Sonderlaboratorium der SS. Zbiór dokumentów polskich i niemieckich z okresu okupacji hitlerowskiej*, vol. 1 (Warsaw, 1977).

Mallmann, Klaus-Michael, 'Vom Fußvolk der Endlösung. Ordnungspolizei, Ostkrieg und Judenmord', in Dan Diner, *Deutschlandbilder* (Gerlingen, 1997), pp. 355–92.

Mallmann, Klaus-Michael, and Martin Cüppers, *Halbmond und Hakenkreuz. Das Dritte Reich, die Araber und Palästina* (Darmstadt, 2006).

Manoschek, Walter, *'Serbien ist judenfrei'. Militärische Besatzungspolitik und Judenvernichtung in Serbien 1941/42* (Munich, 1993).

Massimo, Arico, *Ordnungspolizei: Ideological War and Genocide in the East 1941–42* (Stockholm, 2012).

Matthäus, Jürgen, 'What about the "Ordinary Men"? The German Order Police and the Holocaust in the Occupied Soviet Union', in *HGS* 10/2 (1996), 134–50.

Mentel, Christian, 'Das Protokoll der Wannsee-Konferenz. Überlieferung, Veröffentlichung und revisionistische Infragestellung', in Norbert Kampe and Peter Klein (eds), *Die Wannsee-Konferenz am 20. Januar 1942. Dokumente, Forschungsstand, Kontroversen* (Cologne, Weimar, and Vienna, 2013), pp. 116–38.

Meyer, Ahlrich, 'Der Beginn der "Endlösung" in Frankreich—offene Fragen', *Sozial. Geschichte* 18/3 (2003), 35–82.

Meyer, Ahlrich, '"…daß französische Verhältnisse anders sind als polnische". Die Bekämpfung des Widerstands durch die deutsche Militärverwaltung in Frankreich 1941', in Guus Meershoek and others, *Repression und Kriegsverbrechen. Die Bekämpfung von Widerstands- und Partisanenbewegungen gegen die deutsche Besatzung in West- und Südosteuropa* (Berlin, 1997), pp. 43–92.

Meyer, Beate, *'Jüdische Mischlinge'. Rassenpolitik und Verfolgungserfahrung 1933–1945* (Hamburg, 1999).

Michaelis, Meir, *Mussolini and the Jews: German-Italian Relations and the Jewish Question in Italy, 1922–1945* (Oxford, 1978).

Michman, Dan, 'Waren die Juden Nordafrikas im Visier der Planer der "Endlösung"? Die "Schoah" und die Zahl 700 000 in Eichmanns Tabelle am 20. Januar 1942', in Norbert Kampe and Peter Klein (eds), *Die Wannsee-Konferenz am 20. Januar 1942. Dokumente, Forschungsstand, Kontroversen* (Cologne, Weimar, and Vienna, 2013), pp. 379–400.

Młynarczyk, Jacek Andrzej, *Judenmord in Zentralpolen. Der Distrikt Radom im Generalgouvernement 1939–1945* (Darmstadt, 2007).

Młynarczyk, Jacek Andrzej, 'Treblinka—ein Todeslager der "Aktion Reinhard"', in Bogdan Musiał (ed.), *'Aktion Reinhardt'. Der Völkermord an den Juden im Generalgouvernement 1941–1944* (Osnabrück, 2004), pp. 257–84.

Mommsen, Hans, discussion contribution in Eberhard Jäckel and Jürgen Rohwer (eds), *Der Mord an den Juden im Zweiten Weltkrieg. Entschlußbildung und Verwirklichung* (Stuttgart, 1985), p. 66.

Mommsen, Hans, 'Die Realisierung des Utopischen: Die "Endlösung der Judenfrage" im "Dritten Reich"', in *GG* 9/3 (1983), 381–420.

Moore, Bob, *Victims and Survivors: The Nazi Persecution of the Jews in the Netherlands 1940–1945* (London, 1997).

Moser, Jonny, *Nisko. Die ersten Judendeportationen*, ed. by Joseph W. and James R. Moser (Vienna, 2012).

Moser, Jonny, 'Österreich', in Wolfgang Benz (ed.), *Dimension des Völkermords. Die Zahl der jüdischen Opfer des Nationalsozialismus* (Munich, 1991), pp. 67–94.

Müller, Rolf-Dieter, 'Von der Wirtschaftsallianz zum kolonialen Ausbeutungskrieg', in Horst Boog and others, *Der Angriff auf die Sowjetunion* (Stuttgart, 1983), pp. 98–189.

Musiał, Bogdan, *Deutsche Zivilverwaltung und Judenverfolgung im Generalgouvernement. Eine Fallstudie zum Distrikt Lublin 1939–1944* (Wiesbaden, 1999).

Nachama, Andreas (ed.), *Vor aller Augen. Die Deportation der Juden und die Versteigerung ihres Eigentums. Fotografien aus Lörrach 1940* (Berlin, 2011).

Nationalsozialistische Massentötungen durch Giftgas. Eine Dokumentation, ed. by Hermann Langbein, Adalbert Rückerl, Eugen Kogon, and others (Frankfurt a. M., 1983).

Nesládková, Ludmila (ed.), *The Case Nisko in the History of the Final Solution of the Jewish Problem in Commemoration of the 55th Anniversary of the First Deportation of Jews in Europe 1944* (Ostrava, 1995).

Nolzen, Armin, 'Gerhard Klopfer, die Abteilung III in der Partei-Kanzlei und deren "Judenpolitik"', in Norbert Kampe and Peter Klein (eds), *Die Wannsee-Konferenz am 20. Januar 1942. Dokumente, Forschungsstand, Kontroversen* (Cologne, Weimar, and Vienna, 2013), pp. 303–22.

Ortner, Helmut, *Der Hinrichter Roland Freisler - Mörder im Dienste Hitlers* (Frankfurt a. M., 2014).

Otto, Reinhard, *Wehrmacht, Gestapo und sowjetische Kriegsgefangene im deutschen Reichsgebiet 1941/42* (Munich, 1998).

Pätzold, Kurt, and Erika Schwartz, *Tagesordnung: Judenmord. Die Wannsee-Konferenz vom 20 Januar 1942. Eine Dokumentation zur Organisation der 'Endlösung'* (Berlin, 1992).

Petrick, Fritz (ed.), *Die Okkupationspolitik des deutschen Faschismus in Dänemark und Norwegen (1940–1945)* (Berlin and Heidelberg, 1992).

Piper, Ernst, *Alfred Rosenberg. Hitlers Chefideologe* (Munich, 2005).

Piper, Franciszek, 'Vernichtung', in Wacław Długoborski and Franciszek Piper (eds), *Auschwitz 1940–1945. Studien zur Geschichte des Konzentrations- und Vernichtungslagers Auschwitz*, vol. 3 (Oświęcim, 1999).

Piper, Franciszek, *Die Zahl der Opfer von Auschwitz. Aufgrund der Quellen und der Erträge der Forschung, 1945 bis 1990* (Oświęcim, 1993).

Pohl, Dieter, 'Schauplatz Ukraine. Der Massenmord an den Juden im Militärverwaltungsgebiet und im Reichskommissariat 1941–1943', in Christian Hartmann, Dieter Pohl, and others, *Der deutsche Krieg im Osten 1941–1944. Facetten einer Grenzüberschreitung* (Munich, 2009), pp. 155–98.

Pohl, Dieter, *Nationalsozialistische Judenverfolgung in Ostgalizien 1941–1944. Organisation und Durchführung eines staatlichen Massenverbrechens* (Munich, 1996).

Pohl, Dieter, *Von der 'Judenpolitik' zum Judenmord. Der Distrikt Lublin des Generalgouvernements, 1934–1944* (Frankfurt a. M., 1993).

Polian, Pavel, 'Hätte der Holocaust beinahe nicht stattgefunden? Überlegungen zu einem Schriftwechsel im Wert von zwei Millionen Menschenleben', in Johannes Hürter and Jürgen Zarusky (eds), *Besatzung, Kollaboration, Holocaust. Neue Studien zur Verfolgung und Ermordung der europäischen Juden* (Munich, 2008), pp. 1–20.

Poznanski, Renée, *Jews in France during World War II* (Hanover, NH, 2001).

Pressac, Jean-Claude, *Die Krematorien von Auschwitz. Die Technik des Massenmordes*, 2nd edn (Munich, 1995).

Presser, Jacques, *Ashes in the Wind: The Destruction of the Dutch Jewry* (New York, 1968).

Priamus, Heinz-Jürgen, *Meyer. Zwischen Kaisertreue und NS-Täterschaft: Biographische Konturen eines deutschen Bürgers* (Essen, 2011).

Rautkallio, Hannu, *Finland and the Holocaust: The Rescue of Finland's Jews* (New York, 1987).

Reitlinger, Gerald, *Die Endlösung. Hitlers Versuch der Ausrottung der Juden Europas 1939–1945* (Berlin, 1956).

Reynolds, David, *The Creation of the Anglo-American Alliance, 1937–1941: A Study in Competitive Co-operation* (Chapel Hill, NC, 1981).

Roseman, Mark, '"Wannsee" als Herausforderung. Die Historiker und die Konferenz', in Norbert Kampe and Peter Klein (eds), *Die Wannsee-Konferenz am 20. Januar 1942. Dokumente, Forschungsstand, Kontroversen* (Cologne, Weimar, and Vienna, 2013), pp. 401–14.

Rosenberg, Heinz, *Jahre des Schreckens... und ich blieb übrig, dass ich Dir's ansage* (Göttingen, 1993).

Rosenkranz, Herbert, *Verfolgung und Selbstbehauptung. Die Juden in Österreich 1938–1945* (Vienna, 1978).

Roth, Karl Heinz, '"Generalplan Ost" und der Mord an den Juden. Der "Fernplan der Umsiedlung in den Ostprovinzen" aus dem Reichssicherheitshauptamt vom November 1939', in *1999. Zeitschrift für Sozialgeschichte des 20. und 21. Jahrhunderts* 12/2 (1997), 50–70.

Safrian, Hans, *Die Eichmann-Männer* (Vienna, 1993).

Sandkühler, Thomas, *'Endlösung' in Galizien. Der Judenmord in Ostpolen und die Rettungsinitiativen von Berthold Beitz 1941–1944* (Bonn, 1996).

Scheffler, Wolfgang, 'Das Schicksal der in die baltischen Staaten deportierten deutschen, österreichischen und tschechoslowakischen Juden 1941–1945', in *Buch der Erinnerung. Die ins Baltikum deportierten deutschen, österreichischen und tschechoslowaskischen Juden*, ed. by Wolfgang Scheffler and Diana Schulle, vol. 1 (Munich, 2003), pp. 1–78.

Scheffler, Wolfgang, 'Massenmord in Kowno', in *Buch der Erinnerung. Die ins Baltikum deportierten deutschen, österreichischen und tschechoslowaskischen Juden*, ed. by Wolfgang Scheffler and Diana Schulle, vol. 1 (Munich, 2003), pp. 83–7.

Scheffler, Wolfgang, 'Die Wannsee-Konferenz und ihre historische Bedeutung', in *Erinnern für die Zukunft. Ansprachen und Vorträge zur Eröffnung der Gedenkstätte*, ed. by Gedenkstätte Haus der Wannsee-Konferenz (Berlin, 1992), pp. 17–34.

Schelvis, Jules, *Vernichtungslager Sobibór* (Berlin, 1998).

Schneider, Hubert, *Die 'Entjudung' des Wohnraums—'Judenhäuser' in Bochum. Die Geschichte der Gebäude und ihrer Bewohner* (Münster, 2010).

Schulte, Jan Erik, *Zwangsarbeit und Vernichtung. Das Wirtschaftsimperium der SS. Oswald Pohl und das SS-Wirtschafts-Verwaltungshauptamt, 1933–1945* (Paderborn and elsewhere, 2001).

Schwarz, Angela, 'Von den Wohnstiften zu den "Judenhäusern"', in Angelika Ebbinghaus and Karsten Linne (eds), *Kein abgeschlossenes Kapitel: Hamburg im 'Dritten Reich'* (Hamburg, 1997), pp. 232–47.

Seeger, Andreas, *'Gestapo-Müller'. Die Karriere eines Schreibtischtäters* (Berlin, 1996).

Seidel, Robert, *Deutsche Besatzungspolitik in Polen. Der Distrikt Radom 1939–1945* (Paderborn and Munich, 2006).

Silberklang, David, 'Die Juden und die ersten Deportationen aus dem Distrikt Lublin', in Bogdan Musiał (ed.), *'Aktion Reinhardt'. Der Völkermord an den Juden im Generalgouvernement 1941–1944* (Osnabrück, 2004), pp. 141–64.

Spector, Shmuel, *The Holocaust of Volhynian Jews, 1941–1944* (Jerusalem, 1990).

Steinbacher, Sybille, *'Musterstadt' Auschwitz. Germanisierungspolitik und Judenmord in Oberschlesien* (Munich, 2000).

Strauß, Herbert A., 'Jewish Emigration from Germany: Nazi Policies and Jewish Responses', in *The Leo Baeck Institute Year Book* 25 (1980), 313–61 (I), and 26 (1981), 343–409 (II).

Streit, Christian, *Keine Kameraden. Die Wehrmacht und die sowjetischen Kriegsgefangenen 1941–1945* (Stuttgart, 1978).

Sundhausen, Holm, 'Jugoslawien', in Wolfgang Benz (ed.), *Dimension des Völkermords. Die Zahl der jüdischen Opfer des Nationalsozialismus* (Munich, 1991), pp. 311–30.

Terner, Daniel, *Prophet und Prophezeiung. Zur Geschichte eines Hitler-Zitats 1939–1945*, unpublished Master's dissertation, Historisches Institut, Stuttgart University (1995).

Tomasevich, Jozo, *War and Revolution in Yugoslavia, 1941–1945: Occupation and Collaboration* (Stanford, CA, 2001).

Tregenza, Michael, 'Bełżec Death Camp', in *Wiener Library Bulletin* 30 (1977/8), 8–25.

Tuchel, Johannes, *Am Großen Wannsee 56–58. Von der Villa Minoux zum Haus der Wannsee-Konferenz* (Berlin, 1992).

Ueberschär, Gerd R., and Wolfgang Wette (eds), *'Unternehmen Barbarossa'. Der deutsche Überfall auf die Sowjetunion 1941. Berichte, Analysen, Dokumente* (Paderborn, 1984).

Weber, Wolfram, *Die Innere Sicherheit im besetzten Belgien und Nordfrankreich 1940–1944. Ein Beitrag zur Geschichte der Besatzungsverwaltungen* (Düsseldorf, 1978).

Wegner, Bernd (ed.), *Zwei Wege nach Moskau. Vom Hitler-Stalin-Pakt bis zum 'Unternehmen Barbarossa'* (Munich, 1991).

Wetzel, Juliane, 'Frankreich und Belgien', in Wolfgang Benz, *Dimension des Völkermords. Die Zahl der jüdischen Opfer des Nationalsozialismus* (Munich, 1991), pp. 105–36.

Wildt, Michael (ed.), *Die Judenpolitik des SD 1935 bis 1938. Eine Dokumentation* (Munich, 1995).

Wilhelm, Hans-Heinrich, *Rassenpolitik und Kriegsführung. Sicherheitspolizei und Wehrmacht in Polen und in der Sowjetunion 1939–1942* (Passau, 1991).

Wilhelm, Hans-Heinrich, 'Die Einsatzgruppe A der Sicherheitspolizei und des SD 1941/42. Eine exemplarische Studie', in Helmut Krausnick and

Wilhelm, *Die Truppe des Weltanschauungskrieges. Die Einsatzgruppen der Sicherheitspolizei und des SD 1938–1942* (Stuttgart, 1981), pp. 281–636.

Willems, Susanne, *Der entsiedelte Jude. Albert Speers Wohnungsmarktpolitik für den Berliner Hauptstadtbau* (Berlin, 2002).

Witte, Peter, 'Letzte Nachrichten aus Siedliszcze. Der Transport AX aus Theresienstadt in den Distrikt Lublin', in *Theresienstädter Studien und Dokumente* 3 (1996), 98–113.

Witte, Peter, 'Two Decisions Concerning the "Final Solution to the Jewish Question", Deportations to Łódź and Mass Murder in Chełmno', in *HGS* 9/3 (1995), 318–45.

Yahil, Leni, 'Madagascar: Phantom of a Solution for the Jewish Question', in George L. Mosse and Bela Vago (eds), *Jews and Non-Jews in Eastern Europe, 1918–1945* (New York and elsewhere, 1974), pp. 315–34.

Zellhuber, Andreas, *'Unsere Verwaltung treibt einer Katastrophe zu…': Das Reichsministerium für die besetzten Ostgebiete und die deutsche Besatzungsherrschaft in der Sowjetunion 1941–1945* (Munich, 2006).

Subject Index